AA004311

CYBER 2018

The Third International Conference on Cyber-Technologies and Cyber-Systems

November 18 - 22, 2018

Athens, Greece

CYBER 2018 Editors

Steve Chan, Harvard University/Decision Engineering Analysis Laboratory, USA

Tom Klemas, Decision Engineering Analysis Laboratory-Cambridge, USA

Xing Liu, Kwantlen Polytechnic University, Surrey, B.C., Canada

Keith Joiner, Australian Cyber Security Centre (ACSC), University of New South Wales (UNSW), Canberra, Australia

Michael Massoth, Hochschule Darmstadt - University of Applied Sciences, Germany

Printed from e-media with permission by:

Curran Associates, Inc.
57 Morehouse Lane
Red Hook, NY 12571

Some format issues inherent in the e-media version may also appear in this print version.

Copyright© (2018) by International Academy, Research, and Industry Association (IARIA)
Please refer to the Copyright Information page.

Printed by Curran Associates, Inc. (2019)

International Academy, Research, and Industry Association (IARIA)
412 Derby Way
Wilmington, DE 19810

Phone: (408) 893-6407
Fax: (408) 527-6351

petre@iaria.org

Additional copies of this publication are available from:

Curran Associates, Inc.
57 Morehouse Lane
Red Hook, NY 12571 USA
Phone: 845-758-0400
Fax: 845-758-2633
Email: curran@proceedings.com
Web: www.proceedings.com

Table of Contents

CYBER 2018

Forward

The Third International Conference on Cyber-Technologies and Cyber-Systems (CYBER 2018), held between November 18, 2018 and November 22, 2018 in Athens, Greece, continued the inaugural event covering many aspects related to cyber-systems and cyber-technologies considering the issues mentioned above and potential solutions. It is also intended to illustrate appropriate current academic and industry cyber-system projects, prototypes, and deployed products and services.

The increased size and complexity of the communications and the networking infrastructures are making it difficult the investigation of the resiliency, security assessment, safety and crimes. Mobility, anonymity, counterfeiting, are characteristics that add more complexity in Internet of Things and Cloud-based solutions. Cyber-physical systems exhibit a strong link between the computational and physical elements. Techniques for cyber resilience, cyber security, protecting the cyber infrastructure, cyber forensic and cyber crimes have been developed and deployed. Some of new solutions are nature-inspired and social-inspired leading to self-secure and self-defending systems. Despite the achievements, security and privacy, disaster management, social forensics, and anomalies/crimes detection are challenges within cyber-systems.

The conference had the following tracks:

- Cyber security
- Cyber infrastructure
- Cyber Attack Surfaces and the Interoperability of Architectural Application Domain Resiliency
- Embedded Systems for the Internet of Things
- Cyber resilience

We take here the opportunity to warmly thank all the members of the CYBER 2018 technical program committee, as well as all the reviewers. The creation of such a high quality conference program would not have been possible without their involvement. We also kindly thank all the authors that dedicated much of their time and effort to contribute to CYBER 2018. We truly believe that, thanks to all these efforts, the final conference program consisted of top quality contributions.

We also gratefully thank the members of the CYBER 2018 organizing committee for their help in handling the logistics and for their work that made this professional meeting a success.

We hope that CYBER 2018 was a successful international forum for the exchange of ideas and results between academia and industry and to promote further progress in the domain cyber technologies and cyber systems. We also hope that Athens, Greece, provided a pleasant environment during the conference and everyone saved some time to enjoy the historic charm of the city.

CYBER 2018 Chairs

CYBER Steering Committee

Carla Merkle Westphall, Federal University of Santa Catarina (UFSC), Brazil
Cong-Cong Xing, Nicholls State University, USA
Jean-Marc Robert, Polytechnique Montréal, Canada
Steve Chan, Massachusetts Institute of Technology (MIT), USA
Jan Richling, South Westphalia University of Applied Sciences, Germany
Duminda Wijesekera , George Mason University, USA
Francesco Buccafurri, University Mediterranea of Reggio Calabria, Italy
Syed Naqvi, Birmingham City University, UK

CYBER Industry/Research Advisory Committee

Rainer Falk, Siemens AG, Corporate Technology, Germany
Cristina Serban, AT&T Security Research Center, Middletown, USA
Juan-Carlos Bennett, SSC Pacific, USA
Barbara Re, University of Camerino, Italy
Daniel Kaestner, AbsInt GmbH, Germany
George Yee, Carleton University / Aptusinnova Inc., Canada
Yao Yiping, National University of Defence Technology - Hunan, China
Thomas Klemas, SimSpace Corporation, USA

CYBER 2018
Committee

CYBER Steering Committee

Carla Merkle Westphall, Federal University of Santa Catarina (UFSC), Brazil
Cong-Cong Xing, Nicholls State University, USA
Jean-Marc Robert, Polytechnique Montréal, Canada
Steve Chan, Massachusetts Institute of Technology (MIT), USA
Jan Richling, South Westphalia University of Applied Sciences, Germany
Duminda Wijesekera , George Mason University, USA
Francesco Buccafurri, University Mediterranea of Reggio Calabria, Italy
Syed Naqvi, Birmingham City University, UK

CYBER Industry/Research Advisory Committee

Rainer Falk, Siemens AG, Corporate Technology, Germany
Cristina Serban, AT&T Security Research Center, Middletown, USA
Juan-Carlos Bennett, SSC Pacific, USA
Barbara Re, University of Camerino, Italy
Daniel Kaestner, AbsInt GmbH, Germany
George Yee, Carleton University / Aptusinnova Inc., Canada
Yao Yiping, National University of Defence Technology - Hunan, China
Thomas Klemas, SimSpace Corporation, USA

CYBER 2018 Technical Program Committee

Abdulghani Ali Ahmed, Universiti Malaysia Pahang (UMP), Kuantan, Malaysia
Irfan Ahmed, University of New Orleans, USA
Hamzah Al-Najada, Florida Atlantic University, Boca Raton, USA
Khalid Alemerien, Tafila Technical University, Jordan
Abdullahi Arabo, Centre for Complex and Cooperative Systems - CSCT, UWE Bristol, UK
A. Taufiq Asyhari, Cranfield University, UK
Hannan Azhar, Canterbury Christ Church University, UK
Liz Bacon, University of Greenwich, Old Royal Naval College, UK
Pooneh Bagheri Zadeh, Leeds Beckett University, UK
Hayretdin Bahşi, Tallinn University of Technology, Estonia
Morgan Barbier, GREYC - ENSICAEN, France
Juan-Carlos Bennett, SSC Pacific, USA
Davidson Boccardo, Clavis Information Security, Brazil
Paul Bogdan, University of Southern California, USA
David Brosset, Naval Academy Research Institute, France
Francesco Buccafurri, University Mediterranea of Reggio Calabria, Italy

Steve Chan, Massachusetts Institute of Technology (MIT), USA
Steve Chan, University of Colorado, Boulder, USA
DeJiu Chen, KTH Royal Institute of Technology, Sweden
Albert M. K. Cheng, University of Houston, USA
Michal Choras, University of Science and Technology, UTP Bydgoszcz, Poland
Christos Dimopoulos, European University Cyprus, Cyprus
Jana Dittmann, Otto-von-Guericke-University Magdeburg, Germany
Tadashi Dohi, Hiroshima University, Japan
Levent Ertaul, California State University, USA
Rainer Falk, Siemens AG, Corporate Technology, Germany
James Martin Fellow, Global Cyber Security Capacity Centre - University of Oxford, UK
Eduardo B. Fernandez, Florida Atlantic University, USA
Roberto Ferreira Júnior, Federal University of Rio de Janeiro, Brazil
Massimo Ficco, Università degli Studi della Campania Luigi Vanvitelli, Italy
Daniel Fischer, Technische Universität Ilmenau, Germany
Steven Furnell, University of Plymouth, UK
Kambiz Ghazinour, Kent State University, USA
Michael Goldsmith, Worcester College, University of Oxford, UK
Stefanos Gritzalis, University of the Aegean, Greece
Martin Grothe, complexium GmbH, Germany
Yuan Xiang Gu, Irdeto, Canada
Ao Guo, Hosei University, Japan
Chunhui Guo, Illinois Institute of Technology, USA
Flavio E. A. Horita, University of São Paulo, Brazil
Shaohan Hu, IBM Research, USA
Zhen Huang, University of Toronto, Canada
Shareeful Islam, University of East London, UK
Daniel Kaestner, AbsInt GmbH, Germany
Georgios Kambourakis, University of the Aegean - Karlovassi, Samos, Greece
Tahar Kechadi, University College Dublin (UCD), Ireland
Yvon Kermarrec, IMT Atlantique / Ecole Navale, France
Veena Khandelwal, Rajasthan Technical University, Kota, India
Georgios Kioumourtzis, Center for Security Studies - Ministry of Interior, Greece / European University Cyprus, Cyprus
Thomas Klemas, SimSpace Corporation, USA
Xiangjie Kong, Dalian University of Technology, China
Ah-Lian Kor, Leeds Beckett University, UK
Kevin T. Kornegay, Morgan State University, USA
Fatih Kurugollu, University of Derby, UK
Petra Leimich, Edinburgh Napier University, UK
Rafal Leszczyna, Politechnika Gdańska, Poland
Jianwen Li, Iowa State University, USA
Jing-Chiou Liou, Kean University, USA
Jane W. S. Liu, Institute of Information Science | Academia Sinica, Taiwan

Xing Liu, Kwantlen Polytechnic University, Canada
Mirco Marchetti, University of Modena and Reggio Emilia, Italy
Keith Martin, Royal Holloway, University of London, UK
Carla Merkle Westphall, Federal University of Santa Catarina (UFSC), Brazil
Louai Maghrabi, Kingston University, UK
Imad Mahgoub, Florida Atlantic University, USA
Sayonnha Mandal, St. Ambrose University, USA
Sathiamoorthy Manoharan, UniversityofAuckland, New Zealand
Eduard Marin, KU Leuven, Belgium
Emmanuel Masabo, Makerere University, Uganda
Michael Massoth, Hochschule Darmstadt - University of Applied Sciences / CRISP – Center for Research in Security and Privacy, Darmstadt, Germany
Vasileios Mavroeidis, University of Oslo, Norway
Claudio Miceli de Farias, Federal University of Rio de Janeiro, Brazil
Mahshid R. Naeini, University of South Florida, USA
Syed Naqvi, Birmingham City University, UK
Serena Nicolazzo, University Mediterranea of Reggio Calabria, Italy
Antonino Nocera, University Mediterranea of Reggio Calabria, Italy
Nadia Noori, University of Agder, Norway
Klimis Ntalianis, University of West Attica, Greece
Joshua C. Nwokeji, Gannon University, USA
Ika Oktavianti, Fakultas Ilmu Komputer, Palembang, Indonesia
Flavio Oquendo, IRISA (UMR CNRS) - University of South Brittany, France
Risat Pathan, Chalmers University of Technology, Sweden
Carlos J. Perez-del-Pulgar, University of Malaga, Spain
Stefan Pforte, Institut für grafische Wissensorganisation, Germany
Hao Qiu, Fort Valley State University, USA
Khandaker A. Rahman, Saginaw Valley State University, USA
Barbara Re, University of Camerino, Italy
Antonio J. Reinoso, Alfonso X University, Spain
Leon Reznik, Rochester Institute of Technology, USA
Jan Richling, South Westphalia University of Applied Sciences, Germany
Jean-Marc Robert, Polytechnique Montréal, Canada
Christophe Rosenberger, ENSICAEN, France
Gordon Russell, Edinburgh Napier University, Scotland
Giedre Sabaliauskaite, iTrust Centre for Research in Cyber Security | Singapore University of Technology and Design, Singapore
Cristina Serban, AT&T Security Research Center, USA
Thar Baker Shamsa, Liverpool John Moores University, UK
Zhihao Shang, Free University of Berlin, Germany
Lynsay Shepherd, Abertay University, UK
Sandeep Shukla, Virginia Tech, USA
Kristina Soukupova, I3CAS Ltd., Czech Republic
Angelo Spognardi, Sapienza University of Rome, Italy

Kuo-Feng Ssu, National Cheng Kung University, Taiwan
Marco Steger, Virtual Vehicle research center, Graz, Austria
Eniye Tebekaemi, George Mason University, USA
Aderonke F. Thompson, Federal University of Technology, Akure, Nigeria
Panagiotis Trimintzios, EU Agency for Cybersecurity, Greece
Elochukwu Anthony Ukwandu, Edinburgh Napier University, Scotland
Timothy Vidas, Dell Secureworks, USA
Stefanos Vrochidis, Information Technologies Institute - Centre for Research and Technology Hellas, Greece
Peipei Wang, North Carolina State University, USA
Ruoyu (Fish) Wang, Arizona State University, USA
Duminda Wijesekera , George Mason University, USA
Zhen Xie, Paypal Inc, USA
Cong-Cong Xing, Nicholls State University, USA
Wuu Yang, National Chiao-Tung University, HsinChu, Taiwan
George Yee, Carleton University / Aptusinnova Inc., Canada
Yao Yiping, National University of Defence Technology - Hunan, China
Xiao Zhang, Palo Alto Networks, USA
Piotr Zwierzykowski, Poznan University of Technology, Poland

Copyright Information

For your reference, this is the text governing the copyright release for material published by IARIA.

The copyright release is a transfer of publication rights, which allows IARIA and its partners to drive the dissemination of the published material. This allows IARIA to give articles increased visibility via distribution, inclusion in libraries, and arrangements for submission to indexes.

I, the undersigned, declare that the article is original, and that I represent the authors of this article in the copyright release matters. If this work has been done as work-for-hire, I have obtained all necessary clearances to execute a copyright release. I hereby irrevocably transfer exclusive copyright for this material to IARIA. I give IARIA permission or reproduce the work in any media format such as, but not limited to, print, digital, or electronic. I give IARIA permission to distribute the materials without restriction to any institutions or individuals. I give IARIA permission to submit the work for inclusion in article repositories as IARIA sees fit.

I, the undersigned, declare that to the best of my knowledge, the article is does not contain libelous or otherwise unlawful contents or invading the right of privacy or infringing on a proprietary right.

Following the copyright release, any circulated version of the article must bear the copyright notice and any header and footer information that IARIA applies to the published article.

IARIA grants royalty-free permission to the authors to disseminate the work, under the above provisions, for any academic, commercial, or industrial use. IARIA grants royalty-free permission to any individuals or institutions to make the article available electronically, online, or in print.

IARIA acknowledges that rights to any algorithm, process, procedure, apparatus, or articles of manufacture remain with the authors and their employers.

I, the undersigned, understand that IARIA will not be liable, in contract, tort (including, without limitation, negligence), pre-contract or other representations (other than fraudulent misrepresentations) or otherwise in connection with the publication of my work.

Exception to the above is made for work-for-hire performed while employed by the government. In that case, copyright to the material remains with the said government. The rightful owners (authors and government entity) grant unlimited and unrestricted permission to IARIA, IARIA's contractors, and IARIA's partners to further distribute the work.

A Comparative Evaluation of Automated Vulnerability Scans versus Manual Penetration Tests on False-negative Errors

Saed Alavi, Niklas Bessler, Michael Massoth
Department of Computer Science
Hochschule Darmstadt (h_da) — University of Applied Sciences Darmstadt,
and Center for Research in Security and Privacy (CRISP), Darmstadt, Germany
E-mail: {saed.alavi,niklas.bessler}@stud.h-da.de, michael.massoth@h-da.de

***Abstract*—Security analysis can be done through different types of methods, which include manual penetration testing and automated vulnerability scans. These two different approaches are often confused and believed to result in the same value. To evaluate this, we have build a lab with several prepared vulnerabilities to simulate a typical small and medium-sized enterprise. Then, we performed a real penetration test on the lab, and a vulnerability scan as well, and then compared the results. Our conclusion shows, that the results obtained through both types of security analysis are highly distinct. They differ in time expenditure and false-positive rate. Most importantly, we have seen a remarkable higher false-negative rate in the vulnerability scan, which suggests that automated methods cannot replace manual penetration testing. However, the combination of both methods is a conceivable approach.**

Keywords–Security analysis; penetration test; vulnerability scan.

I. INTRODUCTION

Information technology (IT) security has become more and more important, due to the increasing threat of cybercrime. Therefore the demand for security analysis of information technology infrastructure is constantly growing. The purpose of such a security analysis is to identify threats, estimate likelihood and potential consequences, which makes it possible to determine a risk value eventually. Results are achieved through different methods of security testing. However, these security tests can vary significantly in cost, scope, informative value and other characteristics. In this paper, we distinguish between penetration tests (colloquially known as pentest) and vulnerability scans (abbreviated vuln scan).

The goal of this research is to assess which method of security analysis should be considered to be better relating to false-positives errors as well as false-negative errors. In this paper, we focus on the false-negative rate. The reason for this is, that this type of error is more severe. To accomplish this research goal, we strictly separate the work in isolated work packages as summarized in this section. The overall experimental setup is described in detail in Section IV.

First, one of the authors builds a lab environment, which represents a typical and representative IT infrastructure of a small and medium enterprise. In addition, the computer systems are prepared with various vulnerabilities. Following this, a typical penetration test will be performed by another author, who is in the role of a penetration tester. This happens without any knowledge of the previous work package (preparation of the lab environment). Using this approach, we want to ensure that all vulnerabilities are revealed in a proper way through real pentesting and results are not influenced in any way by prior knowledge. Then, we use two popular vulnerability scanners to generate automated vulnerability reports. We make use of the proprietary software Nessus and the free software framework OpenVAS. In a final step, we validate both manually and automatically generated reports and determine error rates, where we finally consider the knowledge, of building a self-made lab environment, which has been totally absent up to this point.

This paper is organized as follows: Section II gives an overview of the relevant terminology. Section III summarize the research achievement of previous scientific publications on this topic. In Section IV we explain all tasks of the particular work packages in their chronological order. This includes how we build the lab environment, our methodology used in the penetration test and how we configured the two vulnerability scanners. Section V provides our results and analysis. Section VI summarizes our conclusion. Finally, Section VII talks about possible future work.

II. BACKGROUND

In this section, we introduce the terminology. We also define several terms, due to lack of a standardized definitions. Furthermore, we describe the two different error types, explain their meaning in the context of a security analysis and point out their relevance.

A. Security analysis

Security analysis refers to the process of identifying security related issues and determining their estimate of risk as well. The process of looking for vulnerabilities can be either in technical manner, including penetration tests and vulnerability scans. Or it is in organizational manner, e.g., business process analysis or enter into a dialog with employees. We only cover the technical part. Furthermore, all findings shall be assessed in their risk value and include recommendations for appropriate measures. As an example periodic security assessments are required in several security standards such as the Payment Card Industry Data Security Standard (PCI DSS) [1]. It requires quarterly external vulnerability scans and external penetration testing at least annually.

B. Risk

A risk is always associated with potential harm to an infrastructure, respectively to an whole organization. It consists of two factors: the potential impact and the probability of occurrence. Both values should be understood as estimates, which are represented in a quantitative (e.g., amount of money) or qualitative (e.g., low, medium, high) form. Figure 1 shows how we categorized the risk values for the penetration test.

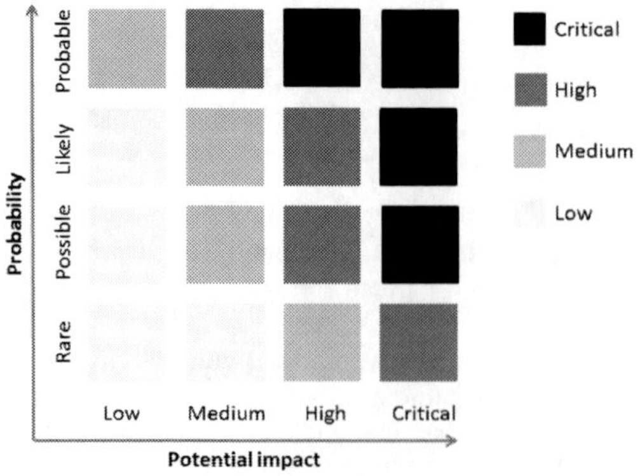

Figure 1. Risk matrix.

C. Penetration test

Penetration testing describes the simulation of a genuine cyber attack. Its goal is to identify vulnerabilities, thereby reducing security risks. This is done using a wide range of attack vectors to cover as much potential vulnerable points as possible. Components of such a test includes especially extensive manual testing and automated tool sets for at least common vulnerabilities. In contrast to a real attack, pentests differentiate in motivation, time expense and legality.

D. Vulnerability scan

A vulnerability scanner is a computer program, which identifies known vulnerabilities in an automated way. Such Vulnerability scans can be performed either unauthenticated or authenticated. Running the scan with corresponding credentials often leads to lower error rates and results of higher quality. Typically a vuln scan is very fast and do not require much technical knowledge, except in interpreting its results. It is a common practice to perform a vulnerability scan and claim it as pentest, although a pentest is actually ordered.

E. Informative base of testing

Black-box testing refers to testing without knowing the internal structure of a system (correlates to the knowledge of external individuals). The opposite is known as White-box test (correlates to the knowledge of (ex-)employees). Something in between we call Grey-box test. In general the informative base determines the knowledge of an attacker, and therefore determine the attack vectors the attacker would be capable of.

F. False-positive error

A false-positive error is a result, that wrongly indicates the presence of a given condition, where the condition is actually absent. It is colloquially known as false alarm. For example, a security report claims a deprecated software version as vulnerable, however a newer version is installed, which is not exploitable anymore. We declare two subtypes of false-positives, which are described more detailed in Section V. This error type is in general not severe, but can slow down the progress of testing.

G. False-negative error

A false-negative error is a result, that wrongly indicates the absence of a given condition, where the condition is actually present. This type of error basically refers to an existing vulnerability, which is not found through testing. False-negative errors are very critical within the context of security analysis, because they result in unreported and thus unfixed vulnerabilities.

III. Related Work

Some research achievement already has been accomplished when it comes to comparing manual and automated methods for security analysis. Therefore, we want to give an overview of the current state of research and show other scientific publications, which address the similar research question.

Austin et al. [2] conducted a case study on two Electronic Health Records (EHR) systems with the objective to compare different approaches of security analysis. In contrast to our research they have chosen two open source EHR systems as subject for study and rather performed a White-box test on computer software, whereas we performed a Grey-box penetration test on a whole IT-infrastructure. In their publication, they distinguish between systematic and exploratory manual penetration testing, static analysis and automated penetration testing. The authors claim, that no single technique discovered every type of vulnerability and almost no individual vulnerabilities were found by more than one type of security analysis. Furthermore, they conclude, that systematic penetration testing was the most effective way. At the same time, static analysis and automated pentesting shouldn't be relied on, because these two methods result in a higher rate of undiscovered vulnerabilities (false-negatives). However, automated penetration testing was the most efficient detection technique, when it comes to found vulnerabilities per hour.

Holm [3] investigated in his research how many vulnerabilities would be remediated if one would follow the recommendations provided by an automated vuln scan. For this purpose both authenticated and unauthenticated scans of seven different network vulnerability scanners were evaluated. The author concludes that "a vulnerability scanner is a usable security assessment tool, given that credentials are available for the systems in the network". However, they do not find all vulnerabilities and likewise do not provide a remediation guideline for every security issue. Furthermore, his research findings suggests that the false-positive rate is relatively low, especially when credentials are given to the scanner. Although false-positives increases with a higher remediation- and detection rate.

Stefinko et al. [4] compared several aspects of manual and automated penetration testing. The comparison was primarily realized in a theoretical way. However, some practical examples are given. The authors come to the conclusion that an automated approach can be less time consuming and highly benefits from reproducibility. Although manual methods are still better, automation can lead to a significant improvement, e.g. by using scripts.

IV. Approach

In this section, we describe the overall experimental setup in detail. Before we assessed any results, we finished the three isolated work packages, which were completed by different authors. The work packages are done in the chronologically order as in this section.

A. *Lab environment*

First, a typical and representative lab environment was build for the experiment. Its conceptual architecture is shown in Figure 2.

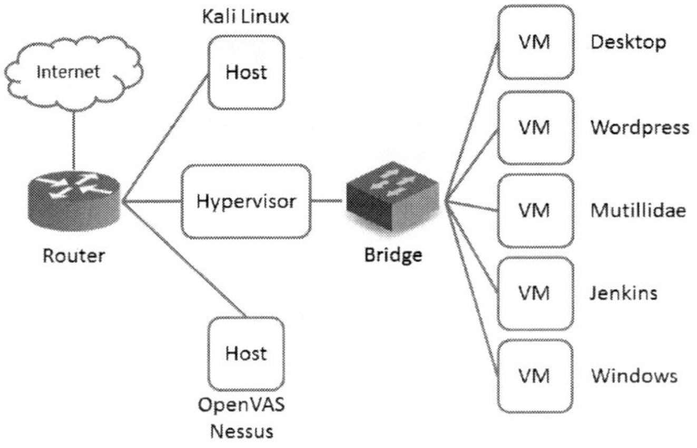

Figure 2. Setup of the Lab Environment.

The lab consists, among others, of two hosts, which main purpose is to perform security analysis. Even in the conceptional architecture of the lab we have already paid attention to the strict separation of the hosts used for penetration testing and automated vuln scans. Therefore, the two techniques are evaluated on independent and isolated hosts. Both hosts have access to the Internet to make research possible on the pentesters side and an easier configuration on the vuln scanners side.

Furthermore we setup one machine as hypervisor, based on VirtualBox. This can be seen as core of the lab running all five guest virtual machines (VM). To ensure none of the virtual machines are able to automatically update themselves, no Internet access is configured to prevent potential auto update mechanisms.

All virtual machines are based on Ubuntu 18.04, except the virtual machine named Desktop, which is running an intendedly outdated version of Ubuntu Linux. One VM is installed with Windows 7. The installed applications are popular and mostly open-source software. They include the automation server Jenkins, the content management system WordPress, the deliberately vulnerable web-application OWASP Mutillidae 2, the web development tool XAMPP and File Transfer Protocol (FTP) services installed on the VM Windows and last but not least a typical linux based desktop computer with lots of outdated components. While Mutillidae is meant to be a vulnerable web application, the other VMs are prepared with either outdated applications, weak credentials or bad misconfiguration. All prepared vulnerabilities are summarized in Table 1. Our selection includes the ten most critical security risks to web applications as postulated in "OWAS Top 10 - 2017" [5]. Additionally, we covered every item on the checklist proposed in the penetration test guideline "Ein Praxis-Leitfaden für IS-Penetrationstests" by the German Federal Office for Information Security (in German Bundesamt für Sicherheit in der Informationstechnik) [6].

The number of detected security issues, which are mentioned in Table 1, will be later considered as criterion for false-negatives. The reason for this is that the amount of false-negatives is potentially uncountable, so we decided to use this scale as an objective measurable criterion. Deeper explanations follows in the result section.

B. *Penetration test of the lab*

The second work package includes comprehensive penetration testing of the lab. It is designed as it would be a genuine pentest in the real world. In order to do this, one of the authors, who has not any knowledge of the lab environment, obtains an Internet Protocol address (IP address) of the bridged network to access the virtual machines. From this point he is permitted to perform pentests on the lab.

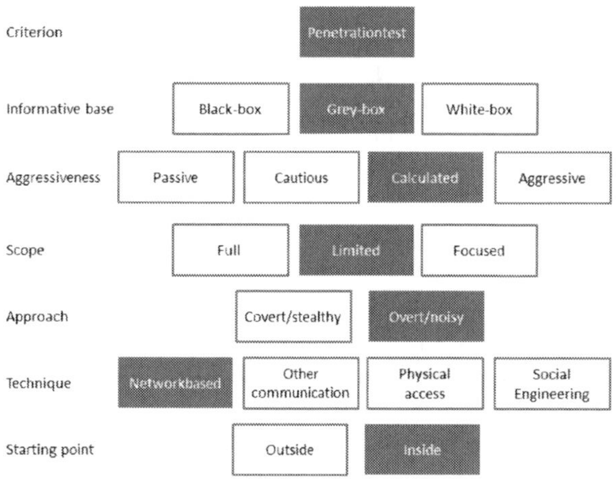

Figure 3. Classification of the penetration test. Criteria based on [7].

Before testing starts, we define the scope of the penetration test. As it is common practice we also clarified underlying conditions. So the penetration tester has permission to test the whole infrastructure for five work days which is the equivalent of 40 hours. Aggressive methods like distributed denial-of-service (DDoS) attacks are forbidden and no value is put to a stealthy approach. Furthermore we let the pentester know that no IPv6 addresses have to be checked, because it is impossible to scan an IPv6 network in an appropriate time. Furthermore we communicated that no User Datagram Protocol (UDP)-based network ports are open, because scanning such ports is very time consuming. Figure 3 illustrates how we would classify the penetration test. To guarantee the highest possible reproducibility the author in the role of the penetration tester strictly followed the methodology proposed by the Federal Office for Information Security (BSI) [7]. By following this guide every penetration tester should find at least the same number of vulnerabilities.

C. *Vulnerability scan of the lab*

Last but not least, we performed the vulnerability scans. In order to do that, we decided to use two popular scanners - one proprietary (Nessus) and one open source tool (OpenVAS). According to the developer Nessus is the most used network assessment tool. It has over 100,000 plugins that contain vulnerability information, a set of remediation actions and algorithms to prove the presence of security issues. OpenVAS is a free software framework of services and tools recommended by the BSI. It offers vulnerability- scanning, assessment and management. It contains over 50,000 Network Vulnerability Tests (NVTs) that are equivalent to the Nessus Plugins.

We performed Address Resolution Protocol (ARP)-, Transmission Control Protocol (TCP)- and Internet Control Message Protocol (ICMP) tests on the default port range of Nessus, that includes 4,790 commonly used ports, including all open ports on our target network. Additionally the following settings were enabled: Probe all ports to find services, perform thorough tests, web applications - and the "enable safe checks" setting was turned off. All available Nessus Plugins were activated.

The OpenVAS default port range includes 4,481 ports and was performed with ICMP-, TCP-ACK Service- & ARP Ping alive tests. The full and very deep scan setting was used, while the Safe Checks" setting was disabled. No UDP ports were scanned, because they are very time consuming and there are no open UDP ports in the test environment as communicated before. Both scanners allow to use credentials for authenticated scans. All virtual machines except of the Mutillidae host were scanned two times, authenticated and unauthenticated.

V. RESULTS

In this section, we want to display our results. We listed the prepared vulnerabilities of the lab and the findings of the pentest and vuln scanners. Furthermore we describe the meaningfulness of the different security analysis methods.

Figure 4 shows the concrete number of findings revealed by the pentest and the vuln scanners. The penetration test includes a total of 73 findings in this work, while we ignored findings with the lowest criticality "Info/Log" in general and also ignored findings by OpenVAS with a quality of detection less than 70%, which is the recommended threshold value. The automated analysis lists 1.5 to 3-times more findings than the manual test. Actually, concluding the automated methods have more findings is a fallacy. The explanation for this is that the pentest report is a sum up of all exploited findings, e.g. it is grouped in categories. The vuln scanners list every single vulnerability, that matches a database entry for the software version or configuration. Those findings can include false-positive errors, which are explained in more detail in Subsection B.

A. Report

The result of every security analysis usually ends up with a structured report. The main part of such a write-up includes the revealed vulnerabilities, their criticality, a proof of concept and recommendations for remedial actions. In this section, we will look at the differences of the reports. A penetration test report includes a comprehensible proof for every listed vulnerability. That could be either a few lines of code, a screenshot or for example a console output, that proofs the existence of a vulnerability, which makes it possible to reproduce the test. OpenVAS and Nessus both have their own way of output format for listed vulnerabilities, denoted as Vulnerability Detection Result (OpenVAS) and Plugin Output (Nessus). The major problem with the outputs of the vuln scanners is, that they are not reproducible, i.e. the output is just a version number of a running service. It is not distinguishable whether the vuln scanners actually exploited the vulnerability or not. Only for web services the scanners reported a comprehensibly and reproducible proof.

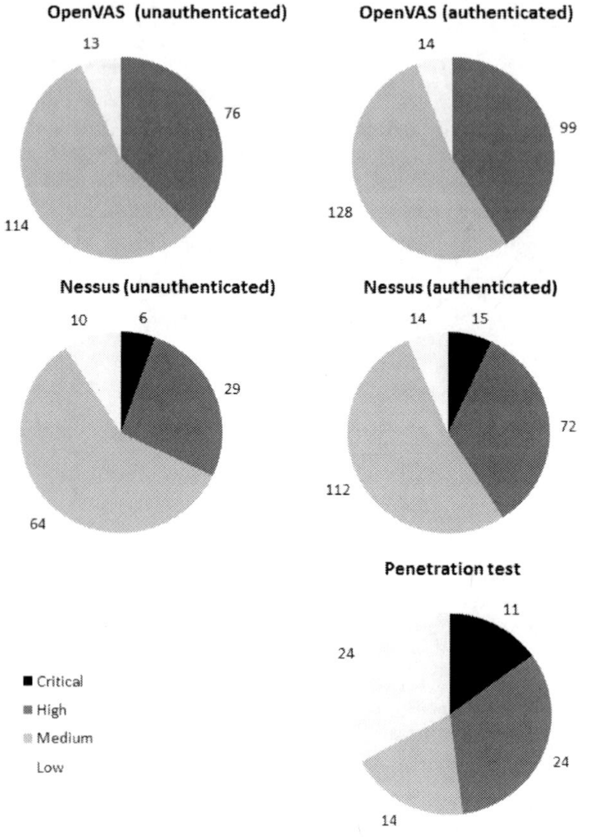

Figure 4. Overall vulnerabilities detected via different methods of security analysis.

A set of vulnerabilities may help the system administrator/network operator to get an overall overview of the tested systems. But it is also important to get recommendations for remedial actions, to fix detected security issues. The manual generated report as well as the automated generated report have recommendations for more than 99% of the findings. Since the pentest report lists a lower number of findings, it also has fewer recommendation treatments. Nevertheless, all the findings of the automated scans are also handled in the manual report.

To get an order for closing weak points, it is recommended to treat the most dangerous vulnerabilities as first. All security analysis evaluate the listings, denoted as criticality. Nessus and our pentest have four evaluation stages between low and critical, meanwhile OpenVAS has three, from low to high. The ISACA Implementation Guideline ISO/IEC 27001:2013 recommends an even number of criticality levels to prevent a more frequently "landing in the middle" for decisions [8].

B. False-positives

As explained in Section II, false-positive errors indicate the presence of given conditions, that are not the case. For vuln scans there are two major kinds of false-positive errors. The first type is a displayed vulnerability that doesn't exist, actually. To classify such errors as true-positives, it is enough to exploit that vulnerability. The inversion in that case doesn't apply. If one cannot exploit that vulnerability it doesn't mean that it's non-existent. Usually it is associated with lots of efforts to check if the reported vulnerabilities are perhaps false alarms. To perform such a classification, you have to examine the affected lines of code to check if an exploiting is impossible, what requires access to the code (White-box testing).

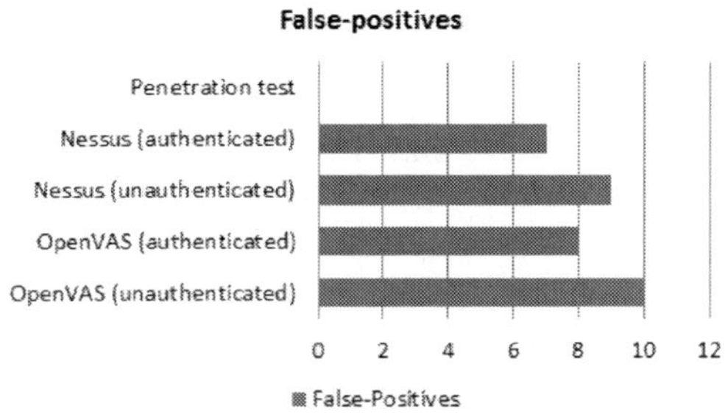

Figure 5. Number of Type II false-positive errors (less is better). Based on the totals findings cf. Figure 4.

The second type, we have identified, is a wrong information about the target systems. For example the report shows misconfiguration of a service, when the configuration is actually fine. To classify such vulnerabilities as true or false positives, you can easily check the affected configuration files. Penetrationtesters usually prove the existence of a security issue and therefore shouldn't be prone to any false positives. In this research, we considered only the second type of false-positive errors, that include incorrect information about the target system. Figure 5 shows the number of false-positives, the scanners have listed. Compared to the total number of findings, false-postive rate in this cases is less than 1%. The authenticated scan has a lower number of false-positives for both scanners, than without providing credentials. The reason is that the vulnerability scanners can access more detailed information. In comparison of other works the false-positive rate is unexpectedly low.

C. Time required

For security analysis the required time is always one major factor to choose between an automated or a manual security assessment. Vulnerability scanners should always have the same scanning time, if utilization factors like network, memory and central processing unit (CPU) are the same. Only the time for setting up varies, depending on the experience of the user. In our case it took approximately 30 minutes for configuring Nessus and approx. 45 minutes for OpenVAS as shown in Figure 6.

Usually, for a penetration test a fixed period of time is scheduled. As in Section II described the penetration test in this case was performed in 40 hours. This time includes preparation, analysis, exploitation and writing the final penetration test report. One huge advantage of the vulnerability scanners is the detection speed and that it provide other useful information about the target systems. Figure 6 shows, that the vuln scanners need only approximately 10% of the time a pentester needs for the full security analysis.

TABLE I. PREPARED VULNERABILITIES.
✓: TRUE-POSITIVES, ✗: FALSE-NEGATIVES

<table>
<tr><th>VM</th><th>Vulnerability</th><th>Criticality</th><th>Nessus</th><th>OpenVAS</th><th>Pentest</th></tr>
<tr><td>Jenkins</td><td>missing authentication for web application</td><td>high</td><td>✓|✓</td><td>✗|✗</td><td>✓</td></tr>
<tr><td>Jenkins</td><td>CMDi-Vulnerability</td><td>high</td><td>✗|✗</td><td>✓|✓</td><td>✓</td></tr>
<tr><td>Jenkins</td><td>file-permission misconfiguration</td><td>critical</td><td>✗|✗</td><td>✗|✗</td><td>✓</td></tr>
<tr><td>Jenkins</td><td>user-permission misconfiguration</td><td>high</td><td>✗|✗</td><td>✗|✗</td><td>✓</td></tr>
<tr><td>Desktop</td><td>outdated linux kernel</td><td>critical</td><td>✓|✓</td><td>✓|✓</td><td>✓</td></tr>
<tr><td>Desktop</td><td>weak user password</td><td>high</td><td>✗|✗</td><td>✗|✗</td><td>✓</td></tr>
<tr><td>Desktop</td><td>weak openSSH configuration</td><td>high</td><td>✗|✗</td><td>✗|✗</td><td>✓</td></tr>
<tr><td>Windows</td><td>outdated XAMPP</td><td>critical</td><td>✗|✗</td><td>✓|✓</td><td>✓</td></tr>
<tr><td>Windows</td><td>vulnerable free-sshd</td><td>critical</td><td>✗|✗</td><td>✗|✗</td><td>✓</td></tr>
<tr><td>Windows</td><td>phpMyAdmin missing authentication</td><td>high</td><td>✓|✓</td><td>✗|✗</td><td>✓</td></tr>
<tr><td>Windows</td><td>FTP-Anonymous user enabled</td><td>medium</td><td>✗|✗</td><td>✓|✓</td><td>✓</td></tr>
<tr><td>Windows</td><td>FTP-unencrypted data transfer</td><td>medium</td><td>✗|✗</td><td>✗|✗</td><td>✓</td></tr>
<tr><td>Wordpress</td><td>XSS vulnerable activity-log Plugin</td><td>high</td><td>✗|✗</td><td>✗|✗</td><td>✓</td></tr>
<tr><td>Wordpress</td><td>CMDi-Vulnerability</td><td>high</td><td>✗|✗</td><td>✗|✗</td><td>✓</td></tr>
<tr><td>Wordpress</td><td>missing HTTP-Only and Secure Flag</td><td>medium</td><td>✗|✗</td><td>✗|✗</td><td>✓</td></tr>
<tr><td>Wordpress</td><td>Wordpress-Admn with weak credentials</td><td>high</td><td>✗|✗</td><td>✗|✗</td><td>✓</td></tr>
<tr><td>Wordpress</td><td>misconfigured ssh private-key</td><td>critical</td><td>✗|✗</td><td>✗|✗</td><td>✓</td></tr>
<tr><td>Wordpress</td><td>sudo commands without password</td><td>critical</td><td>✗|✗</td><td>✗|✗</td><td>✓</td></tr>
<tr><td>Mutillidae</td><td>SQL-Injection/XSS Vulnerabilities</td><td>high</td><td>✓</td><td>✗</td><td>✓</td></tr>
<tr><td>Mutillidae</td><td>CMDi-Vulnerability</td><td>critical</td><td>✓</td><td>✗</td><td>✓</td></tr>
<tr><td>Mutillidae</td><td>missing HTTP-Only and Secure Flag</td><td>medium</td><td>✗</td><td>✗</td><td>✓</td></tr>
<tr><td>Mutillidae</td><td>bypass authentication via authentication token</td><td>high</td><td>✗</td><td>✗</td><td>✓</td></tr>
<tr><td>Mutillidae</td><td>unvalidated redirects and forwards</td><td>medium</td><td>✗</td><td>✗</td><td>✓</td></tr>
<tr><td>Mutillidae</td><td>CSRF-vulnerability</td><td>high</td><td>✓</td><td>✗</td><td>✓</td></tr>
<tr><td>Mutillidae</td><td>Insecure Direct Object References</td><td>medium</td><td>✓</td><td>✓</td><td>✓</td></tr>
<tr><td>General</td><td>missing banner</td><td>low</td><td>✗|✗</td><td>✗|✗</td><td>✓</td></tr>
<tr><td>General</td><td>exploit error routine for information leaks</td><td>medium</td><td>✗|✗</td><td>✗|✗</td><td>✓</td></tr>
<tr><td>General</td><td>no HTTPS</td><td>medium</td><td>✓|✓</td><td>✓|✓</td><td>✓</td></tr>
<tr><td>General</td><td>outdated Software</td><td>low to critical</td><td>✓|✓</td><td>✓|✓</td><td>✓</td></tr>
</table>

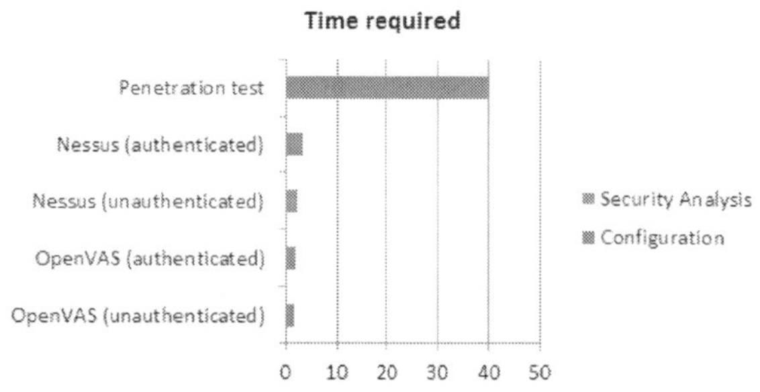

Figure 6. Required time in hours to perform a security analysis.

D. False-negatives

The most important criterion of a security analysis is to reveal vulnerabilities. Therefore every false-negative can lead to a very serious security problem. Nevertheless it is not possible to find all vulnerabilities in a system. To get a measurable rate of false-negative errors, we created the lab with prepared vulnerabilities as listed in Table 1. The table only shows the deliberately implemented vulnerabilities. The list was not completed by found true-positives that was not noted before the tests. The columns of the vulnerability scanners Nessus and OpenVAS are separated in authenticated (left of the pipe) and not authenticated (right of the pipe) results.

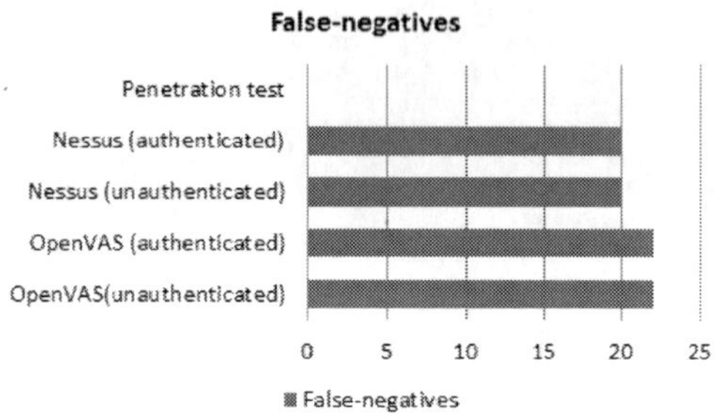

Figure 7. Number of false-negative errors (less is better). Based on the prepared vulnerabilities cf. Table 1.

The author who performed the penetration test found all of those vulnerabilities and had no false-negatives, using the OWASP-Testing guide and the methodology of the Federal Office for Information Security (BSI). Figure 7 shows that Nessus has 20 false-negative errors, that is equivalent to a rate of 69% and OpenVAS 22 erros, that matches 76%. Surprisingly, there is no difference whether the scans were given system credentials or not. The high false-negative shows, that if all vulnerabilities found by the scanners were fixed, the systems would still be prone for security issues.

VI. Conclusion

In general, automated vulnerability scanners detect more security issues than manual penentration testing viewed in a quantitative perspective. However, the results of automated methods significantly lack of quality and have less useful findings. Furthermore, vulnerability scanners do not always prove their concept how a security hole can be exploited. Fortunately, both methods show appropriate remediation recommendation in the reports. When it comes to false-positive errors, we only find a few errors, although we were not able to consider all potential false-positives, as described in the results section and future works. The most important finding of this research is the significant higher false-negative rate of the vulnerability scanners, i.e. many security holes were not detected. It is worth mentioning that automated methods are much faster in performing the security analysis. To sum up, both manual and automated methods can complement each other, but an automated scan cannot replace manual penetration testing these days. A conceivable approach could also be in combining both methods, which can get the best ratio of effort and results.

VII. Future Work

One aspect that would benefit from further research is a better approach to analyze false-positive errors. In our publication we only determined one specific type of this error, although we are fully aware that the false-positive rate is potentially much higher. The problem at this point is that investigation of such errors is not possible in an appropriate time or sometimes completely impossible. If one of the findings is exploitable we have a clear true-positive result, but this doesn't apply vice versa. If a reported security issue is not exploitable this does not prove the presence of a false-positive error. We have found no scientific publication that deals with this potential errors in a smart way.

Acknowledgment

The authors would like to thank the Center for Research in Security and Privacy (CRISP) in Darmstadt for their support and our good friends from the binsec GmbH for sharing best practices in security analysis.

References

[1] PCI Security Standards Council, LLC., "Payment Card Industry (PCI) Data Security Standard, v3.2.1," May 2018.

[2] A. Austin and L. Williams, "One Technique is Not Enough A Comparison of Vulnerability Discovery Techniques," 2011 International Symposium on Empirical Software Engineering and Measurement (ESEM), Sep. 2011, doi: 10.1109/ESEM.2011.18.

[3] H. Holm, "Performance of automated network vulnerability scanning at remediating security issues," Computers & Security, vol. 31, Mar. 2012, pp. 164–175, doi: 10.1016/j.cose.2011.12.014.

[4] Y. Stefinko, A. Piskozub, and R. Banakh, "Manual and automated penetration testing. Benefits and drawbacks. Modern tendency," 2016 13th International Conference on Modern Problems of Radio Engineering, Telecommunications and Computer Science (TCSET), Feb. 2016, doi: 10.1109/TCSET.2016.7452095.

[5] Open Web Application Security Project, "OWASP Top 10 2017," 2017, URL: https://www.owasp.org/images/7/72/OWASP_Top_10-2017_(en).pdf.pdf 2018-06-15.

[6] Federal Office for Information Security (BSI), "Ein Praxis-Leitfaden für IS-Penetrationstests [A guideline for information system penetration tests]," 2016.

[7] Federal Office for Information Security (BSI) , "Study: A Penetration Testing Model," 2003.

[8] ISACA Germany Chapter e.V., "Implementation Guideline ISO/IEC 27001:2013," Apr. 2017, URL: https://www.isaca.de/de/Implementation Guideline ISO/IEC 27001%3A2013 2018-06-16.

A Taxonomy of Attacks via the Speech Interface

Mary K. Bispham, Ioannis Agrafiotis, Michael Goldsmith
Department of Computer Science
University of Oxford, United Kingdom
Email: {mary.bispham, ioannis.agrafiotis, michael.goldsmith}@cs.ox.ac.uk

Abstract—**This paper investigates the security of human-computer interaction via a speech interface. The use of speech interfaces for human-computer interaction is becoming more widespread, particularly in the form of voice-controlled digital assistants. We argue that this development represents new security vulnerabilities which have yet to be comprehensively investigated and addressed. This paper presents a comprehensive review of prior work in this area to date. Based on this review, we propose a high level taxonomy of attacks via the speech interface. Our taxonomy systematises the prior work on the security of voice-controlled digital assistants, and identifies new categories of potential attacks which have yet to be investigated and thus represent a focus for future research.**

Keywords–cyber security; human-computer interaction; voice-controlled digital assistants; speech interface.

I. INTRODUCTION

The introduction of a speech interface represents a potential expansion of a system's attack surface. With regard to voice-controlled digital assistants, there are clearly serious security concerns arising from an increasingly pervasive presence of such agents. Voice-controlled digital assistants are being used to perform an increasing range of tasks, including Web searching and question answering, diary management, sending emails, and posting to social media. Such 'assistants' are intended to act as brokers between users and the vastly complex, often intimidating cyber world. Their functionalities are being expanded from personal to business use [1]. Sarikaya [2] refers to personal digital assistants as a "metalayer of intelligence" between the user and various different services and actions. With the advent of assistants, such as Amazon's Alexa, which can be used to control smart home devices, control of systems via a speech interface has furthermore extended beyond purely virtual environments to include also cyber-physical systems. Pogue [3] describes voice control as a "breakthrough in convenience" for the Internet of Things. Speech interfaces may eventually be used in time-sensitive and even life-critical contexts, such as hospitals, transport and the military [4] [5]. There is some speculation that communication with computers via natural language represents the next major development in computing technology [6].

Notwithstanding its potential benefits, security concerns associated with such a development have yet to be comprehensively addressed. There has been a considerable amount of debate on the threat to privacy from 'listening' devices, highlighted perhaps most dramatically in a recent request for speech data from Amazon's Alexa as a 'witness' in a murder inquiry [7]. By comparison, the security issues associated with voice-controlled assistants have to date received relatively little attention. Such security issues are however significant. A speech interface potentially enables an attacker to gain access to a victim's system without needing to obtain physical or internet access to their device. Thus, the human-like digital personas intended to give users a sense of familiarity and control in interactions with their systems may in reality be exposing users to additional risks. Internet security company AVG pointed out in 2014 the danger of the speech interface being exploited as a new attack surface, demonstrating how smart TVs and voice assistants might respond to synthesised speech commands crafted by an attacker as well as to their users' voices [8]. The reality of this possibility was recently illustrated by a TV advertisement which contained spoken commands for activation of Google Home on listeners' phones for product promotion purposes. The advert was criticised as a potential violation of computer misuse legislation in gaining unauthorised access to listeners' systems [9]. Another example was an instance in which it was shown to be possible to open a house door from the outside by shouting a command to digital assistant Siri (as discussed by Hoy [10]).

This paper provides a review of the research which has been done to date on attacks via the speech interface, and identifies the gaps in this prior work. Based on this review, we propose a new taxonomy of attacks via the speech interface, and make suggestions for further work. The scope of this taxonomy is limited to attacks which gain unauthorised access to a system by sound. It is possible to attack a voice-controlled system other than by sound - in a security analysis of Amazon's Echo, for example, Haack et al. [11] identify three means of attack on such systems. In addition to sound-based attacks, the paper identifies network attacks (e.g., sniffing of speech data in transmission between an individual user's device and a provider's servers) and API-based attacks (which might involve hacking a voice-controlled assistant's API e.g., to change the default wake-up word). However, such attacks not based on sound are not within scope of the taxonomy presented here.

The remainder of the paper is structured as follows. Section II provides general background on human-computer interaction by speech with reference to the current generation of voice-controlled digital assistants. Section III contains a review of prior work relevant to the security of voice-controlled digital assistants as well as some indirectly relevant work in related areas of research. Section IV proposes a new high-level taxonomy of attacks via the speech interface, including attacks which have been demonstrated in prior work as well as attacks which may be possible in the future. Section V concludes the paper and contains some suggestions for future research.

II. BACKGROUND

Speech interfaces which facilitate the execution of particular actions in response to voice commands are referred to as 'task-based' speech dialogue systems, as distinct from 'chatbots', whose purpose is simply to hold a conversation

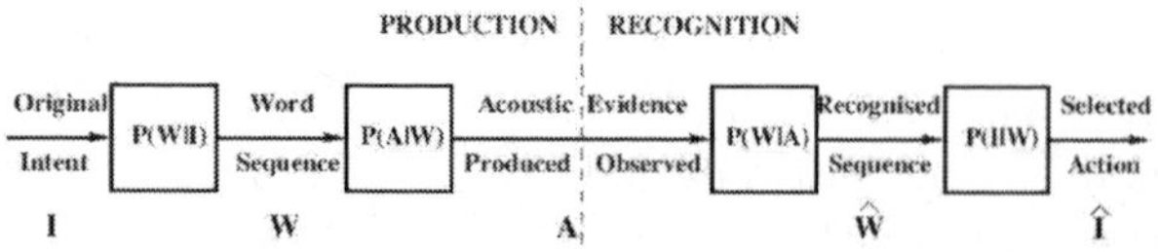

Figure 1. An example of integrated speech and language processing: personal assistance seen as information transmission across a noisy channel [13]

with the user without executing any actions. Current task-based dialogue systems have some similarity with chatbots in that they are often anthropomorphosised, with systems being given the persona of a friendly digital assistant in order to create a sense of communication with a human-like conversation partner. The first voice-controlled digital assistant to be released commercially was Apple's Siri in 2011. Siri was based on an earlier system named Cognitive Assistant that Learns and Organizes (CALO), which had been developed with US defence funding. Siri was followed by the release of Amazon's Alexa in 2014, Microsoft's Cortana in 2015, and most recently in 2016 by Google Assistant [12].

Input to a speech dialogue system is provided by a microphone which captures speech sounds and converts these from analog to digital form. Bellegarda and Monz [13] describe the task of the speech recognition component as the task of extracting from a set of acoustic features the words which generated them, and the task of the natural language understanding component as the task of extracting from a string of words a semantic representation of the user intent behind them. The paper by Bellegarda and Monz conceptualises the process of a user's communication of intent to a speech dialogue system as information transmission across a noisy channel, whereby the user first formulates their intent in words and then vocalises these words as speech, and the dialogue system subsequently extracts from the user's speech the words which generated the speech and then extracts from the words a semantic representation of the intent which generated them. This process is illustrated in the diagram in Figure 1, copied from Bellegarda and Monz's paper.

The typical architecture of a generic speech dialogue system consists of components for speech recognition, natural language understanding, dialogue management, response generation and speech synthesis (see Lison and Meena [14]). The speech recognition and natural language understanding components are the components most likely to be targeted in an attack via the speech interface. Speech recognition is typically performed using Hidden Markov Models (HMMs). HMMs calculate the most likely word sequence for a segment of speech according to Bayes' rule as the product of the likelihood of acoustic features present in the speech segment and the probability of the occurrence of particular words in the sentence context (see for example Juang and Rabiner [15]). HMM-based systems for speech recognition originally used Gaussian Mixture Models (GMMs) for the acoustic modelling and n-grams for the language modelling. In recent years, a shift in modelling methods has been seen with the advent of deep learning. Huang et al. [16] describe recent developments in which Deep Neural Networks (DNNs) have replaced GMMs to extract acoustic model probabilities, and Recurrent Neural Networks (RNNs), a particular type of DNN, have replaced n-grams to extract language model probabilities. Speech recognition technology has become quite advanced. In 2016, Microsoft Research reported that its automatic speech recognition capability had for the first time matched the performance of professional human transcriptionists, achieving a word error rate of 5.9 per cent on the Switchboard dataset of conversational speech produced by the National Institute of Standards and Technology (NIST) in the US (see Xiong et al. [17]).

Natural language understanding in the context of a voice-controlled system is the task of extracting from a user's request a computational representation of its meaning which can be used by the system to trigger an action. The task of mapping a string of words to a representation of their meaning is known as semantic parsing. Liang [18] gives as an example of semantic parsing the instance where a request to cancel a meeting is mapped to a logical form which can be executed by a calendar API. The process of semantic parsing may include syntactic analysis as an intermediate step. Methods of syntactic analysis used in voice-controlled systems include dependency parsing, which is the task of determining syntactic relationships within a sentence, such as verb-object connections (see for example McTear [19]). Current speech dialogue systems typically use semantic representations known as semantic frames (see Sarikaya et al. [20]). Semantic frames provide a structure for representing the meaning of utterances which requires firstly identification of the general domain or concept which a user request relates to (such as travel), secondly determination of the user intent (such as to book a flight), and thirdly slot-filling which involves identifying specific information relevant to the particular request (such as destination city). Sarikaya [2] state that the tasks of domain identification and intent determination in semantic parsing to frames are often performed using support vector machines, whereas slot-fitting is commonly performed using Conditional Random Fields (CRFs). Some recent research has indicated that traditional machine learning methods are now being out-performed in the semantic parsing task for spoken dialogue systems by neural networks, similar to the replacement of n-gram-based systems for language modelling in speech recognition by RNNs. Mesnil et al. [21], for example, present results showing superior performance by RNNs on the slot-filling task for the Air Travel Information System (ATIS) dataset in comparison to the performance of CRFs on the same task. Despite such efforts, it is clear that, unlike in the case of speech recognition, the state-of-the-art in natural language understanding remains far from parity with human capabilities. This is evident in the occasional failure of voice assistants to correctly interpret the meaning of a word in context, despite the correct word or meaning being obvious to any human listener. Stolk et al. [22] give the examples of Apple's assistant Siri mistaking the word 'bank' in the sense of 'river bank' for a financial institution, and of Siri giving directions to a casino when asked about a gambling problem.

Modern voice-controlled digital assistants implement the generic components of speech dialogue systems in the context of a cloud-based service which enables users to interact by voice with smartphones and laptop/desktop computers, as well as to control smart home devices by voice using bespoke hardware. The speech recognition and natural language understanding functionalities of these systems are performed in the

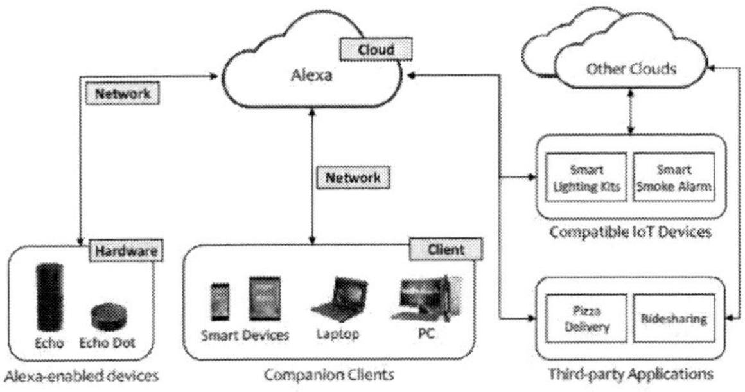

Figure 2. Amazon Alexa Ecosystem [23]

provider's cloud. Chung et al. [23] provide an overview of the typical ecosystem of modern voice-controlled digital assistants in the example of Amazon's Alexa (see Figure 2).

In order to control streaming of audio data to the cloud, current voice-controlled digital assistants include, in addition to the generic speech dialogue system components, an activation component consisting a of wake-up word, which, when spoken by the user, triggers streaming of the subsequent speech audio data to the provider's cloud for processing. Examples of wake-up words include 'Ok Google' for Google Assistant and 'Alexa' for Amazon's Alexa. Wake-up word recognition is the only speech processing capability on users' individual devices, and consists of a short 'buffer' of audio data from the device's environment which is continuously recorded and deleted [24]. Wake-up word activation can be triggered by false positives. Chung et al. [25], for example, refer anecdotally to accidental activation of the Alexa assistant by a sentence containing the phrase 'a Lexus' (see also Michaely et al. [26]), and Vaidya et al. [27] refer to the misrecognition of the phrase "Cocaine Noodles" as "OK Google". False positives in wake-up word recognition may result from misrecognition of a word as the wake-up word, as in the example given by Chung et al., or else from use of a wake-up word in the context of speech not intended to activate a voice assistant, for example the use of the word 'Alexa' as the name of a person in a conversation. Këpuska and Bohouta [28] discuss the latter problem of distinguishing between an 'alerting' and a 'referential' context in wake-up word recognition. It is also possible for voice assistants to be activated by background noise which has frequencies overlapping with those of human speech (see Islam et al. [29]).

The current generation of voice-controlled digital assistants have also introduced platforms for the development of third-party voice applications which can be incorporated in the provider's cloud and made available to users via the assistant's speech interface. Examples of such third-party applications are Alexa Skills and Google Conversation Actions. Third-party applications in systems such as Google Assistant can be accessed by users by asking to 'speak' to the voice app (as named by the developer) [30]. Such apps can be used for example to enable users to access information services or to purchase products.

III. Prior Work

There has been a limited amount of prior work on the security of speech interfaces and voice-controlled digital assistants, as well as some prior work in related areas of research. A review of prior work relevant to attacks via the speech interface of voice-controlled digital assistants is presented, and summarised in Table 1. Whilst the review is concerned with sound-based attacks only, it is recognised that attacks by sound are only a subset of the potential attacks which might be targeted at a voice-controlled digital assistant. The review does not analyse the specific aims of the attacks described in prior work beyond the general goal of gaining unauthorized access to a system via a speech interface.

Several researchers have investigated the ways in which voice-controlled digital assistants might be exploited simply by using standard voice commands. This possibility arises out of the inherently open nature of natural speech. Such potential vulnerabilities associated with speech-controlled systems have been highlighted for example by Dhanjani [31], who describes a security vulnerability identified in Windows Vista which allowed an attacker to delete files on a victim's computer by playing an audio file hosted on a malicious website or sent to the victim as an email attachment. Dhanjani speculates that the potential for such attacks is magnified with the increasing use of speech recognition technology in the Internet of Things. He postulates a hypothetical attack on Amazon's Echo, a device designed to be used for voice control of home appliances via digital assistant 'Alexa', which would potentially cause psychological or physical harm to the victim by controlling their smart home environment. This hypothetical attack involves a piece of malware consisting of JavaScript code which plays an audio file giving a command to Alexa if there has been no user activity on the mouse or keyboard after a certain period of time (thus aiming to play the file at a time when the user may be away from their computer and therefore will not hear the audio command being played). Diao et al. [32] investigate possibilities for gaining unauthorised access to a smartphone via a malicious Android app which uses the smartphone's own speakers to play an audio file containing voice commands. The attacks proposed by the authors include an attack in which the smartphone is manipulated to dial a phone number which connects to a recording device, and then to disclose information such as the victim's calendar schedule by synthesised speech which is recorded by the device. Diao et al. envisage such attacks being executed whilst the victim is asleep and therefore unable to hear the malicious voice command. Such an attack might in fact be executed whilst the victim is neither away from their phone or asleep, but their attention is merely directed elsewhere.

Kasmi and Esteves describe a different type of attack in which voice commands are transmitted silently to a victim's phone via electromagnetic interference using the phone's headphones as an antenna [33]. Unlike plain-speech attacks, this attack is not detectable even if the victim is consciously present at the time of the attack, although for technical reasons the attack can only be performed if the attacker is in close proximity to the victim's device. The types of attack envisaged by Kasmi and Esteves include controlling transmissions from a smartphone by activating or deactivating Wifi, Bluetooth, or airplane mode, and browsing to a malicious website to effect drive-by-download of malware. Young et al. [34] also describe a 'silent' attack on smartphones via the voice command interface which enables an attacker to perform actions such as calling fee-paying phone numbers, posting to Facebook

TABLE I. SUMMARY OF PRIOR WORK RELEVANT TO ATTACKS VIA THE SPEECH INTERFACE

Paper	Attack Target	Attack Category
Dhanjani [31]	speech interface in PC (Windows Vista)	plain speech (overt)
Diao et al. [32]	speech interface in voice-controlled digital assistant (Google Voice Search)	plain speech (overt)
Kasmi and Esteves [33]	voice capture in voice-controlled digital assistant (Google Now, Siri)	silence (covert)
Young et al. [34]	voice capture in voice-controlled digital assistant (Siri)	silence (covert)
Zhang et al. [35]	voice capture in voice-controlled digital assistant (Apple Siri, Amazon Alexa, Microsoft Cortana and others)	silence (covert)
Song and Mittal [36]	voice capture in voice-controlled digital assistant (Google Now, Amazon Alexa)	silence (covert)
Vaidya et al. [27]	speech recognition in voice-controlled digital assistant (Google Now)	noise (covert)
Carlini et al. [37]	speech recognition in voice-controlled digital assistant (Google Now) / speech recognition (CMU Sphinx)	noise (covert)
Iter et al. [38]	speech recognition in speech transcription system (WaveNet)	missense (covert)
Cisse et al. [39]	speech recognition in voice-controlled digital assistant (Google Voice)	missense (covert)
Alzantot et al. [40]	speech recognition in speech transcription system (TensorFlow)	missense (covert)
Carlini and Wagner [41]	speech recognition in speech transcription system (DeepSpeech)	music/missense (covert)
Yuan et al. [42]	speech recognition in speech transcription system (Kaldi)	music (covert)
Papernot et al. [43]	natural language understanding in sentiment analysis system	nonsense (covert)
Liang et al. [44]	natural language understanding in text classification system	missense (covert)
Jia and Liang [45]	natural language understanding in question answering system	missense (covert)

in the victim's name to damage their reputation, accessing email messages, and changing website passwords from the victim's phone. The attack requires a short period of time during which an attacker has unsupervised physical access to the phone in order to to attach a Raspberry Pi-based tool which is recognised by the phone as headphones with a microphone. Zhang et al. [35] and Song and Mittal [36] present methods for injecting voice commands to voice-controlled digital assistants at inaudible frequencies by exploiting non-linearities in the processing of sounds by current microphone technology, which can lead voice-controlled systems to detect a command as having been issued within the human audible frequency range, despite the sound not having been perceptible to humans in reality. Silent attacks such as these target the 'voice capture' stage of voice control, i.e., the process of conversion of speech sounds by the microphone from analog to digital form prior to speech recognition.

There has also been some prior work towards using adversarial machine learning in attacks on voice-controlled digital assistants. The aim of adversarial machine learning is to identify instances in which a machine learning-based system classifies input in a way that a human would regard as erroneous. This is done by some form of systematic exploration of the system's input space with the aim of discovering 'adversarial examples' within that space. Some adversarial machine learning methods involve manipulating inputs based on knowledge of calculations within the classifier (such 'white-box' methods include approaches such as the Fast Gradient Sign Method and the Jacobian-based Saliency Map Approach for altering input to a DNN, as described for example in Goodfellow et al. [46]). Other methods seek to manipulate input on a 'black-box' basis i.e., without knowledge of the inner workings of a target system. McDaniel et al. [47] explain that processes of adversarial machine learning rely on identifying 'adversarial regions' in a classification category which have not been covered by training examples. The exact reasons for the effectiveness of particular adversarial examples are difficult to determine, as the decision-making process in a neural network cannot be precisely reverse-engineered (see for example Castelvecchi [48]). In this sense, whilst some adversarial learning methods require more knowledge of the target network than others, all attacks on DNN-based systems are of necessity 'black-box' attacks, although attacks requiring detailed knowledge of the system's functionality are referred to here as white-box in order to distinguish them from attacks not requiring such detailed knowledge.

Adversarial learning to attack DNN-based systems was first demonstrated in image classification (see for example Szegedy et al. [49]), but has recently also been applied to speech recognition. One example is the work presented by Vaidya et al. [27], who used audio mangling to distort commands issued to precursor to Google Assistant Google Now (this 'mangling' involved reverse MFCC, where MFCC features extracted from a speech sound were used to generate a mangled version of the sound). The mangled commands included commands to open a malicious website, make a phone-call and send a text, in addition to the Google Now wake-up command 'Ok Google'. The work showed that the distorted commands continued to be recognised by the speech recognition system despite being no longer recognisable by humans, who perceived them instead as mere noise. Thus, the distorted commands represented adversarial examples for the target system. The work by Vaidya et al. was expanded by Carlini et al. [37], who also proved the possibility of prompting Google Now to execute mangled commands which had been shown to be unintelligible to humans in an experiment using Amazon Mechanical Turk. The attacks by Vaidya et al. and Carlini et al. on Google Now were 'black-box' attacks i.e., they were constructed without knowledge of the inner workings of the speech recognition system. Carlini et al. additionally conducted a successful 'white-box' attack on Carnegie Mellon University's SPHINX speech recognition system (based on GMMs rather than DNNs), in which 'mangled' adversarial commands were crafted with knowledge of the workings of the system.

Other work on adversarial learning targeting speech recognition includes that by Iter et al. [38], who used two adversarial machine learning methods originally applied in image classification to manipulate a speech recognition system based on Google DeepMind's WaveNet technology to mistranscribe a number of utterances. This included prompting the system to transcribe the utterance "Please call Stella" as "Siri call police". The attacks by Iter et al. are white-box attacks, i.e., they rely on some knowledge of the details of the target neural network. The authors mention the possibility of developing a black-box attack methodology in future work. Similar to Iter et al., Cisse et al. [39] were also able to prompt mistranscription of utterances, including mistranscription by Google Voice in a 'black-box attack', using an adversarial machine learning method called Houdini. Alzantot et al. [40] used a black-box attack method based on a genetic algorithm to engineer misclassification of speech command words, such as 'on', 'off', 'stop' etc, by a machine learning-based speech recognition system. Carlini and Wagner [41] have demonstrated a white-box attack on Mozilla's DNN-based DeepSpeech speech-to-text transcription in which it was shown to be possible to prompt mistranscription of a speech recording as any target phrase, regardless of its similarity to the original phrase, by making perturbations to the original recording which did not affect the original phrase as heard by humans. In contrast to the attacks by Vaidya et al. and Carlini et al., which would be perceived by victims as unexplained noise, attacks based on methods such as those developed by Iter et al., Cisse et al. and Carlini and Wagner would be perceived by victims as ordinary speech and would therefore by more difficult to detect. To date, such work has been limited to speech-to-text transcription i.e., it has not demonstrated mistranscription of voice commands capable of executing an action as yet. In addition to prompting mistranscription of speech, Carlini and Wagner demonstrated the possibility of manipulating music recordings so as to prompt them to be transcribed by DeepSpeech as a given string of words, demonstrating for example that a recording of Verdi's Requiem could be manipulated to be transcribed by DeepSpeech as "Ok Google, browse to evil.com". Yuan et al. [42] similarly demonstrate the possibility of hiding voice commands in music. Unlike the attacks crafted by Carlini and Wagner, the attacks crafted by Yuan et al. are reportedly effective over the air as well as via audio file input, although their attacks are also white-box attacks and are limited to speech-to-text transcription rather than being demonstrated on voice-controlled digital assistants as such.

Adversarial learning has also recently been applied to some areas of natural language understanding, although none of this work has focussed directly on natural language understanding in voice-controlled digital assistants. The generation of adversarial examples in natural language understanding is more complex than the generation of adversarial examples in image or speech recognition. Unlike in the case of continuous data such as image pixels or audio frequency values, adversarial generation of natural language is not a differentiable problem. As word sequences are discrete data, it is not possible to change a word sequence representing an input to a machine learning classifier directly by a numerical value in order to effect a change in output of the classifier. The areas focussed on in prior work include sentiment analysis (see Papernot et al. [43]), text classification (see Liang et al. [44]), and question answering (see Jia and Liang [45]). Papernot et al. [43] use the forward derivative method, a white-box adversarial learning method, to identify word substitutions which can be made in sentences inputted to an RNN-based sentiment analysis system so as to change the 'sentiment' allocated to the sentence. In contrast to adversarial examples in image classification and speech recognition, in which alterations made to the original input are imperceptible to humans, the alterations made to sentences in order to mislead the RNN-based sentiment analysis system targeted in the work by Papernot et al. are easily perceptible to humans as nonsensical, albeit that the attack intent remains hidden. For example, substituting the word 'I' for the word 'excellent' in an otherwise negative review is shown in the paper to lead it to being classified as having positive sentiment, but the altered sentence will appear unnatural to a human. The authors state that this lack of naturalness of adversarial examples in natural language understanding will need to be addressed in future work. By contrast to Papernot et al., Liang et al. [44] demonstrate a linguistically plausible attack on a natural language understanding system. The authors adapt the Fast Gradient Sign Method from adversarial learning in image classification to make human-undetectable alterations to a text passage (by adding, modifying and/or removing words) so as to change the category which is allocated to the passage by a DNN-based text classification system. The attack by Liang et al. is white-box, requiring details of the calculations inside the network. Jia and Liang [45] also demonstrate a linguistically plausible attack in the context of question answering. Their work involves misleading a number of question answering systems by adding apparently inconsequential sentences to text passages from which the systems extract answers to questions. The method works by first choosing a target wrong answer to a given question, and then crafting a sentence containing information leading to this wrong answer which can be inserted into the original passage without noticeably changing its overall import. The attack method proposed by Jia and Liang is a black-box method, not requiring knowledge of the internal details of the target network.

IV. TAXONOMY

Reflecting on the review of prior work above, we propose a high-level taxonomy of categories of attacks via the speech interface. This taxonomy is presented in Figure 3. Table 1 shows the categorization of each of the attacks from prior work in terms of the high-level taxonomy. The taxonomy covers attack types which have been demonstrated in prior work as well as attack types for which potential is implied by related work in other areas. The principle behind the taxonomy is to identify the various categories of non-speech and speech sounds which humans are capable of perceiving, and to group attacks via the speech interface according to these categories, including both attacks which have been demonstrated in prior work as well as attacks which may be possible in the future as implied by prior work in related areas. By applying this principle, the taxonomy fulfils the dual purpose of systematising prior work whilst also identifying new directions for future research. Attacks via the speech interface as categorised under our taxonomy might be targeted at any voice-controlled system, including any voice-controlled digital assistant and any third-party applications accessible through it.

The taxonomy was developed according to established criteria for attack taxonomies, as described for example in Hansman and Hunt [50]. These criteria include the requirement that a taxonomy should be 'complete' i.e., cover all possible attacks within its scope, and unambiguous i.e., it should be possible clearly to allocate every attack to one category within the scope of the taxonomy. In order to meet these criteria, a categorisation principle was chosen for the taxonomy of grouping attacks according to the nature of attacks via the

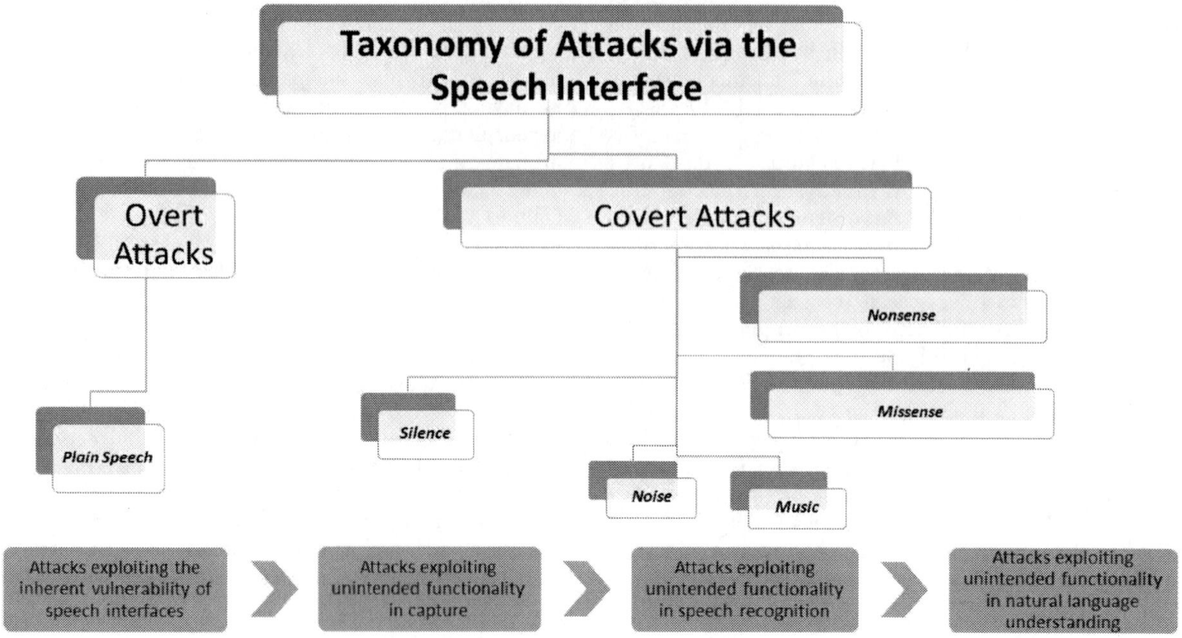

Figure 3. Taxonomy of Attacks via the Speech Interface

speech interface as they might be perceived by a human listener. Within the framework of this categorisation principle, six final categories of attacks via a speech interface were identified, namely attacks consisting of plain speech, silence, music, noise, nonsense, and 'missense', missense being unrelated speech which is misheard or misinterpreted by the target system. These final categories are ordered hierarchically in our taxonomy as detailed below. The principle of categorising attacks according to human perception ensures that the taxonomy is complete, as all attacks via a speech interface can be allocated to one of the six categories. The taxonomy is also unambiguous, in that it is not possible to allocate the same voice attack to more than one of the final categories. To the extent that speech processing by voice-controlled systems mimics human speech processing, the attack categories also reflect vulnerabilities in the different parts of the architecture of voice-controlled systems, as shown at the bottom of Figure 3.

In the taxonomy, the six final categories of voice attacks identified within the categorisation framework are primarily grouped into two categories: 'overt' attacks, which seek to gain unauthorised access to systems using the same voice commands as might be given by a legitimate user and are thus easily detectable by a human, and 'covert' attacks, which seek to gain access using speech commands which have been distorted in some way so as to escape detection by the victim. Another way of characterizing this division is as a distinction between attacks which make illicit use of the intended functionalities of a speech dialogue system, and attacks which exploit unintended functionalities.

Overt attacks exploit an inherent vulnerability in voice-controlled systems which arises from the difficulty of controlling access to a system via the 'speech space'. The plain-speech attacks investigated in prior work, such as that by Dhanjani et al. [31] discussed above, fall into the overt attack category. Covert attacks exploit gaps in the processes of capturing human speech or of translating the captured speech into computer executable actions in a voice-controlled system system. Malicious inputs in covert attacks may include input which consists in human terms of silence, as for example in the attacks demonstrated by Zhang et al. [35], noise, as for example in the attacks demonstrated by Carlini et al. [37], music, as for example in the attacks demonstrated by Yuan et al. [42], missense, as for example in the attacks demonstrated by Carlini and Wagner [41], and nonsense.

Nonsense attacks have yet to be demonstrated with respect to voice-controlled systems directly, although there has been some related work, such as in the attacks on a sentiment analysis system by Papernot et al. [43] by making nonsensical alterations to text. Similar attacks might be demonstrated in the context of voice-controlled digital assistants in future. Prior work on missense attacks in voice-controlled systems has to date been limited to attacks on speech recognition as incorporated in such systems. However, in related work, there have also been examples of missense attacks which target natural language understanding functionality, such the attacks on question answering by Jia and Liang [45] by making apparently inconsequential alterations to text. This suggests that, in the future, missense attacks on voice-controlled systems might target vulnerabilities in natural language understanding as well as in speech recognition. In a missense attack which targets natural language understanding functionality, words might be transcribed correctly by the target system, but their meaning would be misinterpreted. Such missense attacks might seek to exploit the shortcomings of current natural language understanding functionality in voice-controlled digital assistants in terms of being able to identify the correct meaning of words in context.

For missense attacks in the specific context of voice-controlled digital assistants, the need to circumvent the wake-up word activation presents a potential issue of linguistic plausibility. Unlike in the case of attacks hiding commands in silence, noise, or music, it is difficult to incorporate a device's wake-up word as part of an attack based on confusion of meaning. However, due to the known presence of false positives with respect to wake-up word recognition, attacking the activation function of a voice assistant with a missense attack is possible. This possibility was in fact demonstrated in an incident in which an Amazon Alexa device misinterpreted a word spoken in a private conversation as the wake-up word 'Alexa', and subsequently misinterpreted other words in the conversation as commands to send a message to a contact, resulting in a recording of a couple's private conversation in their home being sent to a colleague [51]. Whilst this transmission of private information occurred as a result of error rather than malicious intent, it highlights the potential for missense attacks on voice-controlled systems which include circumvention of the wake-up word.

V. Conclusion

This paper proposes a taxonomy of attacks via the speech interface which covers attacks investigated in prior work as well as attacks which may be possible in the future. The review of prior work in this paper indicates that the potential for attacks via a speech interface has yet to be comprehensively assessed. The scope of attacks via a speech interface can be expected to expand with the increasing sophistication of voice-controlled systems. Consequently, there is a need for further security-focussed research in the area of voice-controlled technology.

Future work should seek more extensively to demonstrate the potential for attacks in the various categories of the proposed taxonomy in the context of different technologies and use-case scenarios. Among the taxonomy categories, nonsense attacks and missense attacks targeting the natural language understanding functionality of voice-controlled systems represent new types of attacks which have yet to be demonstrated in practice, but may become possible in the future. Thus, such attacks should be a special focus of future work. The results of future work should ultimately be used as a basis for the development of more effective defence measures to improve the security of voice-controlled digital assistants and other voice-controlled systems.

Acknowledgment

This work was funded by a doctoral training grant from the Engineering and Physical Sciences Research Council (EPSRC).

References

[1] "Why Amazon's Alexa may soon become your new colleague," 2017, URL: https://www.inc.com/emily-canal/amazon-alexa-for-business.html [accessed: 2018-07-20].

[2] R. Sarikaya, "The technology behind personal digital assistants: An overview of the system architecture and key components," IEEE Signal Processing Magazine, vol. 34, no. 1, 2017, pp. 67–81.

[3] D. Pogue, "At your command," Scientific American, vol. 315, no. 1, 2016, pp. 25–25.

[4] C. Franzese and M. Coyne, "The promise of voice: Connecting drug delivery through voice-activated technology," vol. 2017, 12 2017, pp. 34–37.

[5] "British navy warships 'to use Siri' as technology transforms warfare," 2017, URL: https://www.theguardian.com/uk-news/2017/sep/12/british-navy-warships-to-use-voice-controlled-system-like-siri [accessed: 2018-07-20].

[6] "The Voice-AI Revolution is a Conversational Interface of Everything," 2017, URL: https://medium.com [accessed: 2018-07-20].

[7] "A Murder Case Tests Alexa's Devotion to Your Privacy," 2017, URL: https://www.wired.com/2017/02/murder-case-tests-alexas-devotion-privacy [accessed: 2018-07-20].

[8] "Voice Hackers Will Soon Be Talking Their Way Into Your Technology," 2014, URL: https://www.forbes.com/sites/jasperhamill/2014/09/29/voice-hackers-will-soon-be-talking-their-way-into-your-technology/ [accessed: 2018-07-20].

[9] "Burger King triggers Google Home devices with TV ad," 2017, URL: https://nakedsecurity.sophos.com/2017/04/18/burger-king-triggers-ok-google-devices-with-tv-ad/ [accessed: 2018-07-20].

[10] M. B. Hoy, "Alexa, siri, cortana, and more: An introduction to voice assistants," Medical reference services quarterly, vol. 37, no. 1, 2018, pp. 81–88.

[11] W. Haack, M. Severance, M. Wallace, and J. Wohlwend, "Security analysis of the Amazon Echo," MIT, 2017.

[12] "Google uses Assistant to square up to Siri in AI arms race," 2017, URL: https://www.ft.com/content/f9423056-7efe-11e6-8e50-8ec15fb462f4 [accessed: 2018-07-20].

[13] J. R. Bellegarda and C. Monz, "State of the art in statistical methods for language and speech processing," Computer Speech & Language, vol. 35, 2016, pp. 163–184.

[14] P. Lison and R. Meena, "Spoken dialogue systems: the new frontier in human-computer interaction," XRDS: Crossroads, The ACM Magazine for Students, vol. 21, no. 1, 2014, pp. 46–51.

[15] B.-H. Juang and L. R. Rabiner, "Automatic speech recognition–a brief history of the technology development," Georgia Institute of Technology. Atlanta Rutgers University and the University of California. Santa Barbara, vol. 1, 2005, p. 67.

[16] X. Huang, J. Baker, and R. Reddy, "A historical perspective of speech recognition," Communications of the ACM, vol. 57, no. 1, 2014, pp. 94–103.

[17] W. Xiong et al., "Achieving human parity in conversational speech recognition," arXiv preprint arXiv:1610.05256, 2016.

[18] P. Liang, "Learning executable semantic parsers for natural language understanding," Communications of the ACM, vol. 59, no. 9, 2016, pp. 68–76.

[19] M. McTear, Z. Callejas, and D. Griol, The conversational interface. Springer, 2016.

[20] R. Sarikaya et al., "An overview of end-to-end language understanding and dialog management for personal digital assistants," in IEEE Workshop on Spoken Language Technology, 2016, pp. 391–397.

[21] G. Mesnil et al., "Using recurrent neural networks for slot filling in spoken language understanding," IEEE/ACM Transactions on Audio, Speech and Language Processing (TASLP), vol. 23, no. 3, 2015, pp. 530–539.

[22] A. Stolk, L. Verhagen, and I. Toni, "Conceptual alignment: how brains achieve mutual understanding," Trends in cognitive sciences, vol. 20, no. 3, 2016, pp. 180–191.

[23] H. Chung, J. Park, and S. Lee, "Digital forensic approaches for amazon alexa ecosystem," Digital Investigation, vol. 22, 2017, pp. S15–S25.

[24] "Alexa and Google Home Record What You Say, But What Happens To That Data?" 2016, URL: https://www.wired.com/2016/12/alexa-and-google-record-your-voice/ [accessed: 2018-07-20].

[25] H. Chung, M. Iorga, J. Voas, and S. Lee, "Alexa, can i trust you?" Computer, vol. 50, no. 9, 2017, pp. 100–104.

[26] A. H. Michaely, X. Zhang, G. Simko, C. Parada, and P. Aleksic, "Keyword spotting for google assistant using contextual speech recognition," in Proceedings of ASRU, 2017, pp. 272–278.

[27] T. Vaidya, Y. Zhang, M. Sherr, and C. Shields, "Cocaine noodles: exploiting the gap between human and machine speech recognition," Presented at WOOT, vol. 15, 2015, pp. 10–11.

[28] V. Këpuska and G. Bohouta, "Improving wake-up-word and general speech recognition systems," in Dependable, Autonomic and Secure Computing, 15th Intl Conf on Pervasive Intelligence & Computing, 3rd Intl Conf on Big Data Intelligence and Computing and Cyber Science and Technology Congress (DASC/PiCom/DataCom/CyberSciTech), 2017 IEEE 15th Intl. IEEE, 2017, pp. 318–321.

[29] M. T. Islam, B. Islam, and S. Nirjon, "Soundsifter: Mitigating overhearing of continuous listening devices," in Proceedings of the 15th Annual International Conference on Mobile Systems, Applications, and Services. ACM, 2017, pp. 29–41.

[30] "How to use third-party Actions on Google Home," 2017, URL: https://www.cnet.com/uk/how-to/how-to-use-third-party-actions-on-google-home/ [accessed: 2018-07-20].

[31] N. Dhanjani, Abusing the Internet of Things: Blackouts, Freakouts, and Stakeouts. " O'Reilly Media, Inc.", 2015.

[32] W. Diao, X. Liu, Z. Zhou, and K. Zhang, "Your voice assistant is mine: How to abuse speakers to steal information and control your phone," in Proceedings of the 4th ACM Workshop on Security and Privacy in Smartphones & Mobile Devices. ACM, 2014, pp. 63–74.

[33] C. Kasmi and J. L. Esteves, "Iemi threats for information security: Remote command injection on modern smartphones," IEEE Transactions on Electromagnetic Compatibility, vol. 57, no. 6, 2015, pp. 1752–1755.

[34] P. J. Young, J. H. Jin, S. Woo, and D. H. Lee, "Badvoice: Soundless voice-control replay attack on modern smartphones," in Ubiquitous and Future Networks (ICUFN), 2016 Eighth International Conference on. IEEE, 2016, pp. 882–887.

[35] G. Zhang, C. Yan, X. Ji, T. Zhang, T. Zhang, and W. Xu, "Dolphinattack: Inaudible voice commands," arXiv preprint arXiv:1708.09537, 2017.

[36] L. Song and P. Mittal, "Inaudible voice commands," arXiv preprint arXiv:1708.07238, 2017.

[37] N. Carlini et al., "Hidden voice commands," in 25th USENIX Security Symposium (USENIX Security 16), Austin, TX, 2016.

[38] D. Iter, J. Huang, and M. Jermann, "Generating adversarial examples for speech recognition," Stanford, 2017.

[39] M. Cisse, Y. Adi, N. Neverova, and J. Keshet, "Houdini: Fooling deep structured prediction models," arXiv preprint arXiv:1707.05373, 2017.

[40] M. Alzantot, B. Balaji, and M. Srivastava, "Did you hear that? adversarial examples against automatic speech recognition," arXiv preprint arXiv:1801.00554, 2018.

[41] N. Carlini and D. Wagner, "Audio adversarial examples: Targeted attacks on speech-to-text," arXiv preprint arXiv:1801.01944, 2018.

[42] X. Yuan et al., "Commandersong: A systematic approach for practical adversarial voice recognition," arXiv preprint arXiv:1801.08535, 2018.

[43] N. Papernot, P. McDaniel, A. Swami, and R. Harang, "Crafting adversarial input sequences for recurrent neural networks," in Military Communications Conference, MILCOM 2016-2016 IEEE. IEEE, 2016, pp. 49–54.

[44] B. Liang, H. Li, M. Su, P. Bian, X. Li, and W. Shi, "Deep text classification can be fooled," arXiv preprint arXiv:1704.08006, 2017.

[45] R. Jia and P. Liang, "Adversarial examples for evaluating reading comprehension systems," arXiv preprint arXiv:1707.07328, 2017.

[46] I. Goodfellow, N. Papernot, and P. McDaniel, "cleverhans v0. 1: an adversarial machine learning library," arXiv preprint arXiv:1610.00768, 2016.

[47] P. McDaniel, N. Papernot, and Z. B. Celik, "Machine learning in adversarial settings," IEEE Security & Privacy, vol. 14, no. 3, 2016, pp. 68–72.

[48] D. Castelvecchi, "Can we open the black box of AI?" Nature News, vol. 538, no. 7623, 2016, p. 20.

[49] C. Szegedy et al., "Intriguing properties of neural networks," arXiv preprint arXiv:1312.6199, 2013.

[50] S. Hansman and R. Hunt, "A taxonomy of network and computer attacks," Computers & Security, vol. 24, no. 1, 2005, pp. 31–43.

[51] "Amazon Alexa heard and sent private chat," 2018, URL: https://www.bbc.co.uk/news/technology-44248122 [accessed: 2018-07-20].

Cyber Security Using Bayesian Attack Path Analysis

Remish Leonard Minz, Sanjana Pai Nagarmat, Ramesh Rakesh
Research & Development
Hitachi India Ltd.
Bangalore, India
Email: {remish.minz, sanjana, ramesh.rakesh}@hitachi.co.in

Yoshiaki Isobe
Research & Development
Hitachi Ltd.
Yokohama, Japan
Email: yoshiaki.isobe.en@hitachi.com

***Abstract*—Network security is gaining huge attention in today's world. Attack path analysis provides a comprehensive view of the attack surface for a network infrastructure, thereby assisting decision makers to choose better network protection strategies. Other than several deterministic methods to model the attack graphs, the uncertainty of attacks on the network infrastructure encourages probabilistic modeling which makes the Bayesian network a suitable model to represent the attack graph and to analyze the attack paths. Existing research focuses on representing the network topology into a Bayesian network model and uses a state-of-the-art algorithm to calculate the attack paths. However, practical issues concerning their scalability largely remain unaddressed. In this paper, we provide an efficient modeling mechanism for analyzing the attack paths in the network infrastructure using the Bayesian network. Our approach covers vulnerability identification, collection and mapping, semi-automatic attack graph creation and attack path visualization. In addition to this, we list the bottlenecks in the existing approaches and address some limitations in the existing Bayesian libraries. The details on how we have implemented our approach and conducted the attack path analysis on an enterprise network infrastructure are covered in this paper.**

Keywords–cybersecurity; Bayesian network; attack path analysis; Weka; Py-BBN.

I. INTRODUCTION

Recent cyber-attacks have made headlines due to their enormous impact on business [1]. This has drawn considerable attention to cybersecurity research. Organizations are using considerable resources to protect their network infrastructure. One methodology to protect the network infrastructure is to analyze all the possible paths in a network that an attack can take from an Internet-facing device of the network topology to a target device in the network. This methodology is called the attack path analysis. The representation of the network topology into the graph structure on which analysis is performed is called the *attack graph* [2]. Figure 1 shows an example network topology along with its attack graph. The network topology is shown on the left of the figure and the corresponding attack graph is shown on the right. Vulnerabilities in the devices are represented as nodes *v1*, ..., *v9* in the attack graph. All the paths from the Gateway to any other device in the graph represent attack paths that an attacker can take. Attack paths can be modeled in a deterministic manner to include fine-grain details of the network components as discussed in [2][3]. However, this approach blows up the attack graph making the attack path analysis an NP-Hard problem. In addition to that, the modeling approach misses to include the information about the attackers skill, the device targeted by the attacker, the know-how of the vulnerability used by the attacker to compromise the device. Such an uncertain environment encourages attack path analysis to be modeled in a probabilistic manner rather than a deterministic way. Along with the probabilistic approach, the graph structure of the network infrastructure makes the Bayesian network a suitable tool to model the attack graph and to perform attack path analysis.

Existing research on Bayesian network-based attack path analysis [4] focuses mostly on representation techniques of the network infrastructure. The security conditions of the network and the vulnerabilities in network services are modeled as nodes in the Bayesian network. Vulnerabilities in a device are considered the parent node of the security conditions node. These vulnerabilities are identified either by deploying agents in the network devices or by scanning the open ports of devices on which applications are executed. State of the art Junction Tree algorithm is used in [5] for attack path analysis. The network infrastructure used for attack path analysis in this reference is a synthetic example.

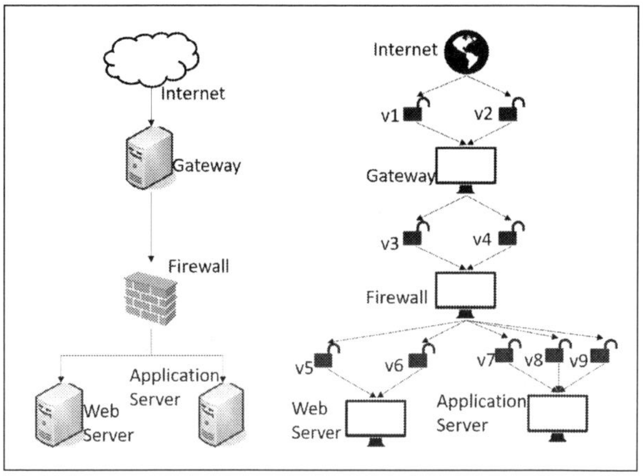

Figure 1. Network topology and attack path

Literature formalizes the modeling of the attack path using Bayesian semantics. However, some design and implementation issues concerning network scalability remain unaddressed. These include implementation concerns of modeling the attack path, assuming the existence of vulnerabilities in the attack graph, visualization as well as a need to qualitatively or quantitatively measure the usefulness of the attack path to the industry. The existing attack paths considered in the literature are fine-grained causing the attack graph to eventually increase in size. Moreover, the existing attack path analysis is done on an example network topology, thus restricting the scale of the network considered.

The remaining part of this paper is organized as follows. Section II discusses the related work in the attack path analysis. Section III describes the details of the technical background which covers the attack path analysis, Bayesian modeling of the attack graph, vulnerability identification, and Bayesian attack path calculation. Section IV describes our approach of Bayesian graph modeling, vulnerability collection, Bayesian attack path calculation and visualization of the attack paths. Section V shows the evaluation of our approach. Section VI describes the conclusion of our approach and we end this paper by acknowledging our collaborating organizations.

II. Related Work

Early work on attack graph modeling can be found in [2][3]. They address the problem of early practice of manual attack graph generation by the Red Teams. Sheyner et al. [2] claim that automating generation of attack graph is exhaustive and succinct. Exhaustive means that the attack graph represents all possible attacks and succinct means that the attack path contains only those state which lies in the actual path of the attacker's goal. The network is modeled in a finite state machine and a model checker tool is used to automatically generate all the possible attack paths. The approach taken in it is symbolic model checking. A similar but scalable approach is taken by Ammann et al. [3]. In this approach again, model checking is used to automatically generate all the possible attack paths. They introduce an assumption on the attacker's behavior. The assumption states that the privilege of the attacker is monotonic in the target network as the attack progresses. This makes the modeling and analysis of attack path less complex. However, model checking approaches suffer from blow up of attack path and do not scale. Recent work in [4][5] uses a probabilistic approach. Both agree that inherent nondeterminism encourages the Bayesian network to be an ideal fit for modeling attack graphs. Frigault et al. [4] focus on modeling a static network infrastructure into a Bayesian network. They have come up with methodologies to model the vulnerabilities in the Bayesian network and ways to handle cycles in it. Further, they also discuss the scenario where the network infrastructure is dynamic. Munoz-Gonzalez et al. [5] discuss various exact inference techniques in the Bayesian network. They talk about, the Variable Elimination technique, Belief Propagation technique, and the Junction Tree technique. Here also, they discuss both static and dynamic network infrastructures. Vulnerability collection is another area of research where [6] evaluates several vulnerability scanning tools and shows that there is a lot of scope to improve the accuracy of the detection of vulnerabilities in both agent-based detection and port scan. A semi-automated way is tried by [7] to address this problem.

III. Technical Details

A. Attack path analysis

An attack path is a trail of vulnerabilities and devices formed from a sequence of attacks an attacker needs to perform on a given network topology, to explore and reach a target device. In the case of the network topology shown in Figure 1, if the attacker intends to target the application server, first, he needs to compromise the Gateway, as it is the only device in the network which can be accessed from the Internet. The attacker does this by exploring the presence of vulnerabilities *v1* and *v2* and exploiting any one of them to get into Gateway. Once the attacker has gained access to the Gateway, he needs to explore the next level of reachable devices in this network and find a way to gain access on those devices. In this example, it is the Firewall. In a similar fashion, the attacker moves step by step to reach the target device. At each step, the attacker needs to know the set of reachable devices in the next level. Once he gains access on a device, he runs a scan to list the reachable devices. After gaining the information of the reachable devices, the attacker finds the vulnerabilities in those devices. One of these vulnerabilities is exploited to gain access to one of the next reachable devices. Referring to the attack graph in Figure 1, an attacker having access to the Gateway can attack the Firewall by exploiting either of the two vulnerabilities *v3* or *v4*. Thus, an example of an attack path will be [Attacker] $\rightarrow$ *v2* $\rightarrow$ [Gateway Server] $\rightarrow$ *v3* $\rightarrow$ [Firewall] $\rightarrow$ *v8* $\rightarrow$ [Application Server].

To protect the network infrastructure, a security operator needs to identify the vulnerabilities present in it. Once the vulnerabilities are identified, the list of vulnerabilities has to be mapped on the services and devices in the network. This comprehensive view also termed the *attack graph* [2][3] helps the operator understand the possible attack paths in the network. The *attack graph* is a standard way to express all the possible attacks from one external facing device in the network to the other potential target devices in the network. However, since information on aspects, such as the expertise of the attacker, vulnerability being exploited by the attacker to gain access to the next device, objective or target device of the attacker, etc. is unknown, a probabilistic approach to modeling the attack graph seems appropriate. Frigault et al. [4] and Munoz-Gonzalez et al. [5], apply the Bayesian network to model the attack graph and analyze the attack paths.

B. Modeling network topology to Bayesian graph

The Bayesian belief network is a probabilistic graphical model that represents a set of variables and their conditional dependencies via a Directed Acyclic Graph (DAG). The network components and the vulnerabilities are modeled as nodes while the edges represent how they are related to each other. Each node in the graph defines a causal relationship of itself with its parents. The step by step attack scenario shows how vulnerabilities have a causal relation among themselves. This makes the Bayesian network a suitable choice for analyzing the attack path. The causal relationship between a node and its parents is encoded in the conditional probability table. Frigault et al. [4] and Munoz-Gonzalez et al. [5], model Bayesian network by considering the attack graph like the one shown in Figure 1. They consider security conditions, where the conditional probability table is constructed using the vulnerability scores provided by the National Vulnerability Database (NVD) [8]. However, instead of devices in the attack graph, there are security conditions. The scores used in modeling the conditional probability table for the security conditions are set to 1.

The semantics of the Bayesian model conveys that, for a vulnerability node to get exploited, all its parent's security conditions must be true. Additionally, for a security condition to be true, any one of its parent vulnerability should be true.

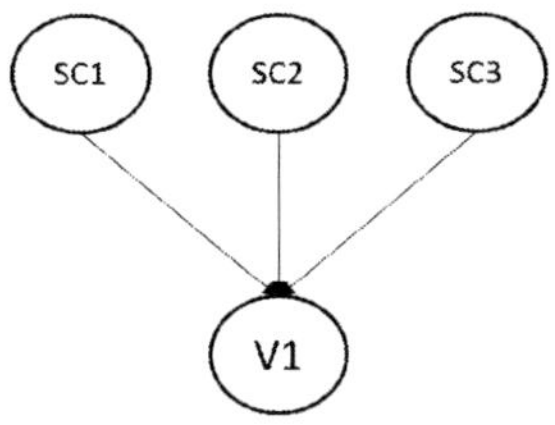

SC1	SC2	SC3	$V1^0$	$V1^1$
0	0	0	1	0
0	0	1	1	0
0	1	0	1	0
0	1	1	1	0
1	0	0	1	0
1	0	1	1	0
1	1	0	1	0
1	1	1	.27	.73

Figure 2. Conditional Probability Table: Conjunction

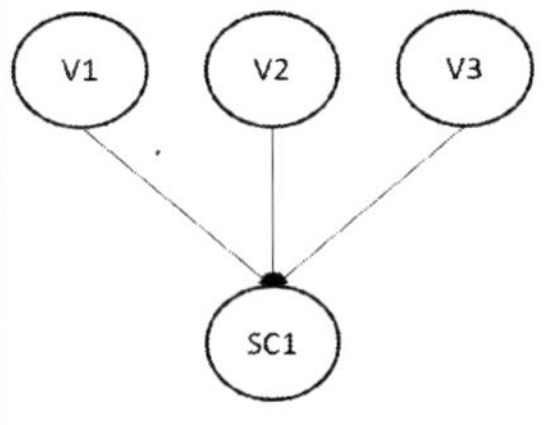

V1	V2	V3	$SC1^0$	$SC1^1$
0	0	0	1	0
0	0	1	0	1
0	1	0	0	1
0	1	1	0	1
1	0	0	0	1
1	0	1	0	1
1	1	0	0	1
1	1	1	0	1

Figure 3. Conditional Probability Table: Disjunction

They call these two semantics as conjunction and disjunction. Figure 2 and Figure 3 show the conjunctive and the disjunctive causal relation between a node and its parents respectively. The disjunctive causal relation is shown for a security condition SC1 and the conjunctive causal relation is shown for a vulnerability V1. The conditional probability of the vulnerability V1 is 0.73. Each row in the conditional probability table shows the probability of the node being true given its parents. As an example, the second row in the table shown in Figure 2 shows variables SC1, SC2, and SC3 are assigned values 0, 0 and 1 respectively. Based on this assignment of the random variables SC1, SC2 and SC3, the probability of child variable V1=0, denoted by $V1^0$ is 1 and the probability of V1=1 denoted by $V1^1$ is 0. Being conjunction causal relation the exploitability score of 0.73 is used only in the case when all three variables SC1, SC2, and SC3 are assigned values 1, 1 and 1. In all other cases, the probability of V1 getting attacked is zero. Similarly, this probability distribution is called the prior probability which represents just the child-parent relationship. However, we need to know how an arbitrary target node is related to the root node in the attack graph. It shows how difficult it is to exploit the target node given that the root node is already compromised. Calculation of marginal probability does the same. Given an observation that a node (observed node) in the network is already compromised, we get the probability of the node (target node) getting exploited in the path from the observed node to the target node. This probability distribution of each node is called posterior probability.

C. Vulnerability Information

Assuming we have a list of vulnerabilities, we create a mapping between the vulnerabilities and services running in the network that contain these vulnerabilities. Vulnerabilities are found by matching the names of the software applications installed in the network devices against a list of vulnerable software in the NVD. This database of vulnerabilities is crowdsourced and maintained by the National Institute of Standards and Technology (NIST). Each reported vulnerability is examined by a team of experts and added to the database with relevant details. The details include an ID for the vulnerability, Description, Vulnerability Score, References, Technical details, Common Weakness Enumeration (CWE) and Common Platform Enumeration (CPE). An example of a vulnerability ID is CVE-2017-1300. Here CVE stands for Common Vulnerability Enumeration. CPE contains a machine-readable format of the reported vulnerable software application. This machine-readable format is called Well-Formed CPE Name (WFN). A CPE entry consists of colon separated values. An example CPE representing Microsoft Internet Explorer 8.0.6001 Beta is wfn[part="a", vendor="microsoft", product="internet_explorer", version=8.0.6001, update=beta]. The Unique Resource Identifier (URI) for the above WFN is cpe:/a:microsoft:internet_explorer:8.0.6001:beta. The names of the services or the software application executing in the network devices need to be matched with the product attribute of WFN.

D. Bayesian network based attack path analysis

There are several algorithms to calculate the posterior probability $p(X_i = x)$ from an attack graph having conditional probabilities for each node. Where X_i is a random variable in the Bayesian network. Belief Propagation and Variable Elimination are the algorithms used for calculating posterior probability for a target node. If X is the set of all random variables in the Bayesian network, $|X| = n$ and $Y = X - X_i$ then posterior probability $p(X_i = x)$ is given by,

$$p(X_i = x) = \sum_{Y} p(Y) = \sum_{Y} \prod_{k=1}^{n} p(X_k \mid X_{k_p})$$

where X_{k_p} is the parent nodes of node X_k. Calculation of posterior probability is an NP-Hard problem. Both Belief Propagation and Variable Elimination provide posterior probabilities for one target security condition. However, these two methods have to be executed for each target device to get all the possible attack paths. On the other hand, the Junction Tree algorithm provides a posterior probability for each target device. The Junction Tree algorithm is a method used in machine learning to extract marginalization in general graphs. It performs Belief Propagation (A message-passing algorithm for performing inference on graphical models, such as Bayesian networks. It calculates the marginal distribution for each unobserved node, conditional on any observed node) on a modified graph called the Junction Tree (In machine learning, tree decompositions are called Junction Trees, Clique Trees, or Join Trees). The steps performed by the Junction Tree algorithm on an attack graph with conditional probability tables for each node are as follows.

1) Graph Moralization
2) Introduction of Evidence
3) Graph Triangulation
4) Junction Tree Creation
5) Belief Propagation

The underlying functionality of this algorithm is summarized in the below steps:

1) Graph Moralization: If the graph is directed, then moralize it to make it undirected. A moral graph is used to find the equivalent undirected form of a DAG. An example is shown in the figure below. The moralized counterpart of a DAG is formed by adding edges between all the pairs of nodes that have a common child followed by making all edges in the graph undirected. An example of Graph Moralization is shown in Figure 4.

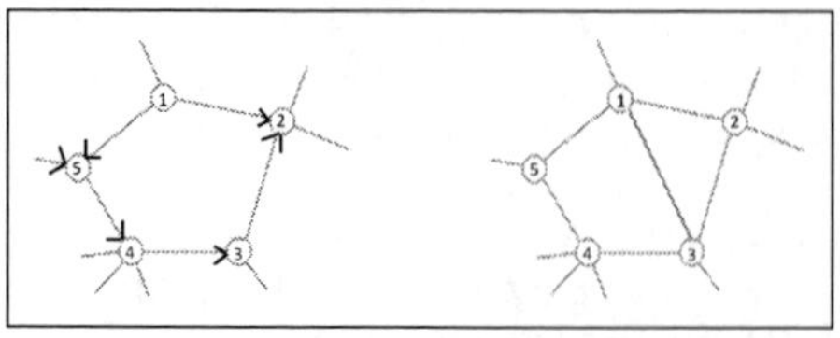

Figure 4. Graph Moralization

In the above graph, we convert the directed edges to undirected edges. Further, node 1 and 3 have a common child, node 2. Thus, in the equivalent moralized graph we introduce an undirected edge between the two parents node 1 and 3.

2) Introduction of Evidence: The second step is setting variables to their observed value. This shows the current event which has occurred. The posterior probability is conditioned on this observed random variable. These variables are also said to be clamped to their value. In case of attack path analysis, the root node of the graph is set as evidence.

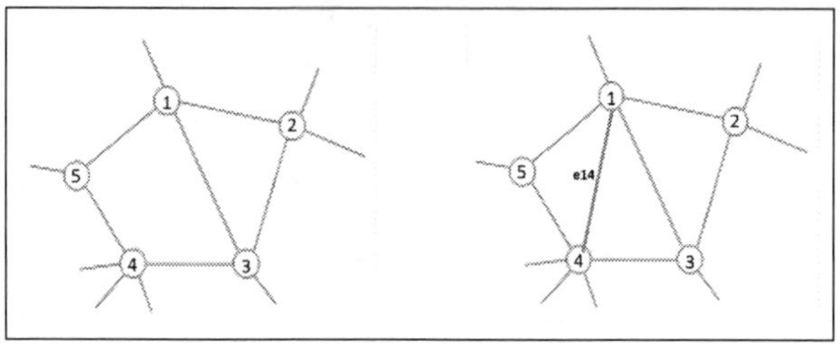

Figure 5. Graph Triangulation

3) Graph Triangulation: Triangulate the graph to make it chordal. The third step is to ensure that the graphs are made chordal if they aren't already chordal. A chordal graph is one in which all the cycles of four or more vertices have a chord, which is an edge that is not a part of the cycle instead connects two vertices of the cycle (A graph in which a cycle of length 4 and above must not exist) An example for graph triangulation is shown in Figure 5.

This graph can be triangulated in many ways. This will result in adding more edges to the initial graph, in such a way that the output will be a chordal graph. Edge (e14) is introduced such that the cycles of 4 or more vertices in the graph have a chord. Here, the cycle is formed by the node set {1, 3, 4, 5}.

4) Junction Tree Creation: Construct a Junction tree from the triangulated graph. The next step is to construct the Junction tree. To do so, we use the graph from the previous step and form its corresponding clique graph. Cliques are a subset of vertices of an undirected graph such that every two distinct vertices are adjacent and its induced subgraph is complete. An example of cliques in a triangulated graph is shown in Figure 6.

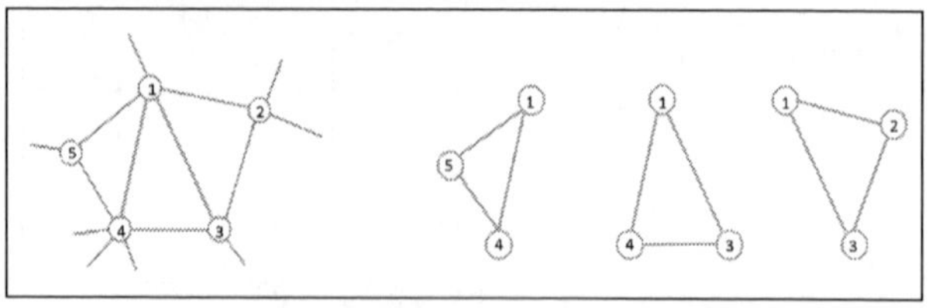

Figure 6. Cliques of Triangulated Graph

In this graph, there are three cliques {1,4,5}, {1,3,4} and {1,2,3}. Additionally, separator sets are sets of common nodes between the adjacent cliques. The total number of separator sets for a graph with n vertices is (n - 1). Therefore, in this case with 3 cliques, there are 2 separator sets {1,4} and {1,3} as shown in Figure 7.

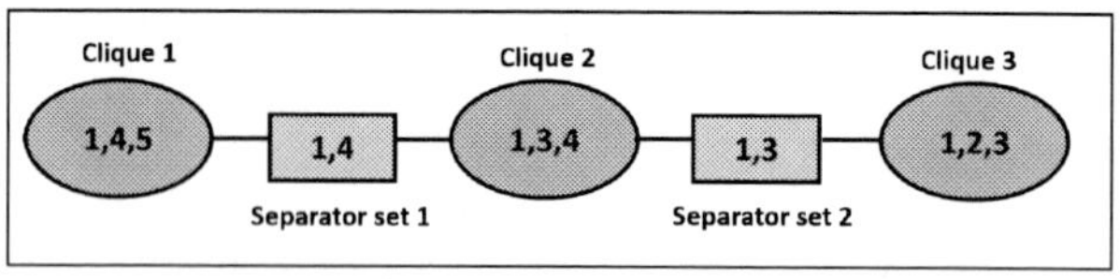

Figure 7. Junction Tree

5) Belief Propagation: Propagate the probabilities along the Junction tree using Belief Propagation algorithm, conditioned on all observed nodes. Marginal Probability for each unobserved node in the Junction Tree is calculated.

Junction Tree algorithm is used in [5] to calculate posterior probabilities which are further used for attack path analysis.

IV. Approach

A. *Modeling Network topology to Bayesian graph*

We performed attack path analysis and identified that the purpose of the analysis is to help an organization take an efficient approach to safeguard their network topology. This boils down to installing patches for the vulnerable software application or services in the right order. To fulfil this requirement, modeling the network devices as attack graph nodes is sufficient, compared to modeling the network services as attack graph nodes. This is because during the patching process, an entire device is patched at a time, mitigating all detected vulnerabilities in that device. This coarse-grained model provides an efficient and concise representation of the network topology. Therefore, to model the Bayesian attack graph from the given network topology, we first draw the network topology and make all the vulnerabilities in a device its parents. This is shown in the attack graph in Figure 1. The conditional probability tables for both vulnerabilities and devices are disjunctive. This is shown in Figure 8 and Figure 9. In the next subsection, we provide a semi-automatic method for the attack graph creation by manually specifying the topology and automatically collecting vulnerabilities.

In Figure 8, as Firewall is the only parent of the vulnerability V5, the conditional probability table of V5 will have two rows. One parent can take only two possible values, 0 or 1 corresponding to each row in the table. As shown in Figure 9, conditional probability table of the Web server has four rows due to two parents V5 and V6.

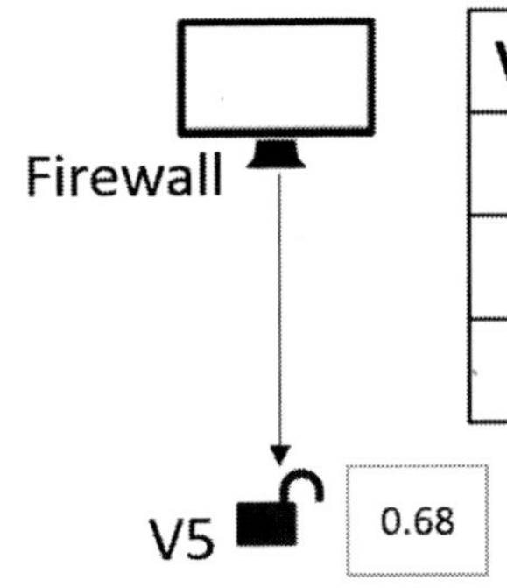

Vulnerability(V5)		
FW	$V5^1$	$V5^0$
1	0.68	0.32
0	0	1

Figure 8. Conditional Probability Table: Vulnerability

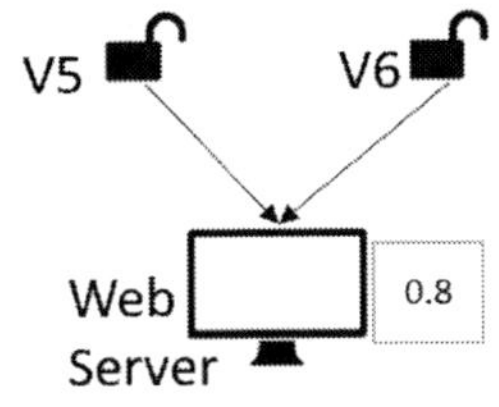

Web Server(ws)			
V5	V6	ws^1	ws^0
1	1	0.8	0.2
1	0	0.8	0.2
0	1	0.8	0.2
0	0	0	1

Figure 9. Conditional Probability Table: Device

B. Vulnerability Collection

Attack path analysis requires topology information and vulnerability information. Figure 1 shows a simple network topology containing a Gateway server connected to the Internet and a Firewall attached to two servers below it. Once we have the topology information, we need to identify the vulnerability information for each device in the network. In this example, we collect software information for Gateway server, Firewall, Web server and Application server. This can be collected automatically, either by agent-based scripts or through port scans. In case of agent-based scripts, a script is executed on a privileged mode on each of the devices. This script collects names of all the software installed in the corresponding devices. It is an exhaustive list of installed software in the device. Once the list of the software is known, vulnerabilities associated with this software list are identified automatically. Since this approach provides an exhaustive list of software, the number of vulnerabilities identified is more.

Agent-based scripts will work only in a network where the operator has privileged access to each device. In the case of a port scan, a network scanning tool is used to scan the ports of each device. This scan provides information on all the open ports and applications running on them. This method only lists the applications currently being executing on an open port. Unlike the former method, this method does not perform an exhaustive check. However, it provides sufficient information of the applications which can be accessed externally. Compared to the agent-based approach, this approach is faster, as it only needs a network command to scan a list of IPs. The list of software names from each of the devices in the topology is automatically matched against a list of vulnerable software application reported in NVD in CPE format.

There is a standardization issue with the naming convention of the software applications. This is a challenge in automating vulnerability detection, as the product name in the CPE does not match with the names of the installed application. For example, in case of Internet Explorer, the application name in Windows registry is 'Internet Explorer'. However, there are two different entries for the same application (Internet Explorer) in the CPE dictionary. These are cpe:2.3:a:microsoft:internet_explorer:11:-:*:*:*:*:*:* and cpe:2.3:a:microsoft:ie:5.5:*:*:*:*:*:*:*. with product name 'internet_explorer' and 'ie' respectively. In this case, the application name does not match with any of the product names. A semi-automated approach is provided in [7]. On the other hand, we use vulnerability scanning software, Nessus [9] to address the challenge. Nessus reports vulnerabilities associated with the applications existing in the devices. Figure 1 shows the detected vulnerabilities in the example topology.

C. Bayesian attack path analysis

We use Weka's [10] implementation of the Junction Tree algorithm to automatically calculate the posterior probabilities of the nodes for attack path analysis. Weka is a generic suite of machine learning software based on JAVA. It provides Application Programming Interface (API) to model and query a Bayesian network. The methods addNode() and addArc() of the EditableBayesNet Class are used to add nodes and edges of the Bayesian network respectively. The prior probabilities in the conditional probability table are set using setDistribution() method of EditableBayesNet Class and the marginal probabilities are retrieved using calcMargin() method of MarginCalculator Class.

We have executed our approach on enterprise networks. A simpler scaled down network is modeled and discussed here. The topology of this simple network consists of one Firewall, four switches and four servers as shown in Figure 10.

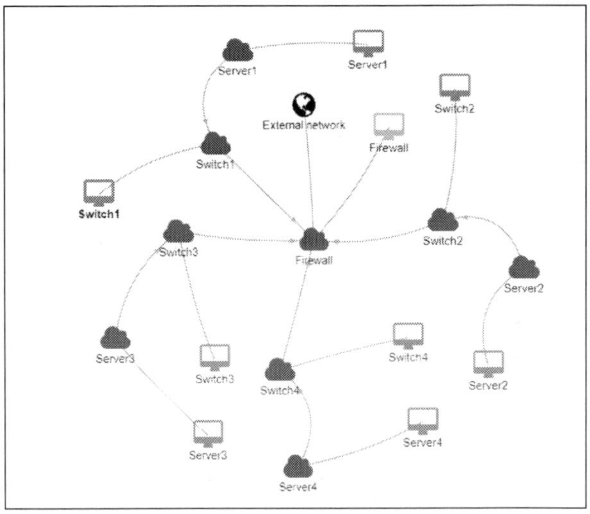

Figure 10. Topology of a sample enterprise network

The attack graph for the modeled network is shown in Figure 11. In this graph, the attack paths are created based on the existence of vulnerabilities in the devices. In the attack graph, there is no path leading to Server1 due to the absence of vulnerabilities in it. However, there are attack paths to other remaining servers.

In this example, in order to protect Server2 from external attacks, a security manager can analyze the attack path and then decide to mitigate the vulnerability in switch2. This will break the attack path from the external facing Firewall device. A security manager can further plan to patch the two vulnerabilities associated with Server2 during off-peak hours of the business. The vulnerabilities in the devices show either the Plugin ID of the vulnerabilities from the Nessus Database or the CVE ID from NVD.

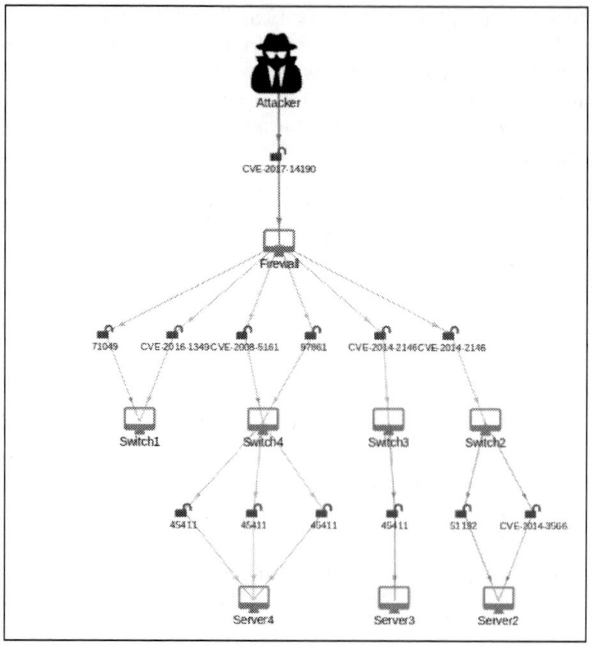

Figure 11. Extended attack graph

During the modeling of the attack path with a larger number of nodes, we identified some issues in Weka. Particularly in our case, when the number of vulnerabilities in the devices was greater than 600, Weka failed to provide appropriate output due to the underflow issue in the JAVA implementation. An underflow situation occurs due to the multiplication of a large number of probability values of the order of 10^{-4}. Particularly, this situation arises when in one level of the attack graph, any device has a large number of child nodes or vulnerabilities. This device along with its child nodes form one wide clique during marginalization. In the Junction Tree algorithm, the prior probability of each node in the clique is multiplied. This led to the generation of Not a Number (NAN) exception in JAVA. We addressed this underflow issue in Weka using a standard approach. Since the change was made in the Weka library, no larger datatype was adopted, neither the formula was converted to the logarithm, due to associated side effects. Rather, the variable collecting the product of a large number of probability values was initialized with a large value in the order of 10^{300}.

Weka holds a General Public License (GPL) license, which restricts the redistribution of the software without making it opensource. We addressed this restriction by replacing Weka with an alternate library, Py-BBN [11]. Py-BBN is an open-source Python implementation of the Junction Tree algorithm, whose implementation is similar to that of Weka. However, during the integration of our application with Py-BBN, we identified some issues in the generated attack path. Py-BBN failed to generate the output in some cases while in few others, it missed to include the leaf nodes or the terminal nodes in the generated attack graph.

On debugging the Py-BBN library, we identified the cause for the above issues and fixed the glitches in the underlying code. Reporting these identified issues along with their fixes in Weka and Py-BBN community for further improvement of the libraries are under progress.

D. *Visualization*

Maximum benefit from an attack path analysis can be achieved if a security manager can visualize the attack path and make appropriate decisions for securing the network topology. Thus, visualization plays an important role in the attack graph modeling and attack path analysis. We show our attack path in an Angular JS [12] based application, where the library used for rendering the attack graph is Vis.js [13]. Figure 10 and Figure 11 show the topology and the extended attack graph for the sample enterprise network respectively. However, the extended attack graph shown in Figure 11 becomes highly cluttered if the number of devices and the vulnerabilities associated with them is large. Due to the scaling issue associated with Vis.js, the browser times out on rendering attack graphs having nodes beyond 1500. To overcome the cluttered representation, we came up with a consolidated view of the attack graph as shown in Figure 12. Both the attack graphs show the same attack paths. However, all the vulnerabilities of a device are grouped into three categories in the consolidated view. These categories represented by red, yellow and grey colored vulnerability icons indicate high, medium and low severities respectively. Each vulnerability icon now shows the count of vulnerabilities along with the sum (cost) of the marginal probabilities of the vulnerabilities in that category.

V. EVALUATION

Despite several benefits of modeling the network topology in a Bayesian network with either Weka or Py-BBN, there are a few challenges that remain unaddressed. Effective modeling of the network devices can only help in analyzing moderately sized networks. However, larger networks still cannot be analyzed with libraries like Weka and Py-BBN. Figure 13 shows how the average execution time changes with the number of nodes in the attack graph. The average execution time roughly grows in a linear manner with the number of nodes in the graph. We do not include the edges in the evaluation as the number of edges depends on the total number of vulnerabilities in the attack graph. Precisely, the number of edges is twice the number of vulnerabilities in the attack graph. As the number of vulnerabilities in each device is random, calculating the distribution is beyond the scope of this work. Further, we assume the graph to be sparse. Vis.js, on the other hand, has its own limitations in rendering graphs. Evaluation of its performance is shown in Figure 14. When the number of nodes reaches close to 500, the time taken to render the attack graph is approximately 50 seconds. Standard browsers like Mozilla and Chrome timeout after 28 seconds of execution.

VI. CONCLUSION

In this work, we modeled each device of the network infrastructure as a node in the attack graph for analysing the overall security of the network. On the other hand, existing

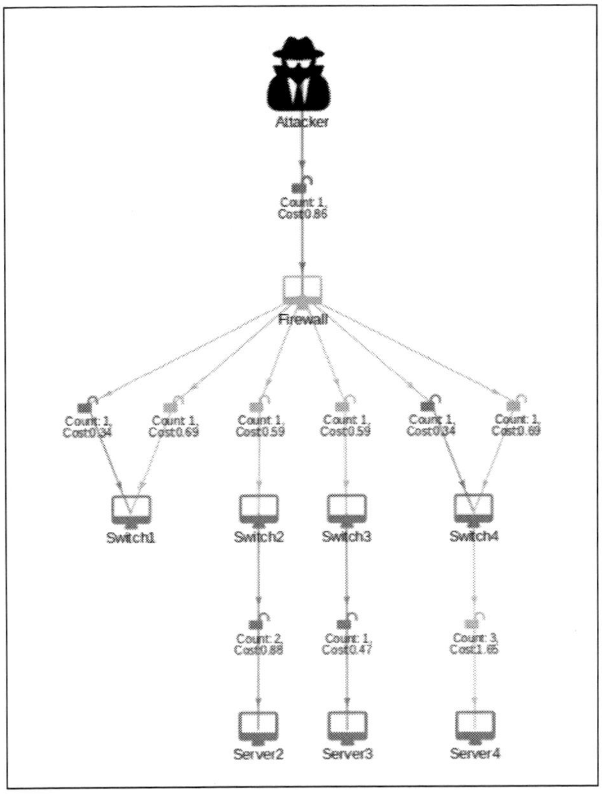

Figure 12. Consolidated view of attack graph

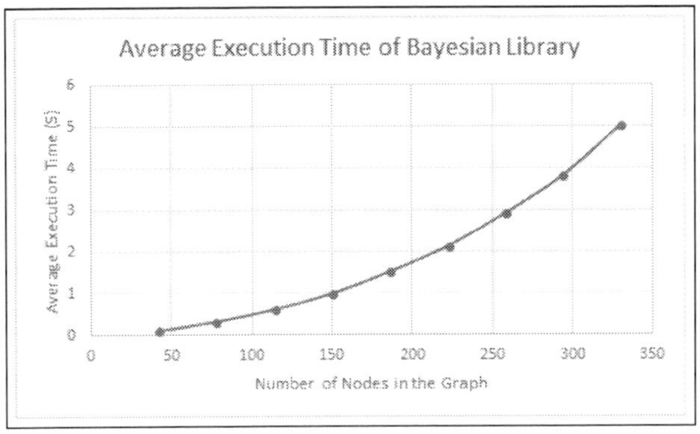

Figure 13. Performance of Py-BBN

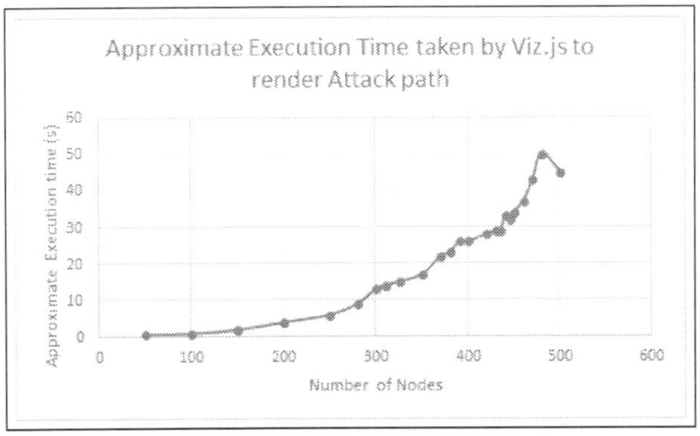

Figure 14. Performance of Vis.js

works model network services as nodes in the attack graph. Based on our evaluation we conclude that device level of modeling of the attack graph is both efficient and sufficient for attack path analysis. We say so as the number of network service is considerably greater than the number of devices in the network. Further, in this work, we identified the challenge in matching software application name with its corresponding product name in the NVD feeds. The existing work on attack path analysis does not discuss this issue. Benthin Sanguino et al. [7] provide a semi-automated approach to address this problem. Inspired by this semi-automated approach, we consider providing an automated approach to address this challenge in our future work. However, in this current work of attack path analysis, we use Nessus to address this challenge. We provide a semi-automatic approach for creating an attack graph by using device level modeling information and information on vulnerabilities collected using Nessus. We have also pointed out practical concerns affecting the scalability of the implementations of the Bayesian network. Scaling issue with Weka, which led to NAN and implementation specific bugs in Py-BBN were identified and fixed. We also plan to report the issues, along with their fixes to the open source communities for their further improvement. An attempt to evaluate the performance of Vis.js library was also made in this paper.

ACKNOWLEDGEMENT

This research is in collaboration with CTI (Center for Technology Innovation) Laboratory, Hitachi Ltd. Research and Development group, Yoshida-cho, Totsuka Yokohama, Japan.

REFERENCES

[1] "National Cyber Security Center," 2018, URL: https://www.ncsc.gov.uk/topics/cyber-attacks [retrieved: November, 2018].

[2] O. Sheyner, J. Haines, S. Jha, R. Lippmann, and J. M. Wing, "Automated generation and analysis of attack graphs," in Proceedings 2002 IEEE Symposium on Security and Privacy May 12–15, 2002, Berkeley, CA, USA. IEEE, Explore Digital Library, May 2002, ISBN: 0-7695-1543-6, ISSN: 1081-6011, URL: https://ieeexplore.ieee.org/document/1004377/.

[3] P. Ammann, D. Wijesekera, and S. Kaushik, "Scalable, graph-based network vulnerability analysis," in Proceedings of the 9th ACM conference on Computer and communication security(CCS'02) November 18–22, 2002, Washington, DC, USA. ACM, Nov. 2002, pp. 217–224, ISBN: 1-58113-612-9, URL: https://dl.acm.org/citation.cfm?id=586140.

[4] M. Frigault, L. Wang, S. Jajodia, and A. Singhal, "Measuring the Overall Network Security by Combining CVSS Scores Based on Attack Graphs and Bayesian Networks," in Network Security Metrics. Springer, Cham, Nov. 2017, chapter 1, pp. 1–23, in Network Security Metrics, Springer, Cham, ISBN: 978-3-319-66505-4,.

[5] L. Munoz-Gonzalez, D. Sgandurra, M. Barrere, and E. Lupu, "Exact Inference Techniques for the Analysis of Bayesian Attack Graphs," in IEEE Transactions on Dependable and Secure Computing. IEEE, 2017, pp. 1–1, in IEEE Transactions on Dependable and Secure Computing, ISSN: 1545-5971.

[6] H. Holm, T. Sommestad, and M. Persson, "A quantitative evaluation of vulnerability scanning," Information Management and Computer Security, vol. 19, 2011, pp. 231–247, ISSN: 0968-5227.

[7] L. A. B. Sanguino and R. Uetz, "Software Vulnerability Analysis Using CPE and CVE," in arXiv May 15, 2017, Cornell University Library, NY, USA. arXiv, May 2017, URL: https://arxiv.org/abs/1705.05347.

[8] "National Vulnerability Database," 2018, URL: https://www.nist.gov/programs-projects/national-vulnerability-database-nvd [retrieved: September, 2018].

[9] "tenable: Nessus, Professional," 2018, URL: https://www.tenable.com/products/nessus/nessus-professional [retrieved: September, 2018].

[10] "Weka," 2018, URL: https://www.cs.waikato.ac.nz/ml/weka/ [retrieved: November, 2018].

[11] "PyBBN," 2018, URL: https://github.com/vangj/py-bbn [retrieved: September, 2018].

[12] "AngularJS," 2018, URL: https://angularjs.org/ [retrieved: November, 2018].

[13] "AngularJS - VisJS," 2018, URL: https://github.com/visjs/angular-visjs [retrieved: September, 2018].

CyberSDnL: A Roadmap to Cyber Security Device Nutrition Label

Abdullahi Arabo

Computer Science and Creative Technologies
The University of the West of England
Bristol UK
Email: abdullahi.arabo@uwe.ac.uk

Abstract—**Security issues mainly evolve from attacking the weakest link within the chain of the ecosystem. One of such weakest links with poor security posture is the smart devices used within a smart space and as Bring Your Own Device (BOYD) for the corporate sector. The main focus of this paper is to briefly highlight the issues and present a roadmap that will facilitate better cyber security footings for smart spaces ecosystems. Based on our findings, we have also proposed a Cyber Security Device nutrition Label (CyberSDnL) conceptual framework as a contribution to the knowledge within this field. Our contributions are threefold: 1) inform the user of the risk associated with their device; this is also a crucial requirement for organization in reference to the development of the new General Data Protection Regulation (GDPR) 2) try to influence manufacturers to change their attitudes towards producing unsecured devices and 3) use this as a platform to create early warning systems to the ecosystem that will be able to stop already infected/insecure devices from proliferating vulnerabilities or risking the entire network/ecosystem from an attack.**

***Keywords*–smart device security; privacy; cyber security; security labels; moving target defense.**

I. Introduction

Communications technologies, devices, and services are becoming more interconnected; hence an enabled future Internet of Things (IoT) connected home. Even though this development offers extensive assistance to home users, it also gives rise to new security threats as this device act as a means of data crowd-sensing agents. The development of ubiquitous computing; IoT to be more specific, has empowered the concept of a connected home ecosystem. This notion is around content anywhere, crowd-sensing and information sharing. Use of IoT devices within connected home ecosystems spawns a cumulative volume of data, habitually lacking the assent of the user, or the user being absolutely cognisant of the insinuations of partaking their personal data. This paper provides a new and easy to use security framework for home devices, with the aim of minimizing the security and privacy threats identified.

Arguably the Internet is one of the utmost human successes in terms of inter-connectivity of things and general telecommunication. However, the development of connected home ecosystems as a result of ubiquitous computing and IoT, promises to make things even more challenging in terms of security and offers more possibilities for improving our way of lives. As a result, users are demanding for seamless inter-connectivity of things to offer countless capabilities to users within their homes and offices. This development is a welcome development, nonetheless, it needs to be noted that it opens up more security and privacy issues for users and critical infrastructure. While we have knowledge of some of the possible vulnerabilities, that are normally only associated with traditional infrastructures, there has been little research and into the individual privacy matters as a result of an interconnected system where devices, with various level of complexity and security, exchange information via a wireless connection to the Internet. Interconnected smart spaces are acting as agent for crowd-sensing. An example of this merging is the control and monitoring of smart grid infrastructures via the use of mobile phones powered either using Android or iOS. Developments within the interconnected ecosystem and demand or seamless and wireless smart grid, coupled with the defencelessness of the smart connected home, will unavoidably lead to consequences in the event of a hacking attack, malware infection or Distributed Denial of Service (DDoS), while the assortment of interconnected systems will likely convert a hub for criminal events, privacy breaches, and other cyber attacks, developing in a life-threatening security hallucination for users [2]. None of these devices used within such environments are developed and deployed with the capability or consideration of being shielded from hacking. Meanwhile, most IoT devices are designed to operate autonomously without considering long periods security protection.

The pace at which they have been spreading is growing exponentially: multiple studies suggest that more than 20 billion smart devices will be circulating by 2020 [9]. Such a complex interconnection and exchange of information requires the development of sophisticated technologies that will allow users, organizations, and the devices themselves, to be reliable, secure and efficient: the main purpose of a smart object is to make the life of the user easier [26]. The growing presence of these devices in our households also points to a level of trust that the consumer has in them. This reliance also led to question the quality, the security of the whole infrastructure, while pointing to the issue of privacy: where is personal information stored? Are they secured? Can we make sure that what we want to keep quiet, will remain private? These and additional questions were at the start of the development of the paper that this paper will explore.

Information security is can essentially be considered a societal problem rather than scientific issues. IoT provides avenues for people to generate snowballing volume of data, often lacking users knowledge, permissions and knowing its consequences. Whereby, this information is either administered by the service provider cloud service or other third parties. The development and inter-connectivity of smart devices within a connected ecosystem will be a vulnerability threat to an individual user or a cumulative community of users. It is only now that society is starting to understand the security implications and costs of privacy, in both its legal and ethical senses [1]. Oberheide and Jahanian [29] have explored when and why it is more difficult to secure mobile devices in comparison to non-mobile equivalents. They derive a set of principles for mobile security.

A major issue that will be addressed is the freedom of information currently being presented on the devices that we use every day. At the present, this information is being shown or heard without any regard to whom that information is related too. The paper will address this issue by attempting to identify insecure apps and devices that not only hide or reveal information while been installed hence providing context-based security solutions, in the other words it will build a system which is privacy aware of its surroundings. Preliminary research found out that the concept of privacy is understood in a different way than the one used in this paper. The literature Xu [25] and Brauchi [6] addresses privacy concerns in a parallel to way to security concern, so privacy of information means that they are not shared outside the household or refers in general to the possible unwanted sharing of personal information as an issue of confidentiality [16]. For the aim of the paper, when talking about privacy, it will indicate the personal users privacy, and his ability to decide whether he wants to share his own information with other users, within the household, or not.

Consequently, we will look at the main cyber security challenges of living in a Smart Home, along with the security and privacy threats that are presented in Smart Home Devices today. The outcome of the research will be used to outline fundamental requirements needed to provide secure and confidential operations in Smart Homes, by providing the user the security rating label for each device used within their ecosystems.

The rest of the paper is structured as follow, in section II we highlight the key state of the art and related work. Section III provides a description of our proposed conceptual framework, with more details on the use of traffic light systems as key to device security nutrition labeling. The proof of concept of the framework is been presented and discussed in section IV, with key findings. Sections V concludes the paper with future research directions in terms of creating a moving target defense for zero trust security in a connected home ecosystem that will further enhance out early results using machine learning.

II. RELATED WORK

A major issue that will be addressed with the paper is the freedom of information currently being presented on the devices that we use every day. At the present, this information is being shown or heard without any regard to whom that information is related too. A number of studies have been conducted in reference to the effectiveness of warning labels on cigarettes and food products [13][15], , etc. Purmehdi [20], has indicated that label effectiveness is contingent on the type of expected behavioral outcome. In response to these problems, Kelley et al [14], proposed a solution for creating an information design that improves the visual presentation and comprehensibility of privacy police viewed online. Their privacy label was inspired by a nutrition label which summarized website privacy policies.

It has been shown that displaying uncertain data visually enables users to understand better. This has been established on food nutrition labels [24]. Supermarkets and food manufacturers have helped users decide between products by using traffic light color-coded labels. Color-coded nutritional information, as shown in Figure 1, gives users at-a-glance information. By the glance, users can quickly see if the food has high (red), medium (orange) or low (green) amounts of fats, saturates, sugars and salt [18].

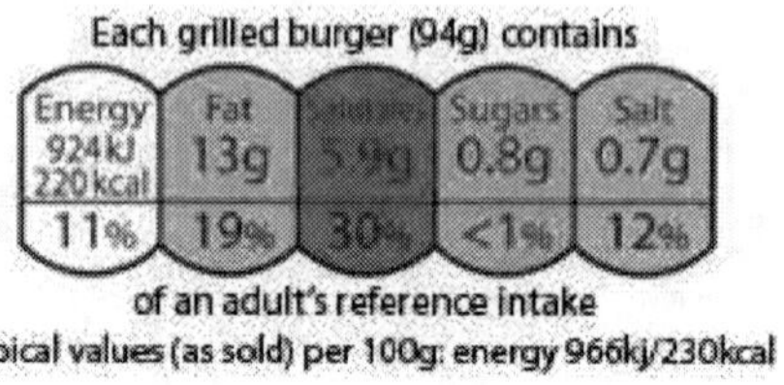

Figure 1. Food Nutrition Label [28]

III. PROPOSED CONCEPTUAL FRAMEWORK

Based upon our research findings, the paper provides a road-map and a visual proposal has been designed for both users and manufacturers which identifies the key issues and vulnerabilities in Smart Devices. This design provides a solution to the key problems of this research which is to extend awareness for both stakeholders. Many users are unaware of what potential threats, vulnerabilities, and issues there are and how many of those Smart Devices contain. By displaying each security component in a red, orange and green color code, users will visually be able to see what risks the device has and whether it is safe to have in their home. Whilst this proposal will be beneficial for users purchasing Smart Devices, it will also help guide manufacturers to make better decisions when designing the product.

Following the food nutritional label, the security nutritional label key and colors are presented in Figure 2. The traffic light color system is well known to users around the world and has been utilized by other industries. Applying the system to our proposal, users can effectively understand what each color represents. In this approach, we are targeting a label system that educates the stakeholder on a safe use of the smart device and the potential risk that such devices can be to other users in the smart ecosystems as a whole.

Information on the label for Smart Devices includes:

- Vulnerability: This will show users an overall estimation of how vulnerable the device is. It will take into consideration the security and privacy aspects and the possible attacks the device is vulnerable to. It will also confirm whether there are default passwords and if so, advising users to change the password straight away
- Operating System (OS): This will state the OS of the device and how vulnerable it is to attacks. It will show if the device updates are automatic or whether users have to update them their selves. A recommended timescale is given to show how often to look.
- Privacy: This will show how much confidential personal data is being collected and used by the manufactures and third-parties

- Threats: This will display the possible threats the device is vulnerable to.

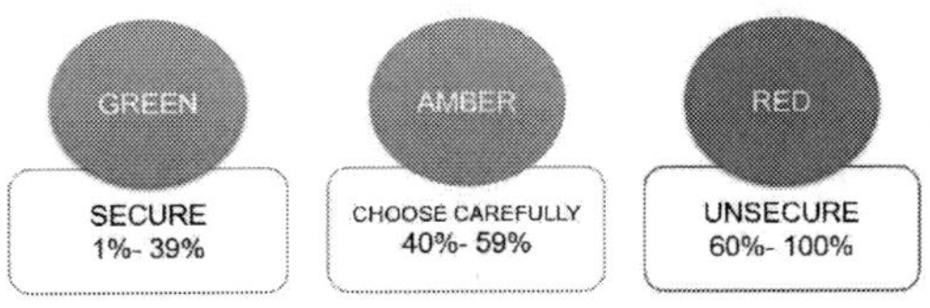

Figure 2. Key and for security food label

This design provides benefits for both users and manufacturers. At first glance, users can automatically see that this device is vulnerable and insecure due to the colors presented. The label informs the users briefly about what threats and privacy issues the device is susceptible to.

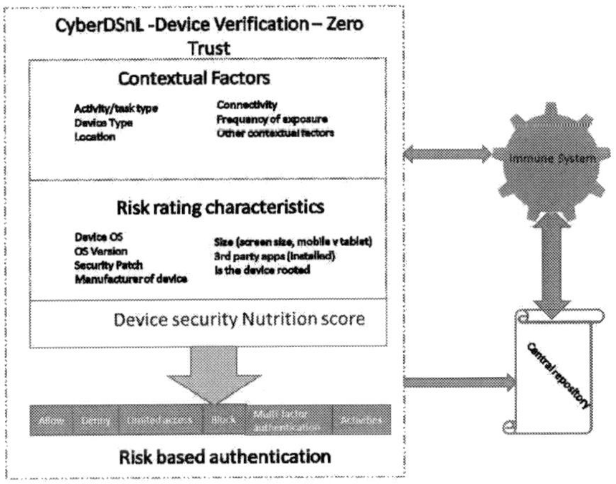

Figure 3. Conceptual Model

Manufacturers will benefit from the use of these labels as it will make them more aware of the designing process. The nutritional label currently seen on food and drink makes users instantly aware as to how sugary it is or how much fat is contained from the colors presented on the label. This type of label on Smart Devices will aid in manufacturer sales whilst boosting user awareness. As manufacturers continuously improve their devices, the awareness will continuously grow until every user is fully aware of the current risks. Convenience will no longer be a priority for an average user. It is important to note that this design is a short-term solution for Smart Devices in homes, as smart technology is continuously evolving over time. Our proposed road-map is based on the conceptual model depicted in Figure 3 which is based on the principles of (VAR) corresponds to VISIBILITY, AWARENESS, and RESPONSE to facilitate a proactive device security nutrition labeling approve. Where we identified some vital contextual factors which have the influence to security risk rating of various devices based on the device features and installed 3rd part applications within the device as well as the context on which the device is been used.

IV. Proof of Concept

As a proof of concept for our proposed road-map and conceptual module, we have developed an Android app that is able to dynamically analysis the contents of the devices that are installed on and is able to inform the user the risk rating or security nutrition label of the device. Where the app is able to dynamically deactivate the access to certain activities within the device and the ecosystem based on the overall security score/rating of the device. To achieve this we have considered the following key context and characteristics:

- Device OS,
- OS version,
- API,
- Security patch last updated,
- Days since the last update,
- Make Model,
- Screen size,
- is the device rooted?

This will then give a device security score. Device score is as follows, and has been worked out using metrics specified below:

- 1 -3 (Green / low-security risk)
- 4-5 (Amber/medium security risk)
- 6-10 (Red / high-security risk)

All devices start out with a score of 1 by default and the score is added to if risks are identified, such as;

- If the device is rooted - score = 6 (automatically high risk)
- If the device hasn't had a security patch in 120 days or more - score = 4
- If the device security patch is over a month old, but not yet 3 months old - score = 3
- If the device OS is out of date (i.e. less than 8) - score = 4
- If the device OS is up to date, but not the latest API (i.e. if it is 8.0, not 8.1) - score = 3

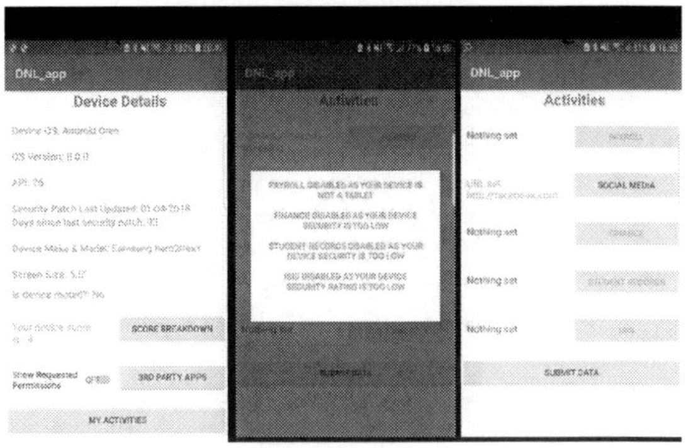

Figure 4. Device Score and a Warning message

The app also looks at the 3rd party apps installed on the phone and their permissions and how many have 40% or more requested permissions than actual permissions as shown in Figure 5 (B).

- If 4 or more 3rd party apps have - score = 4
- If less than 4 3rd party apps have - score = 3 (still Green)
- If none (which would be impossible I feel) then change to the score (still 1).

The app allows the user to launch other activities, which they set themselves (for proof of concept only) based on the following scores, score breakdown and permitted activities are presented in Figure 5

- Payroll allow only when green and bigger screen size (Tablet, so 6" or greater)
- Social media amber or green
- Finance only green
- Student record only green
- ISIS only green, bigger screen size,
- if OS not up to date, automatically deny even if overall rating is green

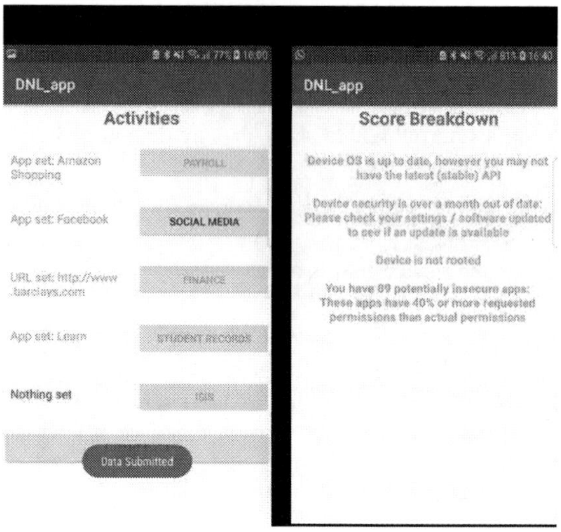

Figure 5. Activity List and Score Breakdown

The end user (admin) can set either a website Figure 4 (C) or app Figure 5 (A) on their phone which is launched when they click the relevant button, assuming the button/activity has not been disabled due to their device score, screen size etc. Lastly, the end user can submit their device data to a Gmail account/form, this submits/lists all the information from the front screen along with how many potentially insecure 3rd party apps are on the device. This data is aim to be used as a training set for the future aspect of this prototype the immune systems depicted in the conceptual model presented in Figure 3.

V. CONCLUSION

IoT is undoubtedly transforming our daily lives by creating opportunities to live better and more efficiently. The increase of Smart Devices is transforming residential homes into Smart Homes. Sooner rather than later, every home will evolve into a Smart Home due to the numerous benefits they provide. However, whilst the benefits of Smart Homes may outweigh the problems for users it is important to address the security-related challenges and concerns within this domain. We have provided a brief description and analysis of the issues of smart device, and the main contribution of our paper is in term of providing a conceptual framework and road-map to a more secure devices security ecosystems based on lessons learned from nutrition labels in both food and tobacco industries. The next step of this paper is to provide a proof of concept that will demonstrate the effectiveness of this framework and road-map to the cyber security ecosystems of smart spaces while highlighting the benefits of the road-map to the three-fold contribution/aims of the paper. This will further be enhanced by providing a proof of concept and more intelligent zero-trust framework for CyberSDnL.

ACKNOWLEDGMENT

The authors appreciate the help and some funding from the CodeWest project, which has supplied some funding for the development of the proof-of-concept presented in this paper. Also, our appreciation goes to the students who helped with the prototype and the background work on the research.

REFERENCES

[1] A.Arabo, I. Brown, F. Musa, "Privacy in the Age of Mobility and Smart Devices in Smart Homes", 2012 ASE/IEEE International Conference on Social Computing and 2012 ASE/IEEE International Conference on Privacy, Security, Risk, and Trust, pp. 803-809, 2014

[2] A. Arabo, "Cyber Security Challenges within the Connected Home Ecosystem Futures." Procedia Computer Science, 61, pp.227-232.

[3] N. Apthorpe, D. Reisman, and N. Feamster, "Closing the Blinds: Four Strategies for Protecting Smart Home Privacy from Network Observers," Cornell University Library. pp. 2. [Accessed 5 October 2018].

[4] N. Apthorpe, D. Reisman, S. Sundaresan, and N. Feamster, "Spying on the Smart Home: Privacy Attacks and Defenses on Encrypted IoT Traffic", arXiv.org [Accessed 11 October 2018].

[5] M. Barnes, "Alexa, are you listening?. MWR InfoSecurity", Available from: https://labs.mwrinfosecurity.com/blog/alexa-are-you-listening/ [Accessed 26 October 2018].

[6] A. Brauchli, D. Li, " A Solution-Based Analysis of Attack Vectors on Smart Home Systems. In:Fei, Security, and Privacy in the Internet of Things (IoTs): models, algorithms and implementation." Taylor Francis Group. pp. 92-106.

[7] S. Bustamante, P. Castro, A. Laso, M. Manana, A. Arroyo, " Smart Thermostats: An Experimental Facility to Test Their Capabilities and Savings Potential " Sustainability. 9 (8), pp. 1462. [Accessed 7 November 2018].

[8] R. L.Finn, D. Wright, and M. Friedewald, "Seven Types of Privacy. European Data Protection: Coming of Age, Dordrecht", Springer, pp3-32.

[9] Gartner "Gartner Says 8.4 Billion Connected "Things" Will Be in Use in 2017, Up 31 Percent From 2016." Available from: https://www.gartner.com/newsroom/id/3598917 [Accessed 4 November 2018].

[10] M. Ghiglieri, M. Volkamer, and K. Renaud, "Exploring Consumers Attitudes of Smart TV Related Privacy Risks [online]". Human Aspects of Information Security, Privacy, and Trust. pp. 656-674. [Accessed 3 October 2018].

[11] W. Haack, M. Severance, M. Wallace, and J. Wohlwend, " Security Analysis of the Amazon Echo [online]". pp. 1-10. [Accessed 7 November 2018].

[12] C. Jackson, & A. Orebaugh, "A study of security and privacy issues associated with the Amazon Echo [online]". International Journal of Internet of Things and Cyber-Assurance. 1 (1), pp. 91-98.

[13] J. Kees, S. J. Burton, C. Andrews, and J. Kozup , "Tests of Graphic Visuals and Cigarette Package Warning Combinations: Implications for the Framework Convention on Tobacco Control." Journal of Public Policy Marketing: Fall 2006, Vol. 25, No. 2, pp. 212-223.

[14] P. Kelley, J. Bresee, L. Cranor, and R. Reeder, " A "nutrition label" for privacy [online]. Proceedings of the 5th Symposium on Usable Privacy and Security" - SOUPS '09. [Accessed 21 October 2018].

[15] N. Khandpur, P.M. Sato, L.A. Mais, A.P.B. Martins, C.G. Spinillo, M.T. Garcia, C.F.U. Rojas, P.C. Jaime, " Are Front-of-Package Warning Labels More Effective at Communicating Nutrition Information than Traffic-Light Labels? A Randomized Controlled Experiment in a Brazilian Sample." Nutrients 2018, 10, 688

[16] H. Lin, N. W. Bergmann, " IoT Privacy and Security Challenges for Smart Home Environments." Information. 7 (44), pp.

[17] R. Miao, R. Potharaju, M. Yu and N. Jain, "The Dark Menace." Proceedings of the 2015 ACM Conference on Internet Measurement Conference - IMC '15. pp. 170. [Accessed 16 October 2018].

[18] NHS "Food labels. [online]". Available from: https://www.nhs.uk/Livewell/Goodfood/Pages/food-labelling.aspx [Accessed 20 October 2018].

[19] A. Prasad, " Exploring the Convergence of Big Data and the Internet of Things." IGI Global.

[20] M. Purmehdi, R. Legoux, F. Carrillat, and S. Senecal , "The Effectiveness of Warning Labels for Consumers: A Meta-Analytic Investigation into Their Underlying Process and Contingencies." Journal of Public Policy Marketing: Spring 2017, Vol. 36, No. 1, pp. 36-53.

[21] SAP National Security Services, Inc " Cracking the conundrum of IoT convenience and security – what's next?. [online]". Available from: https://www.sapns2.com/cracking-conundrum-iot-convenience-security-whats-next/ [Accessed 6 October 2018].

[22] C. Stergiou, K. Psannis, B. Kim, and B. Gupta, " Secure integration of IoT and Cloud Computing." Future Generation Computer Systems. 78pp. 964-975.

[23] Trend Micro "A Look Into the Most Noteworthy Home Network Security Threats of 2017.[online]". Available from: https://www.trendmicro.com/vinfo/au/security/research-and-analysis/threat-reports/roundup/a-look-into-the-most-noteworthy-Home-network-security-threats-of-2017 [Accessed 1 November 2018].

[24] M. Vasiljevic, R. Pechey, and T. Marteau, " Making food labels social: The impact of colour of nutritional labels and injunctive norms on perceptions and choice of snack foods." 91pp. 56-63. [Accessed 20 October 2018].

[25] C. Xu, X. Zheng X. Xiong, " The Design and Implementation of a Low Cost and High Security Smart Home System Based on Wi-Fi and SSL Technologies." Journal of Physics: Conference Series 806 012012.

[26] I. Andrea, C. Chrysostomou, " Internet of Things: Security vulnerabilities and challenges." Computers and Commmunications (ISCC), 2015 IEEE Symposium on. pp. 180-187.

[27] S. Zheng, M. Chetty , and N. Feamster, " User Perceptions of Privacy in Smart Homes" [online]. arXiv.org [Accessed 25 Octover 2018].

[28] Food Standards Agency "Food nutrition label. [online]." Available from: https://www.food.gov.uk/northern-ireland/nutritionni/fop-ni [Accessed 15 October 2018].

[29] J.Oberheide, and F. Jahanian, "When mobile is harder than fixed (and vice versa): demystifying security challenges in mobile environments", Proceedings of the Eleventh Workshop on Mobile Computing Systems Applications, pp.4348.

Prototype Orchestration Framework as a High Exposure Dimension Cyber Defense Accelerant Amidst Ever-Increasing Cycles of Adaptation by Attackers

A Modified Deep Belief Network Accelerated by a Stacked Generative Adversarial Network for Enhanced Event Correlation

Steve Chan
Decision Engineering Analysis Laboratory
San Diego, California U.S.A.
email: schan@dengineering.org

Abstract—**The cycles of adaptation by attackers are ever-increasing. To meet these evolving threats, outsourcing to Managed Security Service Providers (MSSPs) has become prevalent. As these MSSPs contend with a torrent of varied attack vectors, they are increasingly utilizing Artificial Intelligence (AI) to assist them in protecting their clients. Practitioners often assert that systems which provide decisions can be construed as AI; along this vein, this paper presents summary results of a prototype orchestration framework that selects and prioritizes cyber tools to be utilized against a continuous stream of testbed cyber-attacks. This orchestration framework is predicated upon the hybridization of a modified Deep Belief Network (DBN) conjoined with a particular cognitive computing precept (the acceptance of higher uncertainty amidst lower ambiguity for compressed decision cycles); for uncompressed decision cycles, it utilizes a modified Stacked Generative Adversarial Network (SGAN), which serves as a feeder to a Lowering Ambiguity Accelerant (LAA). Results show promise during the 1-5 day period; work has already commenced for improving the performance for day 6+, and uptime is already at 38 days with minimal degradation.**

Keywords-Cyber Attack Accelerants; Orchestration Framework; Uncertainty/Ambiguity Calculus; Deep Belief Network; Generative Adversarial Network.

I. Introduction

Organizations in the Indo-Asia Pacific are currently undergoing a rapid phase of Information Technology (IT) development. Yet, with a large number of companies belonging to the Small and Medium Enterprises (SMEs) segment, there is limited capital available for massive investment into IT infrastructures and manpower. This has resulted in these SMEs (and large industries alike) to turn to third-party Managed Service Providers (MSPs), who can handle the maintenance and monitoring of their mission-critical applications around the clock. This operational tempo for the MSPs has necessitated the use of Artificial Intelligence (AI) to consolidate data and streamline processes in their continuous efforts to defend both SMEs and enterprise level companies. This paper presents a modified Stacked Generative Adversarial Network (SGAN) for uncompressed decision cycles and a modified Deep Belief Network (DBN) for compressed decision cycles. A particular focus is given to the AI accelerant methodology utilized to compress the decision-making cycles of the prototype orchestration framework.

The remainder of this paper is organized as follows: Section II discusses the ecosystem of managed service providers and managed security service providers as well as an exemplar sector (e.g. energy). Subsequently, Section III explores potential accelerants for cyber attackers, which ironically also serve as instruments for cyber defenders. Then, Section IV delves into a posited prototype orchestration framework to help mitigate against accelerated cyber-attacks. Section V posits a cognitive computing precept (e.g. tolerance for higher uncertainty); of note, Section V also provides pertinent background context regarding precision/accuracy and quantitative/qualitative data. The inclusion of Section VA and VB should be clarified. Prodigious amounts of funding have been spent on biomimetic projects, such as attempting to emulate the brain, via synthetic processes. However, in the emulation, oftentimes, certain vital aspects are excluded during the dimensionality reduction of the problem. Indeed, many projects have suffered as they have missed the criticality of the inclusion of certain dimensions, such as morphology. To articulate this "lessons learned" vantage point, this paper focuses upon the underlying logic needed to inform future biomimetic efforts. Section VI posits an artificial intelligence precept (e.g. desire for gestaltian closure); of note, Section VI also provides pertinent background context regarding deeper belief amidst compressed decision cycles, the use of a deep belief network over deep learning amidst compressed decision cycles, and a higher tolerance for uncertainty amidst compressed decision cycles. Furthermore, the topics of Section VI are expounded upon because the hybridization of artificial intelligence precepts with cognitive computing precepts for machine-speed performance is often not treated synchronously. In fact, many projects claim accelerated performance, but often do not incorporate a Deep Belief component for handling decision-making amidst compressed decision cycles. Avoiding the challenge of these trans-disciplinary issues often results in only incremental improvement paradigms. Section VII presents the experimental results from the hybridized computational methodology of Section V and Section VI. Section VIII presents further enhancements to the posited hybridized computational methodology of Section VII. Finally, the paper reviews and emphasizes key points within Section IX, the conclusion.

II. Ecosystem of Managed Service Providers

A. Managed Service Providers (MSPs)

MSPs are, in many cases, an IT services provider that manages a defined set of services for its clients, as agreed prior, or as the MSP (in many cases, not the client) proactively determines. MSP roles have evolved as they have gone from simply maintaining legacy systems (a report by Cisco posits that 65% of IT budgets are allocated for keeping systems functional [1]). In contemporary times, the MSP remotely manages the client's IT infrastructure and/or end-user systems, typically under a subscription model or "pay as you go" pricing model. According to MarketsandMarkets, the global MSP market is forecast to grow from USD$107.17 billion in 2014 to USD$193.34 billion by 2019 [2], and the market is expected to increase as more clients are focusing on their core competencies rather than on IT maintenance and troubleshooting issues. The current compound annual growth rate (CAGR) is 12.5% [2], and this CAGR is expected to rise quickly as IT expenditures shift from a capital expenditure (CapEx) to operational expenditure (OpEx) model.

B. Managed Security Service Providers (MSSPs)

MSP responsibilities are increasingly shifting from repairs, patches, delivery of new software, and incorporation of cloud services to that of data-related security services. According to Gartner, a new class of MSP, the Managed Security Service Provider (MSSP), has emerged to provide outsourced monitoring and management of security devices and systems. Prototypical managed services now include, among others, managed firewall, virtual private network, vulnerability scanning, anti-viral services, and intrusion detection. Outsourcing to MSSPs has typically improved the client ability to deter cyberthreats, and among other assessments, the *Gartner Magic Quadrant (MQ) for Managed Security Service Providers* and the *International Data Corporation (IDC) MarketScape: Worldwide Managed Security Services 2017 Vendor Assessment* compares and contrasts MSSPs. MSSPs have burgeoned not only in industries that have experienced massive compromises in recent times (e.g., healthcare), but also in areas that are at unprecedented levels of risk (e.g., energy sector).

C. MSPs and MSSPs for the Energy Sector

By leveraging available high-speed Internet connections and user-friendly Software-as-a-Service (SAAS) interfaces, MSPs within the energy sector are helping building owners and operators lower energy usage, increase building operations efficiency, and optimize the climate control conditions in tenant working spaces. These MSPs are endeavoring to leverage cloud-based software and the more granular control of Internet of Things (IOT) devices to deliver their managed services. This paradigm has yielded new vulnerabilities within the cyber domain, such as in Figure 1.

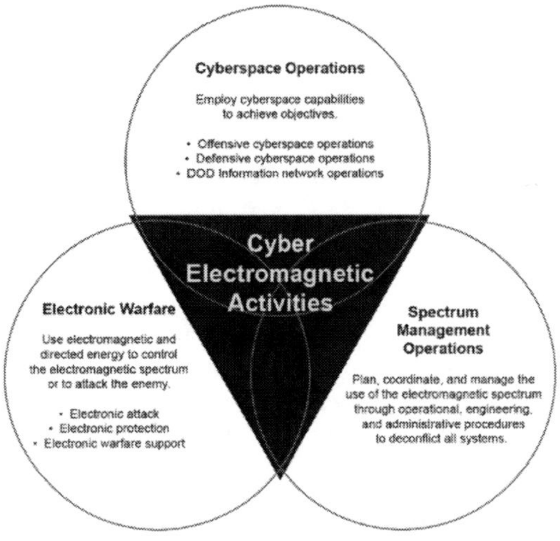

Figure 1. Cyber Electromagnetic Vulnerabilities [3].

MSSPs, such as within the energy sector, are scrutinizing the attack surface problem — the exposure or exploitable vulnerabilities that exist within a system — particularly at the "weak links in the chain" (which represents the weakest members of a system, and because of these points of failure, the entire system may fail). It is well known that the three most common attack surfaces include: (1) human attack surface (e.g., social engineering, insider threat, errors of omission or commission), (2) network attack surface (e.g., open ports on outward-facing Web servers, code listening on those ports, and services available on the inside of the firewall), and (3) software attack surface (with a focus on Web applications).

Putting aside the large issue of human attack surfaces, the SANS Technology Institute asserts that the amalgam of network attack surfaces and software attack surfaces constitute high exposure dimensions. With regards to software attack surfaces, an ever-increasing amount of funding is being spent on developing an escalating number of Web applications that are mission-critical. Concurrently, attackers are becoming more adept at exploiting Web applications. There is a plethora of penetration testing (a.k.a. pen testing) tools and Web application security assessment tools that help identify known and unknown vulnerabilities. These tools can assist in: (1) reducing the amount of code executing (i.e. turning off certain features), (2) reducing the volume of code that is accessible to users (i.e. establishing user privileges), (3) constraining the damage, if code is indeed exploited (i.e. damage control rule sets). However, there are limitations to these prototypical tools. Pen testing itself is limited in scope, and most organizations are not able to exhaustively test the entire portfolio of their systems due to resource constraints and practicality. Also, as pen testing involves a particular set of tests over a certain amount of time, attackers can plan and execute over a longer time frame. Furthermore, pen testing is limited to the models that are created, and the attack surface might be at higher exposure than anticipated. There are also limitations to the automated tools for Web application security scanning. While scanners can identify the more serious technical flaws within applications, they are not able to identify logical (e.g., architectural, design) flaws that were introduced before the coding, authentication, and authorization took place.

III. ACCELERANTS FOR CYBER ATTACKERS

Cyber attackers are becoming increasingly adept. Just as MSPs and MSSPs are leveraging early warning indicators, such as the National Vulnerability Database (NVD) and Sentient Hyper Optimized Data Access Network (SHODAN), cyber attackers are also leveraging these assets for exploitation opportunities and as attack accelerants.

A. NVD

The National Institute of Standards and Technology's (NIST) NVD lists various known vulnerabilities. The NVD utilizes a Common Vulnerability Scoring System (CVSS), which provides an open framework for communicating the characteristics and impacts of IT vulnerabilities. A sample vulnerability and CVSS score is shown in Table 1.

TABLE 1. CHARACTERISTICS OF A NATIONAL VULNERABILITY DATABASE (NVD) VULNERABILITY

Characteristics of an NVD Vulnerability	Description
CVSS 2.0 Base Score	***High*** 7.8
Vulnerability Type(s)	Denial of Service
Availability Impact	***Complete*** (there is a total shutdown of the affected resource. The attacker can render the resource completely unavailable).
Access Complexity	***Low*** (specialized access conditions or extenuating circumstances do not exist. Very little knowledge or skill is required to exploit).
Authentication	***Not required*** (authentication is not required to exploit the vulnerability).

The NVD's CVSS Specification Documents provide severity explanations. For this example, a CVSS Base Score of 7.8 is high, whether it is for the CVSS v2.0 Specification Document or for the CVSS v3.0 Specification Document, as is articulated (bolded and italicized) in Table 2 and Table 3.

TABLE 2. CVSS V2.0 RATINGS

Severity	Base Score Range
Low	0.0 - 3.9
Medium	4.0 - 6.9
High	***7.0 – 10.0***

TABLE 3. CVSS V3.0 RATINGS

Severity	Base Score Range
None	0.0
Low	0.1 - 3.9
Medium	4.0 - 6.9
High	***7.0 - 8.9***
Critical	9.0 - 10.0

B. SHODAN

Unlike traditional search engines that obtain information on the World Wide Web (WWW), SHODAN endeavors to obtain data from the ports of Internet-connected devices accessible by the WWW. Hence, cyber attackers can exploit SHODAN to find various technologies including the Supervisory Control and Data Acquisition (SCADA)/Industrial Control Systems (ICS) of the energy sector. Attackers can accelerate their attack by performing bulk searching and processing of SHODAN queries, via software called SHODAN Diggity, which provides a list of 167 search queries in a dictionary file, known as the SHODAN Hacking Database (SHDB). The described process, as shown in Figure 2, is streamlined and enhanced by SearchDiggity, which is a Graphical User Interface (GUI) application developed for the Google Hacking Diggity Project. It serves as a front-end to SHODAN Diggity. In essence, an attack surface area may be at greater exposure due to the combinatorial of elements (e.g., Search Diggity, SHODAN, SHODAN Diggity, SHDB, etc.) that may be utilized maliciously by an attacker as accelerants.

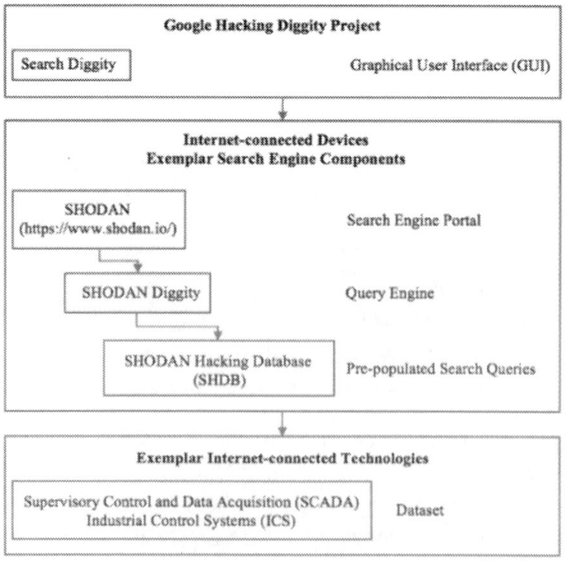

Figure 2. Interplay among the Components of an Internet-connected Devices Search Engine and Exemplar Internet-connected Technologies.

There are many other potential attack accelerants in addition to SHODAN.

IV. A PROTOTYPE ORCHESTRATION FRAMEWORK TO MITIGATE AGAINST ACCELERATED CYBER ATTACKS

As MSPs and MSSPs are determining the services that are needed by their clients, particularly within the energy sector, they are increasingly prototyping various cyber defense frameworks and tools. According to MSP Alliance (an international association of cloud computing providers and MSPs) contributor Charles Weaver, "the most advanced tools become feathers in the caps of service providers" [4].

This paper focused upon a research project that involved devising a prototype orchestration framework, which focused upon Intrusion Detection Systems (IDS) (a security technology originally built for detecting vulnerability exploits), Network Intrusion Detection Systems (NIDS) (a device or software application that monitors a network of systems), Host Intrusion Detection System (HIDS) (a system of monitoring and analyzing the internals of a computing system, as well as the network packets at its network interfaces), Network System Monitors (NSM) (a system that constantly monitors a network for slow or failing components, and in many cases, an assigned tool(s) will try to recover the problem by running a system administrator-defined program or by restarting a process), and Host System Monitors (HSM) (a more localized non-network monitoring agent). This is delineated in Figure 3. Within this figure, various Off-the-Shelf (OTS) tools are organized under IDS. Some of the presented tools include the following.

- *Snort.* Free, open source NIDS software. Entered InfoWorld's Open Source Hall of Fame as one of the "greatest open source software of all time" [5];
- *OSSEC.* Free, open source HIDS software;
- *Wireshark.* Free, open source NSM packet analyzer. Acclaimed by IDG Research as the "world's leading network traffic analyzer" [6];
- *Server Health Monitor.* Free HSM software.

The tools are further organized as follows: (1) NIDS (with NSM sub-category), and (2) HIDS (with HSM sub-category) categories. For example, "Snort" is categorized under NIDS, "OSSEC" under HIDS, "Wireshark" under NSM, and "Server Health Monitor" under HSM.

The discussed prototype orchestration framework does indeed endeavor to recognize the type of cyber-attack, but the focus is on how it procedurally recommends certain tools to be run against the attack vector (refer to Figure 4), recommends accelerant tools (third-party enhancements) based upon the decision cycles available (please refer to Figure 5), and further recommends tools based upon the effectiveness of the prior tools utilized (please refer to Figure 6). In essence, the involved prototype orchestration framework is predicated upon the hybridized computational methodology discussed herein.

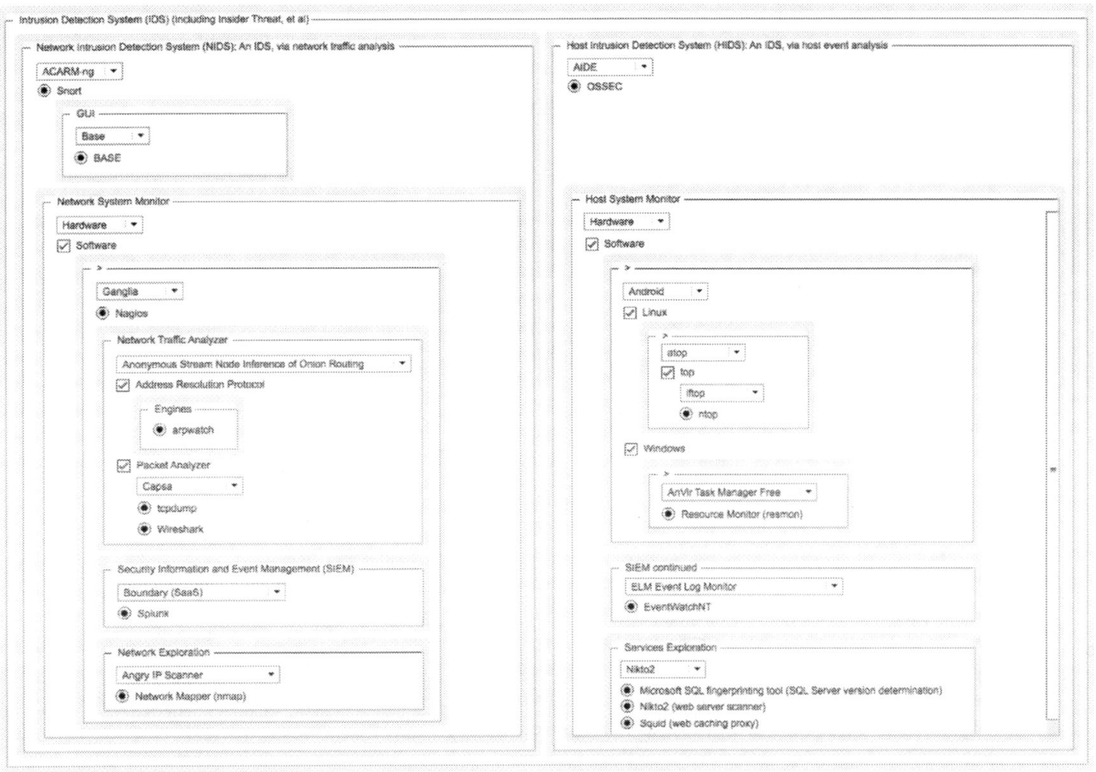

Figure 3. Prototype Orchestration Framework for IDS: NIDS (with NSM) & HIDS (with HSM).

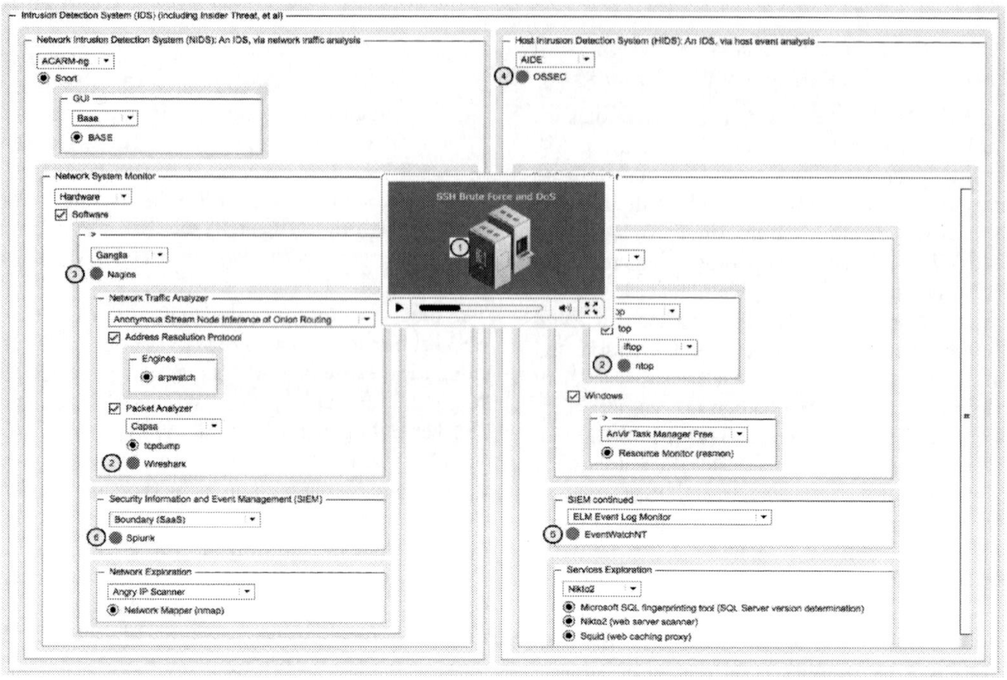

Figure 4. Prototype Orchestration Framework identifies the attack vector (e.g., Secure Socket Shell [SSH] Brute Force as well as Denial-of-Service [DoS]) and procedurally recommends certain tools.

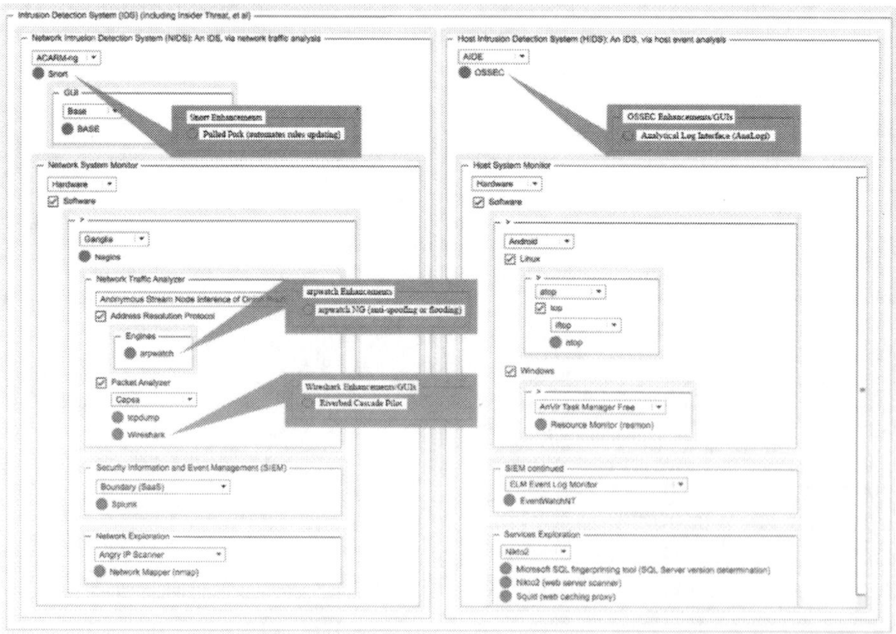

Figure 5. Prototype Orchestration Framework recommends accelerant tools based upon the decision cycles available.

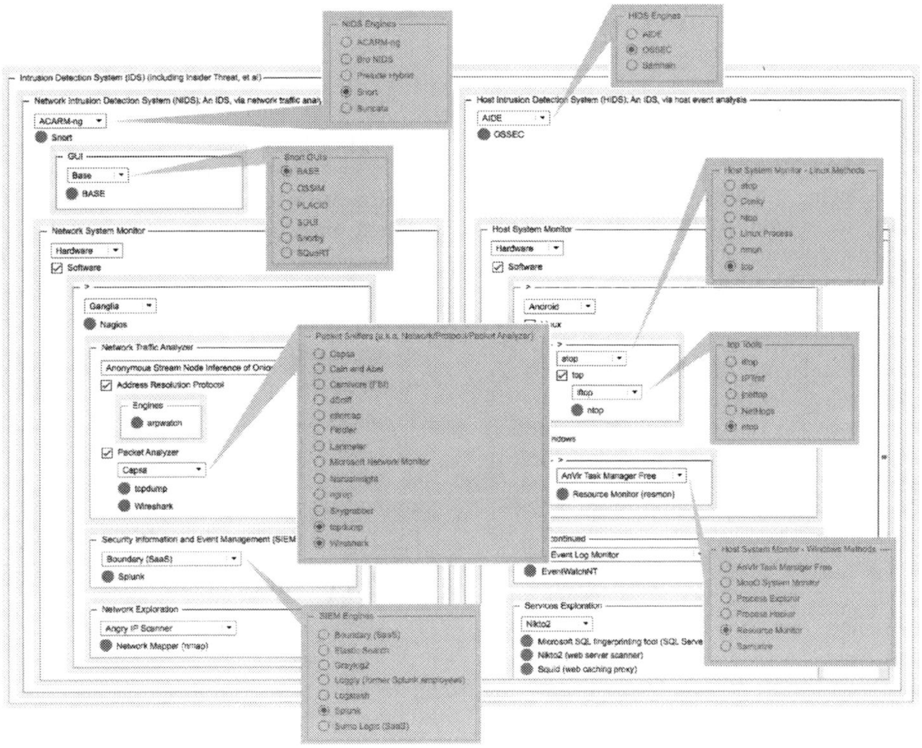

Figure 6. Prototype Orchestration Framework recommends further tools based upon the effectiveness of the prior tools utilized.

V. Posited Cognitive Computing Precept: A Tolerance for Higher Uncertainty

Cognitive computing aims to solve problems with naturalistic processes (e.g., human thinking). For example, a naturalistic process would segue into a decision (and manifestation) of "fight" or "flight." With funding from the Defense Advanced Research Projects Agency (DARPA), Dharmendra Modha of IBM's Almaden Research Center reverse engineered a monkey (type: macaque) brain so as to engineer one of their own, via a project called Systems of Neuromorphic Adaptive Plastic Scalable Electronics (SyNAPSE). "In May 2009, the team managed to simulate a system with 1 billion neurons, roughly the brain of a lower mammal," but the key exception was that the brain only operated at one-thousandth of real time, not enough to perform what Modha referred to as the essentials: food, fight, flight, and mating [7]. In this section, a similar case study — that of the Tyot Alba — is presented, and a supposition is put forth (as a cognitive computing precept), as to how best contend with the problem faced by Modha.

A. Precision and Accuracy

In 2009, a strain of the human influenza virus combined by random chance with a strain of swine influenza in rural Mexico, and the swine flu epidemic (involving the H1N1 influenza virus) was born. After the epidemic breached the U.S.-Mexico border, two teams of scientists offered predictions of how broadly the virus would spread throughout the U.S. Although the teams had worked independently, they produced strikingly similar results, and policy makers and scientists alike took that similarity as a sign that their predictions were accurate. Even more convincing to many were the methods by which they produced those predictions. Both groups processed prodigious amounts of data on human mobility (e.g., understanding human mobility patterns, via mobile phone records) and face-to-face interactions so as to produce a time-varying model of the nation's face-to-face social network.

To produce their predictions, both groups simulated the infection dynamics on that social network using the widely accepted Susceptible-Infected-Recovering (S-I-R) model of viral transmission. This model consisted of a set of coupled differential equations (a mathematical equation for an unknown function of one or several variables) with a small number of free parameters, and the simulation teams obtained estimates of those parameters from the Centers for Disease Control and Prevention (CDC), which seemed to be, from a *provenance* perspective, the best possible source of epidemiological statistics. Based upon all these efforts, both teams confidently concluded that about 1,000 people across the country would become infected with swine flu in the following month. Yet, by the end of that month, the number of infections was well over 100,000. The question then arose as to how the teams' estimates were askew by an error margin of 10,000%.

It turned out that the estimates of the disease's virulence, which the researchers had obtained from the CDC, were far too low. Even though the estimates had excellent *provenance*, they had poor *pedigree*; the estimates were based on reports coming out of rural Mexico, where, it turned out, many people infected with swine flu had not sought medical treatment at the facilities monitored by the public health agencies, who had then produced the estimates.

Despite the tremendous sophistication of both teams' contextual models, the models were highly sensitive to the underlying parameters. Since both teams had used the same CDC numbers for their simulations, they had produced nearly identical answers. Hence, while the estimates had excellent *precision*, they had poor *accuracy*; the teams' models consistently produced the same results, thereby demonstrating reproducibility or repeatability, but the results were far afield from the actual values.

B. Quantitative and Qualitative Data

Since the 19th century, scientists have known that the brain consists of many interacting neurons, and they have suspected that brains (hence, people) behave in the way they actually do because of the specific properties pertaining to the neuronal cells and their concomitant networked interactions. As the 20th century progressed, neuroscientists studied these properties in greater detail. They learned that electrical currents flow through neurons and across their enclosing membranes, and they studied which molecules control those currents as well as even the precise chemical processes that allow these molecules to do so. They also learned that neurons interacted at small, specific locations—synapses—at which the enclosing membranes of the neuron nearly touched. These synapses were asymmetric; one "upstream" neuron would release one of a small set of "neurotransmitter" molecules from its side of the synapse, and these molecules bound to proteins on the other neuronal cell's side of the synapse, which, in response to this binding, allowed electric current to flow into the cell. When enough electric current flowed into the cell within a relatively short period of time (**about 1 millisecond**), it triggered the downstream cell to release neurotransmitter molecules from a different set of synapses for which *it* was the upstream cell. In terms of overall architecture, all the neurons in the brain are linked by an intricate Web of these synapses, which is sufficiently complex to produce the complex set of behaviors that include memory recall on how to perform a specific action.

However, for the neuroscientist, it was difficult to measure the strength of the interaction between two cells grown in a lab, and it was even harder to measure the connection strengths within an intact brain. Subsequently, scientists adopted a simple model of this complex biophysical system, which they termed a *neural network*. This simplified model included a set of neurons, a listing of which particular neurons had made synapses onto each other, as well as a listing of the strength and sign of those synapses (whether they caused current to flow in or out of the downstream cell). Various *neural network models* used more or less complex models to describe the biophysics within neurons: (1) some used a discrete-time process, for which, at each time-point, all the neurons would simultaneously update the signals they sent out of their upstream synapses, based upon the signals they received at the previous time point; (2) more complex approaches used differential equations to model the interactions of incoming signals from different times and non-linear response functions (such as the work of Stanford University School of Medicine's Harley H. McAdams) to calculate the neuron's output from its time-weighted input.

Unfortunately, neuroscientists did not have access to all the requisite information needed to construct even minimalistic models for a real brain (the human brain has ~100 billion neurons and ~100 trillion synapses). However, through careful behavioral experiments, paired with measurements of some of the connections within certain parts of the brain, and the electrical currents flowing through those neurons, scientists have been able to apply the *neural network model* to offer possible explanations for many brain functions.

To provide some insight into the complexity, Knudsen and Konishi's 1978 work on the Tyot Alba (a.k.a. "barn owl" or "common barn owl") is introduced; a series of careful behavioral experiments in the 1980s revealed that barn owls have the ability to very precisely locate the source of a sound, via interaural time difference and interaural level difference. In essence, the barn owl achieves the requisite and apropos "right-left" sound localization (ability to identify the location or origin of a detected sound in direction and distance [8]) by calculating the time difference between sounds arriving at its two ears. A very quick calculation reveals that the time difference will be less than **.1 milliseconds**, meaning that for the barn owl to utilize the changes within that difference to calculate position, it must be sensitive to differences an order of magnitude smaller or even beyond (e.g., approximately **.01 milliseconds**). However, as described previously, neurons in the neural network model respond to inputs averaged at roughly **1 millisecond and beyond**, meaning that the *neural network model* does not adequately explain the barn owl's aural system.

The explanation turns out to involve the interplay of the spatial organization of the connections between the neurons within the system coupled with subtle biophysical differences between the effect of signals that arrive through adjacent synapses as well as the signals that arrive at distant synapses. Hence, to understand how barn owls locate sounds, it is necessary to know not only which neurons are connected to each other, but also their specific biophysical properties, the exact spatial locations in which they connect, and the detailed shapes of the neurons within the network as well as the overall shape of the [neuronal] network. In other words, it is essential to have a comprehensive knowledge of the *morphology*, *epistemology*, and *praxis* of the system [9];

attempts to simplify the description too much results in a loss of ability to explain the effect being studied.

In modern times, it has been noted that many elegant quantitative models do not well describe natural phenomena, and the notion of quantitative (in)exactitude has challenged the promise of exponential increases in computing power. After all, data comes in two forms: *quantitative data* (data that can be measured) and *qualitative data* (data that can be observed, but not necessarily definitively measured — e.g., textures, smells, tastes). However, for both cases, the processed data still constitutes information.

C. Uncertainty and Ambiguity

Oftentimes, the desire to lower *uncertainty* (a lack of information) and achieve quantitative definiteness "overshadows" the need to lower *ambiguity* (a lack of clarity or context around the information). While reducing *uncertainty* is linear, reducing *ambiguity* is iterative. By way of example, an answer in response to a question temporarily reduces *ambiguity*. However, in answering the question, it leads to more questions, with more questions begetting more answers, and so on. Each answer is responsive to that specific question, but by being successive (and iterative), it only slightly reduces the *ambiguity* around the initial query.

Within these environs of ambiguity, decision-making typically occurs before the full context and consequences are known, as much of learning is derived from retrospection, and any delays may render the information-at-hand out-of-date. Hence, for decision-making amidst compressed decision cycles, it is preferable to have lower *ambiguity* and higher *uncertainty* so as to more closely approximate real-time responsiveness. Given this *uncertainty-ambiguity* paradigm, if an orchestration framework can successfully leverage reduced *ambiguity* for an isomorphic problem (i.e., similar to a previous problem, which has been solved) from another situation, higher *uncertainty* will be tolerated assuming the lower *ambiguity*. Hence, the criticality of a repertoire of veteran methodologies and tools (at machine-speed) to achieve this lower *ambiguity* should be axiomatic. Indeed, if this is accomplished (the ability of computer systems to stimulate and complement human cognitive abilities of decision-making), a subtle advance in cognitive computing will have been made.

VI. Posited Artificial Intelligence Precept: Desire for Gestaltian Closure

The Turing Archive for the History of Computing defines AI as "the science of making computers do things that require intelligence when done by humans" [10]. Practitioners often explain the relationship among AI, Machine Learning (ML), and Deep Learning (DL) as follows: AI is the idea that came first, ML blossomed afterwards, DL is driving AI's explosion, and Deep Belief is currently of keen interest.

A. Deeper Belief amidst Compressed Decision Cycles

In accordance with the Shannon-Weaver sender/receiver model of communication, a receiver makes a zeroth-order approximation of the sender's intended connotational meaning, wherein connotational meaning is determined from semantic context (e.g., historical, cultural, political, institutional, social, et al), such as the sender's social behavior (e.g., inflection, facial expressions, body language, proxemics, et al). Then, utilizing what Richard Palmer termed the "constant process of interpretation" [11], the receiver recursively makes higher-orders of approximation as more semantic contextual information becomes available. For all practical purposes, there are finite successive interpretants because, according to linguist Louis Hjelmslev, the interpretation of the sender's intended meaning is constitutive of, and thereby limited to, the receiver's life experiences. Consequently, according to the founder of analytical psychology, psychiatrist Carl Jung, while the symbol may be apprehended by the receiver at the conscious level, the archetypes, which inform it, exist only at the unconscious level; these archetypes are representative of unlearned tendencies, similar to the concept of instincts discussed by the founder of psychoanalysis, neurologist Sigmund Freud, to experience things in an individualized fashion, and in most cases, the receiver's desire for "Gestaltian Closure" leads to an assignment of a low-order approximation based upon these inherent biases or archetypes. Given compressed (i.e. reduced) decision cycles, a special variant Deep Belief Network (DBN) may be leveraged as a "Gestaltian Closure" accelerant to expedite matters.

B. DBN over DL for Gestaltian Closure admist Compressed Decision Cycles

- *Artificial Intelligence (AI).* According to Steve Hoffenberg of VDC Research, "In an artificial intelligence system, the system would have told ... [us] ... which course of action to take based on its analysis. In cognitive computing, the system provides information to help ... [us] ... decide" [12];
- *Machine Learning (ML).* Some AIs utilize ML. This subset of AI is predicated upon algorithms that can learn from and make predictions based upon data; instead of following a specific set of rules or instructions, these algorithms are trained to detect patterns within large amounts of data;
- *Deep Learning (DL).* In general, DL furthers ML by taking the processed information output from one layer and feeding it as input for the next layer;
- *Deep Belief Network (DBN).* Generally speaking, DBNs are Generative Neural Networks (GNN) that stack Restricted Boltzmann Machines (RBMs). While DBS can become complex, in many cases, they still outperform many existing methods of prediction.

C. Higher Tolerance for Uncertainty amidst Compressed Decision Cycles

As discussed previously in Section V, higher *uncertainty* will be tolerated assuming lower *ambiguity*. This cognitive computing precept may be leveraged as an accelerant to expedite matters amidst compressed decision cycles. When combined with a special variant DBN, which may also be leveraged as an accelerant, a unique pathway for decision-making is presented, as shown in Figure 7. By way of explanation, data is ingested by two disparate pathways: (1) Uncompressed Decision Cycles (UDC), and (2) Compressed Decision Cycles (CDC). For UDC, the data is passed for Deep Learning (DL) as well as a paradigm of "Higher Ambiguity and Lower Uncertainty" (HALU) (i.e. more data is desired). In contrast, for CDC (the entire pathway is shown in red within Figure 7), data will be passed to a Deep Belief Network (DBN) and a "Lower Ambiguity and Higher Uncertainty" (LAHU) module. For the UDC pathway, DL and HALU pass their votes to a modified N-Input Voting Algorithm (NIVA) 1 module [13], whose output is then passed along to a modified Voting Algorithm for Fault Tolerant Systems (VAFTs) module for further processing [14] prior to a decision being reached. For the CDC pathway, DBN and LAHU pass their votes down a fast track pathway that has its own modified NIVA 2 module, an additional "Lower Ambiguity Accelerant (LAA)," and a resultant decision. It should be noted that the NIVA modules (NIVA 1, NIVA 2) are custom coded variants. The VAFTS module is also a custom coded variant. It should further be noted that the multi-threaded custom coding (as contrasted to single-threaded) and the inclusion of glue code constituted a non-trivial endeavor.

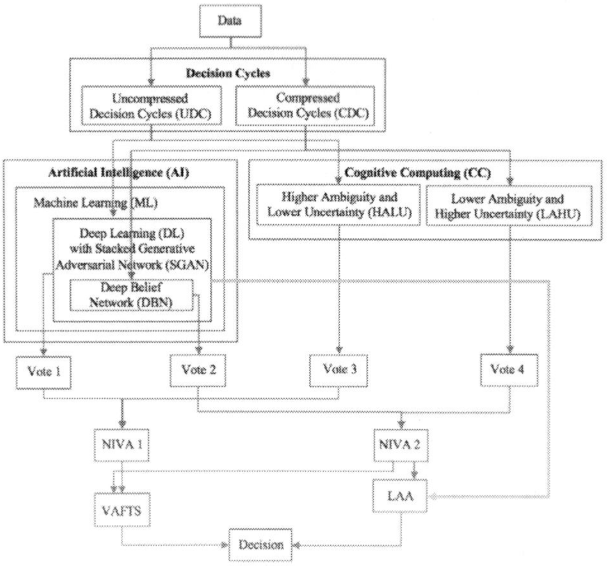

Figure 7. Hybridization of a "Lower Ambiguity and Higher Uncertainty" precept with a "Deeper Belief amidst Compressed Decision Cycles" precept.

Overall, the cognitive computing precept accelerant, when hybridized with a special variant DBN accelerant, yielded a unique pathway for decision-making.

VII. Experimental Results from the Hybridized Computational Methodology

The goal of the experimental testing was to ascertain how the prototype orchestration framework performed when benchmarked against acknowledged performance metrics. Two separate cyber testbeds on a single cyber range, as well as a designated cyber platform for education, training, evaluation and exercise (ETEE) were utilized for the experiment. The results from the two testbeds were averaged for the purposes of Figures 8 and 9 below. Stable operations for the prototype orchestration framework equated to less than 6 days. Results for the Months/Years category were not applicable, as the various iterations were all less than a week (i.e. 1-5 days); likewise, results for the Weeks category were not applicable. Nevertheless, when benchmarked against some percentages from the well-known Verizon Data Breach Investigations Report (whose results have been combined in some cases — e.g., months with years — for the purposes of benchmarking), sub-week results were promising. The time from "initial compromise to discovery" shifted to minutes rather than hours or days. The time from "discovery to containment or restoration" shifted to minutes rather than days. The time from "initial attack to initial compromise" was pushed out to days rather than minutes, and the time from "initial compromise to data exfiltration" was pushed out to days rather than minutes or hours. Further investigation is needed with regards to the slight degradation in performance after several days (i.e. 6+ days) against the programmed advanced persistent threats (APTs) of the involved testbeds.

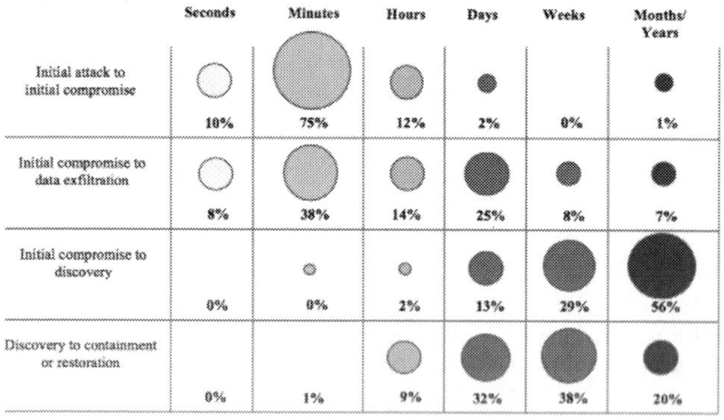

Figure 8. Verizon Data Breach Investigations Report (VDBIR) (whose results have been combined in some cases — e.g., months and years — for the purposes of benchmarking).

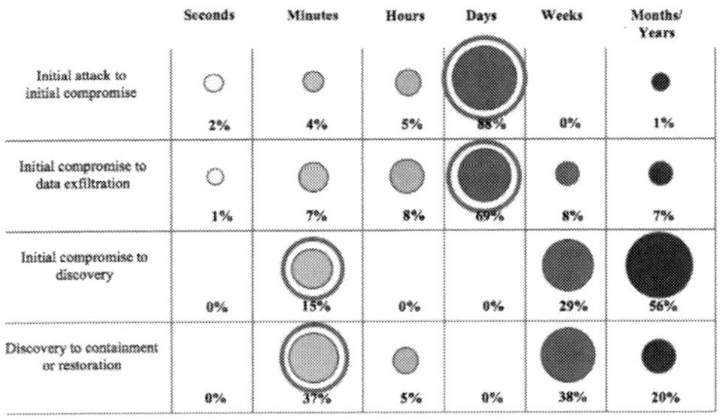

Figure 9. Performance Results of the Prototype Orchestration Framework Benchmarked against the Results of the Verizon Data Breach Investigations Report.

Overall, the experimental testing demonstrated that the prototype orchestration framework, which incorporated, among other notions, an artificial intelligence precept with a cognitive computing precept (i.e., hybridization of the LAHU precept with a DBN precept), proved promising (as demonstrated by the aforementioned results) when benchmarked against the acknowledged performance metrics.

VIII. Posited Key DL Paradigm and LAA Feeder

A. DL with SGANS Paradigm

The contributory DL vote stems from modified [Deep Convolutional] Generative Adversarial Networks (GANs) [15], each of which is comprised of two *neural networks,* which are pitted against each other (hence, the "adversarial" aspect in an unsupervised machine learning paradigm). The generative aspect is best described by contrasting it to a discriminative aspect. Whereas discriminative models endeavor to learn the boundary between classes (given the labels y and features x, the formulation p(y|x) equates to "the probability of y given x"), generative models endeavor to model the distribution of individual classes (the focus is on "how you get x," and the formulation p(x|y) equates to "probability of x given y" or the probability of features given a class). GANs are well known for being able to, for example, find the roads on an aerial map, fill in the missing details of an image (up sampling, given the edges), and construct an image, which postulates how a person might look when they are older [16]. For this experiment, the GANS are stacked; hence the paradigm is that of Stacked Generative Adversarial Network (SGAN).

B. LAA, via DL Feeder

As previously discussed, the higher need for cognitive closure [17] drives a tolerance for higher *uncertainty* given a state of relatively lower *ambiguity* (a repertoire of examples of successively handling similar problems). A key factor for achieving this steady state of relatively lower *ambiguity* resides in the ongoing learnings of the SGAN in the DL module. This feeder mechanism, which is comprised of the SGAN in the DL as well as the LAA, was previously shown in orange within Figure 7.

IX. Conclusion

This paper presents the benchmarked performance results of a prototype orchestration framework. The premise for devising such a system was predicated on the ever-increasing cycles of adaptation of cyber-attackers leveraging an array of potential accelerants (e.g., NVD, SHODAN, etc.). The presented system utilizes several accelerants in an attempt to mitigate, via a cyber defense accelerant for particular high exposure dimensions (e.g., network, software attack surfaces). For the UDC pathway, DL and HALU passed their votes along to a modified NIVA 1 module and VAFTS variant. For the CDC pathway, DBN and LAHU pass their votes down a fast track pathway; this pathway is facilitated by a LAA, which has been continuously informed by the SGAN from the DL module. The described work has been benchmarked, via an ETEE, against various permutations generated by the testbeds of the involved cyber range and compared to the presented VDBIR. The preliminary results of the modified SGAN-DBN-NIVA-VAFTS amalgam seem promising. Future work necessitates a further investigation of any degradation in performance, as well as the potential involvement of other useful algorithmic modifications. Collaboration MSSPs have concurred that the discussed modified DBN (within the AI->ML->DL paradigm) and LAHU as well as their modified SGAN-fed LAA, particularly amidst CDC, warrant further research.

Acknowledgment

The author would like to thank the Decision Engineering Analysis Laboratory (DEAL) for its encouragement and motivation throughout the process of pursuing and completing this research. Without their initial and continuing assistance, as well as the ideas, feedback, suggestions, guidance, resources, and contacts made available through that support, much of this research would have been delayed. The author would also like to thank VT & IE²SPOMTF. This is part of a paper series on enhanced event correlation. The author would like to also thank USG leadership (e.g., the CAG). In addition, the author would like to thank ICE Cyber Security for the opportunity to serve as Chair, Scientific Advisory Board. The author would further like to thank the International Academy, Research, and Industry Association (IARIA) for the constant motivation to excel as well as the opportunity to serve as a contributing IARIA Fellow within the cyber and data analytics domains, particularly in the area of mission-critical systems.

References

[1] "What You Need to Know About Managed Services," CISCO Public, p. 3, 2017.

[2] "Managed Services Market Worth $193.34 Billion by 2019," PR Newswire, pp. 1-4, 7 January 2015.

[3] "FM 3-38 Cyber Electromagnetic Activities," Department of the Army, pp. 1-2, 12 February 2014.

[4] E. Tabor, "3 Ways Managed Services Provide Access to the Most Advanced IT Tools," ISG Technology, pp. 1-2, 11 January 2017.

[5] D. Dinely, "The Greatest Open Source Software of All Time: InfoWorld's Open Source Hall of Fame Recognizes the 36 Most Important Free Open Source Software Projects in History (and Today)," InfoWorld, pp. 1-2, 17 August 2009.

[6] J. Porup, "What is Wireshark? What This Essential Troubleshooting Tool Does and How to Use It," CSO, IDG Research, pp. 1-8, 17 September 2018.

[7] R. Kay, "Cognitive Computing: When Computers Become Brains," Forbes, pp. 1-5, 9 December 2011.

[8] B. Nelson and T. Takahashi, "Independence of Echo-Threshold and Echo-Delay in the Barn Owl," PLOS One, pp. 1-11, 31 October 2008.

[9] G. Ritter, "An Introduction to Morphological Neural Networks," Pattern Recognition, Proceedings of the 13th International Conference on Pattern Recognition, vol. 4, pp. 709-717, 1996.

[10] D. Evans, "Cognitive Computing Vs. Artificial Intelligence: What's the Difference?" Tech Innovation, pp. 1-11, 28 March 2017.

[11] R. Palmer, Hermeneutics: Interpretation Theory in Schleiermacher, Dilthey, Heidegger, and Gadamer. Northwestern University Press, 1969, p. 283.

[12] S. Hoffenberg, "IBM's Watson Answers the Question, 'What's the Difference Between Artificial Intelligence and Cognitive Computing'," IDC Research, pp. 1-3, 24 May 2016.

[13] A. Karimi, F. Zarafshan, and A. Ramli, "A Novel N-Input Voting Algorithm for X-by-Wire Fault-Tolerant System," The Scientific World Journal, pp. 1-9, 2014.

[14] S. Latif-Shabgahi, "An Integrated Voting Algorithm for Fault Tolerant System," 2011 International Conference on Software and Computer Applications, International Proceedings of Computer Science and Information Technology (IPCSIT), vol. 9, pp. 1-17, 2011.

[15] A. Radford, L. Metz, and S. Chintala, "Unsupervised Representation Learning with Deep Convolutional Generative Adversarial Networks," ArXiv, pp. 1-16, 7 January 2016.

[16] C. Liu, X. Wu, and X. Shu, "Learning-Based Dequantization for Image Restoration Against Extremely Poor Illumination," ArXiv, pp. 1-10, 20 March 2018.

[17] P. Iannello, A. Mottini, S. Tirelli, S. Riva, and A. Antonietti, "Ambiguity and Uncertainty Tolerance, Need for Cognition, and Their Association with Stress," Medical Educadtion Online, vol 22(1), pp. 1-17, 2017.

Prototype Open-Source Software Stack for the Reduction of False Positives and Negatives in the Detection of Cyber Indicators of Compromise and Attack

Hybridized Log Analysis Correlation Engine and Container-Orchestration System Supplemented by Ensemble Method Voting Algorithms for Enhanced Event Correlation

Steve Chan
Decision Engineering Analysis Laboratory
San Diego, California U.S.A.
email: schan@dengineering.org

Abstract—**A prototypical solution stack (Solution Stack #1) with chosen Open-Source Software (OSS) components for an experiment was enhanced by hybridized OSS amalgams (e.g., Suricata and Sagan; Kubernetes, Nomad, Cloudify and Helios; MineMeld and Hector) and supplemented by select modified algorithms (e.g., modified N-Input Voting Algorithm [NIVA] modules and a modified Fault Tolerant Averaging Algorithm [FTAA] module) leveraged by ensemble method machine learning. The preliminary results of the prototype solution stack (Stack #2) indicate a reduction, with regards to cyber Indicators of Compromise (IOC) and indicators of attack (IOA), of false positives by approximately 15% and false negatives by approximately 47%.**

Keywords-Threat Intelligence Processing Framework (TIPF); Security Orchestration (SO); Log [Analysis] and Correlation Engine (LCE); Container-Orchestration System (COS); Dynamic Service Discovery (DSD).

I. INTRODUCTION

At an Advanced Computing Systems Association (a.k.a. Unix Users Group or USENIX) Enigma Conference, Rob Joyce, the head of the National Security Agency's (NSA) Tailored Access Operations (TAO) hacking team noted that, "If you really want to protect your network, you have to know your network, including all the devices and technology in it." He went on to add that a successful attacker will often know networks better than the people who designed and run them [1]. The onus of Joyce's statement is very much, in contemporary times, carried by Managed Security Service Providers (MSSPs). The increasing level of cyber threats has obligated MSSPs to use a defense-in-depth methodology of layering various security appliances, and it has been noted that much of the successful commercial software applications in this arena is principally comprised of either the original or variants of Open-Source Software (OSS) projects. Interestingly, commercial offerings have, in some cases, become black boxed. The ensuing risk is that 41% of cyber-security applications contain high-risk open source vulnerabilities [2], and according to the 2018 Open Source Security and Risk Analysis (OSSRA) report by Black Duck of Synopsys, these risks are increasing. Without a firm understanding of the innards, MSSPs cannot readily ascertain the risk of the black boxed commercial offering itself. Accordingly, MSSPs are endeavoring to put forth their own offerings (also for market differentiation), in a white box fashion; for the purposes of adhering to Joyce's recommendation, the white box approach can be, in some cases, more effective than the black box approach, but it is a much more difficult pathway in terms of the sophistication needed to understand and appropriately orchestrate the various involved subsystems. By way of example, a Verizon Data Breach Report had articulated that those with robust log analysis and correlation were least likely to be a cyber victim; yet, legacy approaches to this particular challenge are often highly manual in nature, thereby creating complex workflows and extending the time needed for implementation (rather than decreasing the time needed, as desired by the MSSPs). To further the complexity, while various security appliances are quite successful at detecting and logging attacks and anomalous behavior, contemporary threats are characterized by being distributed in nature, acting in concert across varied systems, and employing advanced detection evasion techniques. Accordingly, MSSPs are turning to various means of automation, correlation, and orchestration. This paper presents preliminary findings from an experiment conducted, which focused upon comparing a prototypical solution stack with one that was enhanced by hybridized tools and supplemented by select modified algorithms.

This paper describes an experiment of clustering by class and hybridizing tools within the same class with certain decision-support accelerants to improve detection and decision-making. The paper first presents a solution stack (Solution Stack #1) with chosen OSS and then presents an enhanced solution stack (Solution Stack #2) aiming to reduce false positive and false negative of cyber alarms. It then proposes a method of leveraging inputs channeled via multiple OSS components (within the same class) for various classes and utilizes ensemble method machine learning. Solution Stack #1 is an original contribution as it combines OSS comments via glue code. Solution Stack #2 is an original contribution as it utilizes hybridized amalgams not discussed robustly elsewhere in literature or implemented as described herein. The N-Input Voting Algorithm (NIVA) and Fault Tolerant Averaging Algorithm (FTAA) algorithms utilized are variants from the originals and have unique architecture and glue code to effectuate their implementation; indeed, the implementation was quite challenging. The paper is organized as follows: Section II discusses the trending toward the increasing utilization of MSPs, specifically MSSPs. The discussion also reviews the increasing level of cyber threats, which have obligated MSSPs to use a defense-in-depth methodology of layering various security appliances as well as their own differentiated solution stack offerings. Subsequently, Section III discusses the acknowledged layers of a MSSP solution stack, regardless of the diversification. The layers range from Remote Monitoring and Management to Dynamic Service Discovery. Then, Section IV delves into the predilection of OSS for the experiment of this paper and the preferred licenses, which include, among others, the classic GNU General Public License as well as the Affero General Public License. Section V discusses the OSS components utilized for the first phase of the experiment (as part of Solution Stack #1). The OSS projects discussed range from Project-Open to GOSINT. Section VI discusses various OSS amalgams, which have been hybridized for enhanced performance. Amalgams include Kubernetes, Nomad, Cloudify, and Helios. Section VII presents a posited hybridized solution stack, which includes the hybridized OSS amalgams from Section VI for the second phase of the experiment (as part of Solution Stack #2). Section VIII provides the experimental results from Solution Stack #1 (constituting Phase 1 of the experiment) as well as Solution Stack #2 (constituting Phase 2 of the experiment). In essence, the preliminary results indicate a reduction of false positives from Phase 1 of the experiment, Solution Stack #1 to Phase 2 of the experiment, Solution Stack #2 by approximately 15% and a reduction of false negatives by approximately 47%. Finally, the paper reviews and emphasizes key points in Section IX, the conclusion.

II. MANAGED SECURITY SERVICES PROVIDER TREND

According to International Data Corporation (IDC), at least 50% of the global [Gross Domestic Product] GDP will be digital by 2021 [3]. Yet, digital business has inherent cybersecurity risks, and this was articulated by the Digital Business World Congress. According to Klynveld Peat Marwick Goerdeler (KPTM), Chief Executive Officers (CEOs) view cybersecurity as their top risk and innovation challenge. As digital business (e.g., Internet of Things [IOT], Bring Your Own Device [BYOD], mobile computing, cloud computing, etc.) increases in its applications, new exploitable vulnerabilities for cybercrime will emerge. Along this vein, Cyveillance's "Cyber Intelligence Report" asserts that cybercriminals are constantly finding new ways to exploit cyber vulnerabilities [4]. Cybercrime damage costs are expected to reach USD$6 trillion annually by 2021 [5]. According to the Ponemon Institute, 98% of business respondents reported that they will spend over a million dollars in 2017 on cybersecurity; however, many of the systems and people in place are still not able to handle either simplistic or complex contemporary cyber threats [6].

According to Gartner, organizations are expected to increase spending on enterprise application software this year, shifting more of their budget to Software as a Service (SaaS), via the managed services market [7]. MarketsandMarkets asserts that the global managed services market is approximately USD$152.45 billion [8], and it is expected to grow to nearly USD$257.84 billion by 2022 [9]. According to Allied Market Research, the global market for SaaS or managed cyber security services by Managed Services Providers (MSPs) – or, more specifically, Managed Security Services Providers (MSSPs) – is expected to garner USD$40.97 billion by 2022 [10]. According to Gartner, "The EU General Data Protection Regulation (GDPR) has created renewed interest, and will drive 65 percent of data loss prevention buying decisions today through 2018," "security services will continue to be the fastest growing segment, especially IT outsourcing, consulting, and implementation services," and "by 2020, 40 percent of all managed security service (MSS) contracts will be bundled with other security services and broader IT outsourcing projects, up from 20 percent today" [11]. Between 2018-2025, "The security services segment is expected to grow at a [Compound Annual Growth Rate] CAGR of over 18%" and "the Asia Pacific is expected to be the fastest-growing region over the forecast period, ...[due] ... to the growing adoption of ... managed services by the small and medium-sized enterprises [SMEs], which are expected to drive the market growth" [12] (albeit large enterprises are still significant as they are establishing branch offices at remote locations and outsourcing to MSPs and/or MSSPs as well).

Hiscox, a cyber insurance company, states that less than 52% of small businesses have a clearly defined cyber security strategy, 65% of small businesses have failed to act following a cyber security incident, and less than 21% of small businesses have a standalone cyber insurance policy, compared to more than half (58%) for large companies [13]. According to the Ponemon Institute, 61% of small businesses experienced a breach in 2017, and, according to the National Cyber Security Alliance, 60 percent of Small and Medium Businesses (SMBs) that suffer a cyber-attack are out of business within six months of a breach [14]. Given the risk, these SMEs or SMBs are treating their exposures more seriously. Trends are changing, and according to Allied Market Research, SMBs will spend approximately USD$11 billion on remotely managed security services as well as represent the primary driver for the global remotely managed security services market's projected growth [15]; after all, many SMBs have minimal IT staffing to handle the ever-increasing complex threats on the cyber landscape. Hence, the desire and need for MSSPs is ever-increasing.

III. Layers of a MSSP Solution Stack

The following sections discuss the universally acknowledged layers of a MSSP solution stack, regardless of the differentiation.

A. Remote Monitoring and Management (RMM)

Digital business has necessitated automation, and MSPs have strived to provide Professional Services Automation (PSA) tools to meet this need. Digital business has also required remote access (e.g., mobile phones, tablets, laptops). Likewise, MSPs have deployed RMM tools to meet this need. PSA tools are fundamental for any MSP, as they may keep track of customer information, track workflow, and generate invoices from that work. Most of this described work will involve those things performed and managed through the RMM; in essence, PSA is the tool to track the work, and RMM is the tool to help effectuate that work.

B. Machine Learning (ML) for the RMM

As the RMM is a backbone for the MSP, among other applications, Atera (a company that produces software for MSPs) CEO Gil Pekelman envisions incorporating ML to assist MSPs with tasks, such as how to program an RMM. According to Pekelman, with regards to monitoring tasks, there are "hundreds of things to choose from … how do you know what are the right things to monitor" [16]? Pekelman further notes that, in the past, such decisions were based upon the MSP's experience, intuition, and suggestions from peers [16]. Current thinking centers upon the fact that ML can enhance RMM by shifting from subjective (e.g., intuition) to objective (e.g., empirically-based logic) monitoring paradigms.

C. Intrusion Detection System (IDS) and Intrusion Prevention Systems (IPS)

For cyber security, monitoring should be a central tenet of any strategy, so a robust monitoring strategy seems axiomatic. However, as the time required to operationalize a robust paradigm is non-trivial, it is often de-prioritized. A classic example involves one of the most notable security breaches to date, which involved Equifax, a consumer credit reporting agency. More than 145.5 million people were affected by the attack [17], which exploited the Apache Struts Vulnerability (CVE-2017-5638) [18]. Notably, this attack was carried out over time and 30 malicious web shells were uploaded over the course of four months [19]. Ultimately, this catastrophic breach resulted from a failure to monitor and act upon security incidents early enough in the cyber-attack lifecycle.

Among other monitoring paradigms, IDS and IPS work by actively monitoring network traffic for unusual patterns or aberrant behavior. For example, an unusually high volume of data being directed to an external Internet Protocol (IP) address (e.g., an IP address located in a country in which the organization does not perform work) might trigger an IDS or IPS alert. The following are some general approaches.

1) Signature-Based: will monitor packets on the network and compare them against a database of signatures (i.e., attributes) from known cyber-threats (i.e., similar to an antivirus approach). The deficiency is that there will be a lag between the time a new threat is discovered in the wild and when the signature for detecting that threat is applied.

2) Anomaly-Based: will monitor network traffic and compare it against an established baseline. The baseline will reflect what constitutes normal for that network (e.g., bandwidth, protocols, ports, devices, etc.). An alert is provided when traffic that is anomalous from the baseline is detected.

3) Passive: will simply detect and alert. When anomalous network traffic is detected, an alert is provided. However, human intervention is needed to take an action.

4) Reactive: will not only detect anomalous traffic and provide an alert, but will also respond by taking pre-defined, proactive actions (e.g., blocking the user or source IP address from accessing the network, etc.).

The principal difference between IDS and IPS is that while IDS will indeed provide an alert based upon anomalous network traffic, it is typically a passive system that does not prevent or terminate activity; in contrast, IPS typically undertake action. They are broadly classified as follows:

1) Network Intrusion Detection Systems (NIDS): are placed at strategic points throughout the network to monitor traffic to and from all devices. Pragmatically, although monitoring all inbound and outbound traffic seems ideal, doing so might create a bottleneck that would impair the overall speed of the network.

2) Host Intrusion Detection Systems (HIDS): are run on individual hosts or devices on the network and monitor the inbound and outbound packets to and from the device only.

D. Unified Threat Management (UTM)

In an attempt to simplify and unify matters, UTM devices typically integrate a range of security devices, such as firewalls, gateways, and IDS/IPS into a single device or platform. The consolidation of these functions can simplify management tasks and training requirements; however, it can also create a single point of failure.

E. Security Information and Event Management (SIEM)

SIEM works differently from the UTM. Rather than replacing antivirus, firewalls, or IDS/IPS, SIEM operates in a complementary fashion with these devices to collect and correlate information from the log and event data produced by the disparate systems (e.g., devices, applications) on the network. While individual devices or point applications may provide various fragments of information, the SIEM assists in assembling higher order vantage points to identify security risks, which individual devices and applications may not identify. Via this defense-in-depth methodology, the SIEM can help identify attacks during the initial stages of the cyber kill chain rather than the final stages.

1) Security Incident Indicator of Compromise (IOC)

To avoid security incidents from occurring, MSSPs are increasingly leveraging IOCs (e.g., malware, exploits, vulnerabilities, IP addresses, etc.). These IOCs are typical of the evidence left behind when a breach has occurred. Utilizing IOCs forensically constitutes a reactive posture.

2) Indicator of Attack (IOA):

In contrast, the utilization of IOAs (e.g., code execution, command and control, lateral movement) segue to a proactive stance, as cyber defenders actively hunt for early warning signs that an attack may be underway.

F. Threat Intelligence Platform (TIP) and Threat Intelligence Processing Framework (TIPF)

IOCs and IOAs are amalgamated from heterogeneous external sources (e.g., Spamhaus) by TIPs, which endeavor to aggregate, correlate, and analyze threat data from multiple sources in real-time to support defensive actions. The advantage of disparate sources is that each will have varied techniques and tools for operationalizing various compliance regimes. In turn, TIPFs can, in some cases, study IOCs and IOAs so as to capture cross-incident trends. TIPFs effectively translate collected IOCs and IOAs into actionable controls for enforcement on security devices.

G. Optimizing SIEM with Security Orchestration (SO)

The SIEM is unable to, inherently, reduce the number of false positives (i.e., if the SIEM sends thousands of false alarms every day, it becomes nearly impossible to keep pace, ascertain the alerts that matter, and respond in a timely fashion). By leveraging SO, the SIEM can focus on collecting data and correlating alerts, while SO (considered an enhancement to SIEM) actions, taken across the entire security product stack, can scale SIEM capabilities by automating tasks (e.g., IP lookups, log queries, etc.) and streamlining the alert ingestion from multiple sources (e.g., TIPs, TIPFs) so as to produce tailored response playbooks, as automated, orchestrated security responses (as well as potentially handling the investigation and remediation process), such as the following:

1) Firewall

- Proactively blocks IP addresses of recognized attacks (e.g., ransomware) and/or attackers;
- Proactively blocks newly detected attackers discovered by peers within the trusted circle;
- Automatically blocks the IP address of an attacker, a compromised device from outbound communication, etc.;

2) Network Device

- Automatically takes a snapshot image of the suspected device;
- Automatically removes or quarantines the device from the network;

3) User Account

- Automatically locks an account for a period of time;
- Automatically forces the password reset of a suspicious account.

The described automated actions assist in reducing false positives and better illuminating those alerts, which require further human investigation.

H. Log [Analysis] and Correlation Engine (LCE) as a Monitoring Strategy

The "Verizon Data Breach Report: Detective Controls by Percent of Breach Victims" highlighted the fact that 71% of the breach victims were those that relied predominantly upon System Device Logs, 30% for Intrusion Detection Systems, 20% for Automated Log Analysis, 13% for SIEM, and 11% for Log Review Process [20]. In essence, a comprehensive log review process or analysis (perhaps a combination of manual and automatic log analysis) very much minimizes cyber breaches. Indeed, per various Verizon Data Breach Reports, investigators noted that a substantive portion (e.g., 66%) of victims had sufficient evidence available within their logs to discover the breach had they been more diligent in analyzing such resources [21]. Accordingly, in addition to extrospection (e.g., TIPs and TIPFs), there should be a particular emphasis placed on introspection at the log level, such as by the SIEM and SO.

Aggregating security log data, via Vulnerability Scanners (VS), further streamlines the analysis of network vulnerabilities. In general, software security updates endeavor to address vulnerabilities; with the escalating vulnerabilities populating the cyber landscape, software update deployment velocity is increasing. To address this phenomenon, DevOps (a portmanteau of "Development" and "Operations") has surged. Among other solutions, containerization is often used in DevOps; containerization supports the ability to package application dependencies with the application itself, thereby ensuring that the application will perform in a consistent fashion wherever it is deployed; these applications can be modularized further into a collection of loosely coupled services called microservices, each in a container. Containers enable instant scale, as they take microseconds to instantiate, as contrasted to a virtual machine (VM), which can take minutes. Also, VMs generally support one application per Operating System (OS), due to potential conflicts with dependencies (e.g., differing versions of external Dynamic Link Libraries [DLLs]). Virtualization has optimized IT work flow processes, via the capability of running multiple OS on a single server or system. For the discussed experiment, the container approach was utilized, as containers make it possible to deploy applications on generic VMs that do not have to be preconfigured to support the involved applications. This provides more flexibility, as the VMs can be treated generically (not specifically, as in the traditional case), thereby providing the ability to leverage any of the VMs (i.e., not just ones that are prepared to accept a specific application).

Containers are, in turn, run by a Pod, which represents a running process, as it encapsulates an Application (App) container (which contains the program code and its activity) or, in some cases, multiple containers. For a Pod that runs a single container, the Pod can be construed as a wrapper, and the Pods are the managed entity rather than the containers directly. For a Pod that encapsulates an application composed of multiple co-located containers (that are tightly coupled and form a single cohesive unit of service, such as for the case of a container serving files from a shared volume, while a separate "sidecar" container refreshes those files), the Pod serves as a wrapper for both the containers and storage resources, together, as a single manageable entity. This paradigm is shown in Figure 1.

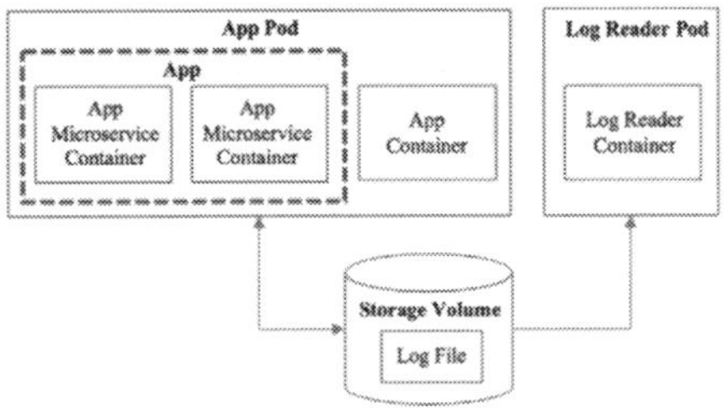

Figure 1. Exemplar Pod, Container, Volume Paradigm for Log Files

LCEs involve logging components (e.g., log reader), which can be deployed as App containers (within Pods) inside a cluster, which can refer to running an application in multiple processes (i.e., Pods), all receiving requests on the same port. In general, contemporary software applications (e.g., service-oriented architecture or SOA) are composed of multiple services; this entails multiple containers or services comprising a single App that needs to be deployed as a distributed system; such a system is complex to scale and manage. To move beyond the simple management of individual containers of simple Apps and move toward larger enterprise applications with microservices, it is necessary to utilize container-orchestration platforms.

I. Container-Orchestration System (COS)

For scalable, multi-container Apps, COS are generally utilized to automate the deployment, scaling, and management. In other words, COS will automatically start containers, scale-out containers with multiple instances per image, suspend them or shut them down as needed, and control how they access resources, such as network and data storage. Whatever the design for the COS, the task is to provide optimization for the involved container-based distributed system [22].

J. Dynamic Service Discovery (DSD)

Service discovery is a key component of most distributed systems and SOAs, as clients seek to determine the IP address port for a service that exists on multiple hosts. For a simple network, static configuration of IP addresses and ports might suffice. However, as more services are deployed, the complexity increases. For a high-performance operational system, service locations can change quite frequently as a result of automatic or manual scaling, new deployments of services, and hosts failing or being replaced; for this situation, dynamic service registration and discovery becomes much more important to avoid service interruption. Indeed, DSD is a key factor in achieving an adaptable, loosely-coupled, and more resilient SOA [23].

IV. OPEN-SOURCE PREDILECTION FOR THE EXPERIMENT

Having performed several iterative deployments of the stacks discussed herein, one experiential learning, among others, has been that past performance may not be an indicator of future results. Sometimes, commercial solutions may quickly advance to the forefront, but in some cases, many are overtaken by OSS projects. Among various reasons, innovation, particularly as pertains to the commercial offerings, may decrease after the product reaches a certain level of maturity. In several other cases, the more successful commercial solutions are comprised of either the original or variants of open-source projects. For this experiment, only OSS projects under the following licenses were utilized.

A. GNU General Public License (GPL)

GPL is a widely used free software license, which guarantees end users the freedom to run, study, share and *modify* the software.

B. MIT License (MITL)

The MIT License is another widely used free software license, which grants end users the freedom to deal with the software without restriction, including without limitation the rights to use, copy, *modify*, merge, publish, distribute, sublicense, and/or sell copies of the software.

C. Apache License

The Apache License is yet another utilized free software license that allows the user of the software the freedom to use the software for any purpose, to distribute it, to *modify* it, and to distribute modified versions of the software, under the terms of the license, without concern for royalties (of special note, Apache License Version 2.0 requires preservation of the copyright notice and disclaimer).

D. *Affero General Public License*

The Affero General Public License (a.k.a. Affero GPL, Affero License) is either of two distinct, though historically related, free software licenses: (1) Affero General Public License Version 1.0 (AGPLv1), which is based upon the GNU General Public License Version 2.0, and (2) Affero General Public License Version 2.0 (AGPLv2), which is a transitional license for an upgrade path from AGPLv1 to the GNU Affero General Public License, which is compatible with GNU GPL Version 3.0. Both versions of the Affero GPL were designed to close a perceived Application Service Provider (ASP) loophole in the GPL (i.e., using, but not distributing software, left copyleft provisions untriggered).

E. *Mozilla Public License*

The Mozilla Public License (MPL) defines rights as passing from "Contributors" who create or modify source code, through an auxiliary distributor (themselves a licensee), to the licensee. It grants copyright and patent licenses allowing for free use, *modification*, distribution, and exploitation of the work, but it does not grant the licensee any rights to a contributor's trademarks.

There are various solution stacks [24], but Figure 2 constitutes one exemplar and is what was utilized for the first phase of the experiment. As shown, TIPF fed its output back to the SIEM, and VS fed its output to the LCE (orange pathway).

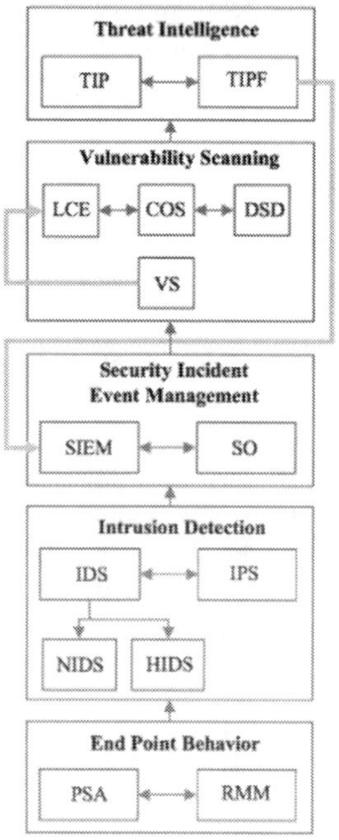

Figure 2. Exemplar Solution Stack for the First Phase of the Experiment: Solution Stack #1

V. COMPONENTS UTILIZED FOR THE EXPERIMENT

The various components utilized for the experiment included the following, which are presented in Subsections A-K.

A. *PSA*

1) Project-Open (commodity modules): free | open-source | GNU GPL Version 3.0 | PSA | application.

B. *RMM*

1) Comodo One: free | open-source | MIT License | RMM | platform. Comodo One is produced by Comodo, a cyber security company that is known for being the world's second largest Certificate Authority (CA) and was, at one time, the largest issuer of Secure Sockets Layer (SSL) certificates.

C. *IDS*

1) Security Onion: free | open-source | GNU GPL Version 2.0 | NIDS | platform.

2) OSSEC & Wazuh: free | open-source | GNU GPL Version 2.0 | HIDS | system.

3) Sagan: free | open-source | GNU GPL Version 2.0 | NIDS + HIDS | engine.

D. *IPS*

1) Suricata: free | open-source | GNU GPL Version 2.0 | IPS | engine. Suricata was developed by the Open Information Security Foundation (OISF). It is partly funded by the Department of Homeland Security's Directorate for Science and Technology and is designed to work with Snort rulesets.

E. *SIEM*

1) OSSIM: pseudo-free | open-source | GNU GPL Version 3.0 | SIEM | platform. The OSSIM project began in 2003, and in 2008, it became the basis for AlienVault. The commercial variant of OSSIM is entitled, "AlienVault Unified Security Management."

F. *SO*

1) PatrOwl: free | open-source | Affero General Public License | SO | platform.

G. *LCE*

1) Sagan: free | open-source | GNU GPL Version 2.0 | LCE | engine.

2) OpenVas: free | open-source | GNU GPL | VS | framework. OpenVAS is a member project of the Software in the Public Interest (SPI), which has hosted Wikimedia Foundation board elections and audited tallies as a neutral third party.

H. COS

1) Kubernetes: free | open-source | Apache 2.0 | COS | platform. It was originally designed by Google and is now maintained by the Cloud Native Computing Foundation. At the core, coordination and storage is provided by etcd.

2) Nomad: free | open-source | Mozilla Public License 2.0 | COS | tool.

3) Cloudify: free | open-source | Apache 2.0 | COS | platform. It is a software cloud and NFV orchestration product originally created by GigaSpaces Technologies (an Israeli company focused on space-based architectures [e.g., tuple spaces]), and then spun out.

4) Helios: free | open-source | Apache 2.0 | COS | platform. Spotify created Helios, which is a key component of their scalability strategy. Helios has the capacity to perceive when a "container is dead;" if a mission critical container is accidentally closed down, Helios quickly loads one back up.

I. DSD

1) Consul: free | open-source | Mozilla Public License 2.0 | DSD | tool. Consul is designed for multi-datacenter service discovery.

J. TIP

1) MineMeld: free | open-source | Apache 2.0 | TIP | platform. As part of its commitment to the security community and mission of driving a new era of threat intelligence sharing, Palo Alto Networks released MineMeld to the community-at-large.

2) HECTOR: free | open-source | GNU GPL Version 3.0 | TIP | platform. HECTOR is an open source initiative originally sponsored by the University of Pennsylvania School of Arts & Sciences (SAS).

K. TIPF

1) GOSINT: free | open-source | GNU GPL Version 3.0 | TIPF | framework. As part of its commitment to the security community and mission of driving a new era of threat intelligence sharing, CISCO release GOSINT to the community-at-large.

The aforementioned components were utilized in both the first and second phases of the experiment. Figure 3 presents the previously presented exemplar solution stack with the various components; each component is represented in accordance to its classification herein. For example, OSSEC & Wazuh would be C-2, Suricata would be D-1, OSSIM would be E-1, Kubernetes would be H-1, and MineMeld would be J-1.

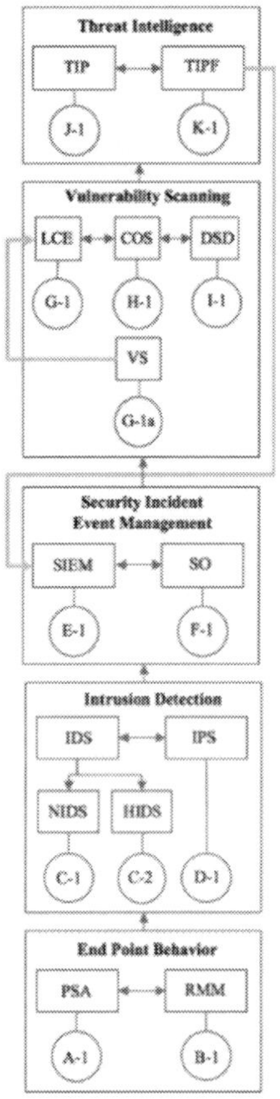

Figure 3. Exemplar Solution Stack with specified Components for the First Phase of the Experiment: Solution Stack #1

The experiment leveraged the open-source Elasticsearch, Logstash, Kibana (ELK) stack for supporting certain functionality. Logstash is a server-side data processing pipeline, which ingests data from multiple sources simultaneously, transforms it, and then sends it to a search and analytics engine, such as Elasticsearch. Kibana supports visualization analytics within Elasticsearch.

VI. HYBRIDIZING FOR ENHANCED PERFORMANCE

Preliminary results from the exemplar solution stack were obtained. It was posited that the results could be improved by enhancing the exemplar solution stack with complementary tools and supplemented by select modified algorithms. The hybridizations are discussed below.

A. Suricata and Sagan

Although Snort may be the world's most deployed IPS, its current limitation is that it, for all intents and purposes, is fundamentally single-threaded; hence, it does not take advantage of multi-core machines without special configurations. Furthermore, results show that a single instance of Suricata is able to deliver substantially higher performance than a corresponding single instance of Snort or multi-instance Snort [25]. However, Sagan utilizes a multi-threaded architecture and encompasses both NIDS and HIDS while Snort and Suricata are just NIDS [26]. In brief, Sagan was utilized to complement Suricata.

B. *Kubernetes, Nomad, Cloudify and Helios*

While Kubernetes is specifically focused on Docker, Nomad is more general purpose. Nomad supports virtualized, containerized, and standalone applications. Kubernetes is wrapped by Application Programming Interface (API) controllers, which are consumed by other services that, in turn, provide higher level APIs for features (e.g., scheduling). Kubernetes documentation states that it can support clusters greater than 5,000 nodes and can support a Multi-Availability Zone (AZ)/multi-region configuration; however, Nomad has operationally proven to scale to cluster sizes that exceed 10,000 nodes in real-world production environments [27]; Nomad is designed to be a global-scale scheduler and natively supports multi-datacenter and multi-region configurations [27]. Cloudify is quite good at hybrid cloud deployment, and Helios is very good at removing single points of failures, as "numerous Helios-master services can react … at the same time" [28]. In brief, Kubernetes, Nomad, Cloudify and Helios were utilized together as a hybridized amalgam.

C. *MineMeld and Hector*

The consolidation and correlation functions performed by MineMeld can be nicely complemented, via HECTOR, which allows for correlation between otherwise unrelated security data points and metrics to extrapolate context. In brief, Hector was utilized to complement MineMeld.

VII. Posited Hybridized Solution Stack

The prototypical exemplar solution stack with the specified components for the experiment was as delineated in Section V, Figure 3. The solution stack was revised to include the hybridized groupings of Section VI. Of the 18 components included, the sponsor organizations self-described these components as: an application (1), system (1), tool (2), framework (2), engine (3), and platform (9). The revised, prototype solution stack with hybridized groupings and modified algorithms for ensemble ML is shown in Figure 4. As can be seen in Figure 4, each set of groupings passed their outputs to modified N-Input Voting Algorithm (NIVA) modules [31], which acted in concert with a modified Fault Tolerant Averaging Algorithm (FTAA) module [32], via ensemble method ML. For Intrusion Detection, C-1, C-2, and C-3 passed their outputs to NIVA-1, whose output was refined by FTAA and the resultant was N-1 (red pathway). For Vulnerability Scanning, H-1, H-2, H-3, and H-4 passed their outputs to NIVA-2, whose output was refined by FTAA and the resultant was N-2 (red pathway). For Threat Intelligence, J-1 and J-2 passed their outputs to NIVA-3, whose output was refined by FTAA and the resultant was N-3 (red pathway).

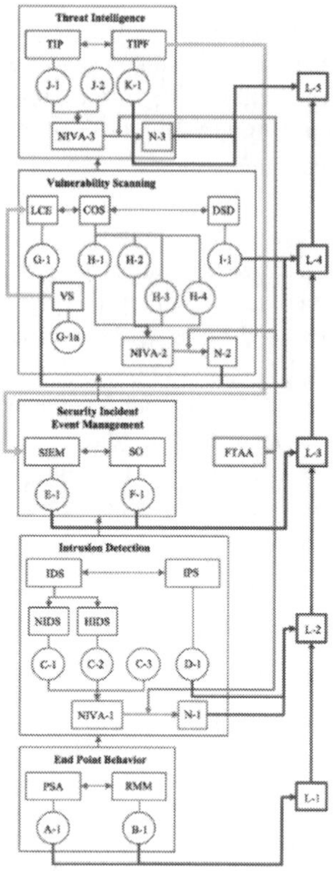

Figure 4. Revised, Prototype Solution Stack with specified Hybridized Components for the Experiment and NIVA, FTAA mechanisms: Solution Stack #2

The FTAA refinement pathways are illuminated (green pathway). The various interim steps were as follows: (A-1)&(B-1)->(L-1), (N-1)&(D-1)->(L-2), (E-1)&(F-1)->(L-3), (G-1)&(N-2)&(I-1)->(L-4), and (K-1)&(N-3)->(L-5). Each layer of the solution stack passed its output to the layer above; hence, End Point Behavior (L-1) -> Intrusion Detection (L-2) -> Security Incident Event Management (L-3) -> Vulnerability Scanning (L-4) -> Threat Intelligence (L-5) (purple pathway). Of course, the TIPF fed its output back to the SIEM, and the VS repertoire fed its output to the LCE (orange pathway).

VIII. Experimental Results

Two separate cyber testbeds on a single cyber range were utilized to conduct the experiment; for the purposes of this paper, the results from the two testbeds were combined and are presented together. The preliminary results, as shown in Figure 5, indicate a reduction of false positives from Phase 1 of the Experiment (Solution Stack #1) to Phase 2 of the Experiment (Solution Stack #2) by approximately 15% (from 82% to 67%) and a reduction of false negatives by approximately 47% (from 78% to 31%).

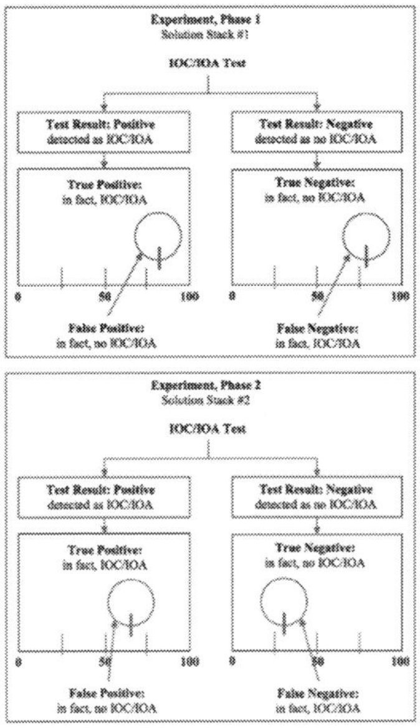

Figure 5. Results of the Experiment, Phase 1 & 2. From Solution Stack #1 to Solution Stack #2, the False Positive and False Negative rates have decreased.

For the experiment, Figure 5 was also recast, so as to be verified, with common performance measurements that were as follows: True Positive (TP), False Positive (FP), False Negative (FN), and True Negative (TN). The False Positive Rate (FPR) was calculated as FP/(FP+TN), and the True Positive Rate (TPR) was calculated as TP/(TP+FN). The Matthews Correlation Coefficient (MCC) was utilized and is shown in (1):

$$MCC = (TP)(TN)-(FP)(FN)/D \quad (1)$$

where D is defined in (2) below:

$$D=\sqrt{E} \quad (2)$$

and where E is defined in (3) below:

$$E = (TP+FP)(TP+FN)(TN+FP)(TN+FN) \quad (3)$$

The Probability Excess (PE) formula was also utilized and is shown in (4):

$$PE = (TP/P)-(FP/N) \quad (4)$$

where P and N are defined in (5) and (6) below:

$$P = TP+FN \quad (5)$$

$$N = FP+TN \quad (6)$$

The combination of MCC and PE are commonly utilized to evaluate performance of prediction methods (e.g., determining an IOC or IOA) [33].

IX. CONCLUSION

A prototypical solution stack (Solution Stack #1) with chosen OSS components for an experiment was enhanced by hybridized amalgams (e.g., Suricata and Sagan; Kubernetes, Nomad, Cloudify and Helios; MineMeld and Hector) and supplemented by select modified algorithms (e.g., modified NIVA and FTAA variants) leveraged by ensemble method ML. The preliminary results of the prototype solution stack (Solution Stack #2) indicate a reduction, with regards to IOC and IOA, of false positives by approximately 15% (from 82% to 67%) and a reduction of false negatives by approximately 47% (from 78% to 31%).

It appears that the use of complementary components conjoined with modified NIVA and FTAAs variants, leveraged by ensemble ML, shows promise. An extensive review of the prior work related to the described components, NIVAs for fault-tolerant systems, and efficient FTAAs based upon an assortment of techniques has been conducted. Future work will involve a review of updated techniques for benchmarking purposes as well as the potential involvement of other useful algorithmic modifications. Other future work, which has already commenced, will include enhancements, such as Rudder, an open-source audit and configuration management utility, which facilitates system configuration. Also, the ELK stack will be complemented with the open-source projects Sawmill and Apollo (both released by Lozi.io) to scale the log analysis environments.

ACKNOWLEDGMENT

The author would like to thank the Decision Engineering Analysis Laboratory (DEAL) for its encouragement and motivation throughout the process of pursuing and completing this research. Without their initial and continuing assistance, as well as the ideas, feedback, suggestions, guidance, resources, and contacts made available through that support, much of this research would have been delayed. The author would also like to thank VT & IE^{2}SPOMTF. This is part of a paper series on enhanced event correlation. The author would like to also thank USG leadership (e.g., the CAG). In addition, the author would like to thank ICE Cyber Security for the opportunity to serve as Chair, Scientific Advisory Board. The author would further like to thank the International Academy, Research, and Industry Association (IARIA) for the constant motivation to excel as well as the opportunity to serve as a contributing IARIA Fellow within the cyber and data analytics domains, particularly in the area of mission-critical systems.

REFERENCES

[1] I. Thomson, "NSA's Top Hacking Boss Explains How to Protect Your Network from His Attack Squads," The Register, pp. 1-2, 28 January 2016.

[2] D. Winder, "41% of Cyber-Secuirty Apps Contain High-Risk Open Source Vulnerabilities," SC Magazine, pp. 1-2, 15 May 2018.

[3] "Global Interconnection Index – Digital Economy Outlook," Equinix, pp. 1-9, 2018.

[4] H. Kenyon, "Cybercriminals Find New Ways to Exploit Vulnerabilities," SIGNAL, pp. 1-2, March 2010.

[5] S. Morgan, "Top 5 Cybersecurity Facts, Figures, and Statistics for 2018," Cybersecurity Business Report, pp. 1-11, 23 January 2018.

[6] "Security Practices Need to Evolve in Order to Handle Complex Threats," Help Net Security, pp. 1-4, 9 February 2017.

[7] C. Saran, "Enterprise Software Spending Set to Grow Thanks to AI and Digital Boost," Computer Weekly, pp. 1-6, 16 January 2018.

[8] J. Cinelli, "Five Trends to Impact Managed Service Providers in 2018," Cloud Jumper, pp. 1-11, 2018.

[9] "Managed Services Market 2017 – Global Forecast to 2022 – Research and Markets," BusinessWire, Berkshire Hathaway, pp. 1-3, 13 September 2017.

[10] N. Rajput, "Managed Security Services Market by Deployment Mode (Hosted or cloud-based MSS and On-premise or customer-premise equipment) and Application (Managed IPS and IDS, Distributed Denial of Services, UTM, SIEM, Firewall management, Endpoint Security and Others) - Global Opportunity Analysis and Industry Forecast, 2014 – 2022," Allied Market Research, pp. 1-3, August 2016.

[11] "Gartner Says Worldwide Information Security Spending Will Grow 7 Percent to Reach $86.4 Billion in 2017," Gartner, pp. 1-7, 16 August 2017.

[12] "Cloud Managed Services Market Size, Share & Trend Analysis Report By Service Type (Business, Network), By Deployment, By End-user, By Vertical, By Region, And Segment Forecasts, 2018 - 2025," Grand View Research, pp. 1-7, April 2018.

[13] "2018 HISCO: Small Business Cyber Risk Report," Hiscox, pp. 1-9, 2018.

[14] J. Loughlin, "Why Cyber Insurance is No Longer Optional for Restaurants," FSR Magazine, pp. 1-7, May 2018.

[15] D. Kobialka, "MSP Research: SMBs Spend $11 Billion on Managed Security Services," MSSP Alert, pp. 1-3, 16 August 2018.

[16] A. Brown, "Machine Learning Gains Momentum in MSP Space," Channel Futures, pp. 1-2, 3 Feburary 2017.

[17] S. Cowley, "2.5 Million More People Potentially Exposed in Equifax Breach," The New York Times, pp. 1-2, 2 October 2017.

[18] "CVE-2017-5638," National Vulnerability Database, National Institute of Standards and Technology, pp. 1-5, 22 September 2017.

[19] "The Power of SIEM: Reducing Detection and Response Time in the Attack Chain," Akamai, pp. 1-14, May 2018.

[20] W. Baker et al., "2009 Data Breach Investigations Report," Technical Report, Verizon Business RISK Team, pp. 1-52, 2009.

[21] M. Grimaila, J. Myers, R. Mills, and G. Peterson, "Design and Analysis of a Dynamically Configured Log-based Distributed Security Event Detection Methodology," The Journal of Defense Modeling and Simulation: Applications, Methodology, Technology, vol. 9(3), pp. 1-34, 2012.

[22] J. Ellingwood, "Architecting Applications for Kubernetes," DigitalOcean, pp. 1-10, 20 June 2018.

[23] H. Samset and R. Braek, "Dynamic Service Discovery Using Active Lookup and Registration," 2008 IEEE Congress on Services, pp. 545-552, 25 July 2008.

[24] "Nomad vs. Kubernetes," Nomadproject.io, HashiCorp, pp. 1-2, 2018.

[25] J. White, T. Fitzsimmons, and J. Matthews, "Quantitative Analysis of Intrusion Detection Systems: Snort and Suricata," Proceedings of SPIE - The International Society for Optical Engineering," pp. 1-13, 2013.

[26] S. Cooper, "10 Top Intrusion Detection Tools for 2018," Comparitech, pp. 1-30, 29 June 2018.

[27] S. Suhy, "NetWatcher Managed Detection and Response (MDR) Cyber Security Service," NetWatcher, pp. 1-2, 11 August 2017.

[28] "9 Best Orchestration Open Source Docker Tools," CodeCondo, pp. 1-8, 19 May 2018.

[29] A. Draffin, "Methodology Vs Framework – Why Waterfall and Agile Are Not Methodologies," IT Strategies, pp. 1-2, 7 April 2010.

[30] A. Bridgwater, "What's the Difference Between a Software Product and a Platform?" Forbes, pp. 1-2, 17 March 2015.

[31] A. Karimi, F. Zarafshan, and A. Ramli, "A Novel N-Input Voting Algorithm for X-by-Wire Fault-Tolerant Systems," The Scientific World Journal, pp. 1-9, 2014.

[32] S. Latif-Shabgahi, "An Integrated Voting Algorithm for Fault Tolerant System," 2011 International Conference on Software and Computer Applications, International Proc. of Computer Science and Information Technology, vol. 9, pp. 1-17, 2011.

[33] M. Vihinen, "How to Evaluate Performance of Prediction Methods? Measures and Their Interpretation in Variation Effect Analysis," BMC Genomics, vol. 13(4), pp. 1-16, 2012.

Prediction of Underground Fire Behavior in South Sumatra

Using Support Vector Machine with Adversarial Neural Network Support

Ika Oktavianti Najib
Center for Research on IoT, Data Science, and Resiliency
Sriwijaya University, Computer Science Department
Palembang, Indonesia
inajib@cridr.org

***Abstract*— Fires, which are the basic cause of smoke haze, can happen due to several reasons, such as the common practice of burning agricultural land, deforestation and delayed rainy seasons (e.g., unusual climatic conditions in the last 20 years, such as El Nino). For plantation companies, land burning is a quick and easy way of preparing land for planting new seeds. Fires that occur in peatlands (peat is a soil composed of partly decaying plant material formed within wetland areas), tend to be under the old soil, generate a great deal of smoke, and are difficult to extinguish. Forest crises and land fires occurring in South Sumatra typically begin in early July, and a fog condition typically lasts until mid-November. According to statistical data, in 2014-2015, 60% of burned land was peatland. In the event of fire, the Government strives to extinguish the fire on peatlands with water bombing, making canals, and others with a variety of local and international aid. However, the most effective way is prevention and/or early intervention. Early intervention is done by installation of aerial and subsurface sensors. Aerial sensors not only detect forest fires in one way, but also detect some additional elements, such as levels of ozone, carbon dioxide, carbon monoxide, and other elements associated with forest fires. Subsurface sensors detect fires below the ground that were previously undetectable. The result of this research is to provide an enhanced baseline analysis for regions of the province of South Sumatra and to determine the probability of fire for particular areas as well as the escalation potential.**

Keywords—forest fire; peatland; smoke; haze; aerial sensor; subsurface sensor.

I. INTRODUCTION

Forest fires have become a world phenomenon. The impacts from these forest fires are very dangerous, not only for the directly affected community, but also for the adjacent environments. As has just happened in Greece in July 2018, it was reported that this wildfire was the worst forest fire in over a decade that occurred in a small resort town near Athens. This tragedy killed at least 74 people, injured almost 200 people, and forced hundreds more to rush on to beaches and into the sea as the blaze devoured houses and cars [1].

Elsewhere in the world, the illegal burning of forests and agricultural land, such as across Indonesia, has blanketed much of Southeast Asia in a dangerous haze, leading to one of the most severe regional (e.g., Association of Southeast Asian Nations or ASEAN) problems in years. The neighbors of Indonesia have complained. For example, Malaysian Prime Minister Najib Razak, has demanded that Indonesia take decisive action again those plantation companies generating the noxious smoke and ensuing haze [2]. The fires, which are the root cause of the haze, stem from a convergence of factors: the prevalent practice of burning agricultural land, deforestation, and a delayed rainy season (due to the most unusual climatic conditions in the past 20 years, such as El Nino). Unfortunately, it is difficult for the plantation companies to stop, for the burning of land is a quick and easy way to prepare soil for new seed. The fires, most of which are burning in peatlands, tend to produce long-lasting, smoky, massive underground blazes. The effects of these blazes are having widespread public health impacts, contributing to respiratory ailments and premature deaths throughout Southeast Asia [3].

In Singapore, news websites post near-hourly updates on the danger of being outside and exposed to the pollution. Some stores in Singapore are providing free masks for children and elderly people. The National Environment Agency in Singapore stated that the haze has entered an "unhealthy range," and to underscore this point, races for the swimming world cup – the Fédération Internationale de Natation[A] (FINA) (English: International Swimming Federation) Swimming World Cup 2017 in Singapore – were cancelled. A marathon in Malaysia was also cancelled, and all schools were closed as a result of the haze [4].

The South Sumatra forest and land fire crisis of 2015 commenced at the beginning of July. There were some warning symptoms by way of an increase in hotspots; the number of hotspots increased until the haze had spread to areas well outside of South Sumatra. This haze condition lasted until mid-November. Based upon the information provided by the Citra Landsat satellite, forest and land fires affected almost 613 thousand hectares and nearly all the districts and cities within the areas of Musi Banyuasin, Ogan Komering Ilir (OKI), Ogan Ilir, and Banyuasin. The cause of these forest and land fires were principally human-induced, and the ensuing widespread unbridled fires were further fueled by the vastness of the peatland areas. As a statistic, between 2014 and 2015, 60% of these unbridled fires occurred within peatlands [5].

Due to the severity of forest fires in 2015, the President of Indonesia decided to establish a "presidential office" in the Ogan Komering Ilir (OKI) district, which is a region of South Sumatra. The OKI district had experienced more forest fires than any other region at that time. This "presidential office" served as an Emergency Operations Center for the President to personally conduct emergency fire-fighting operations. The President also created a task force and various governmental posts to serve as a dedicated force for the handling of forest fires. The task force could request water bombing and direct law enforcement to stop the perpetrators of forest fires. To the surrounding communities, the President articulated the impacts of the fires, such as the impact on the health of the people. Examples raised included Acute Respiratory Infection (ARI) [6].

In 2015, the Governor of South Sumatra asserted that there can be no further forest and land fires in the province of South Sumatra. In 2016, the Governor took steps to ensure that there would be a way to contend with these fires. Accordingly, he established a forest and land fire taskforce (Satgas Karhutlah). However, fires continued to occur throughout 2017. In 2017, an extended drought aggravated the situation [7].

In order to avoid similar events, the focus shifted to the effective pathway of forest fire prevention. In this research, sample data from the installation of various aerial sensors and subsurface sensors in particular regions will be utilized, and this data will be processed by various mechanisms, including an analytical engine.

In this study, efforts that have been made by the government in dealing with forest fires will be explained in Section II. The research methodology will be presented in Section III, which consists of data mining and classification. Then, the data processing will be presented in Section IV, which explains how the data is processed using several methods, as well as delineating some types of sensors that can produce more complete and accurate data. Then, the conclusion and follow-up as to what future work will be done are summarized in Section V.

II. GOVERNMENTAL STUDY AS A BASIS

Much research has been done on forest fires in Indonesia, particularly regarding the prevention, as well as root causes of the forest fires themselves. Every year, the province of South Sumatra experiences wildfires; the impacts are classified as mild, moderate, to severe. To better understand these incidents, a governmental study was conducted by the South Sumatra Forest Fire Management Project (SSFFMP), and it examined the causes of forest fires occurring annually in South Sumatra [8].

This research was conducted for 5 years from 2003 to 2007, involving many parties such as the National Government (Ministry of Forestry and Bappenas), and Provincial Governments (Forestry, Planning, and Environment Department), and District/Municipal Governments (Forestry, Planning, and Environment Department). The main objectives of this research were to reduce the level of forest fires and to cope with the impacts of forest and land fires. This included the environmental damage caused by smoke that also affects the territory of Indonesia as well as the territory of neighboring countries. Accordingly, this study was utilized as a launching pad upon which to build this paper. This paper builds upon the study by combining existing sensor data with that of other newly deployed sensors and utilizes Support Vector Machines (SVM) and an Adversarial Neural Network engine (a component of Analytics on Analytics or A2O) support to analyze that data. Our methodology is presented below.

III. METHODOLOGY

A. Data Mining

Data mining is a process of automatically searching for useful information in large data storage [9]. Other terms often used include Knowledge Discovery [mining] in Database (KDD), knowledge extraction, data / pattern analysis, data archeology, data dredging, information harvesting, and business intelligence. Data mining techniques are used to examine large databases as a way to discover new and useful patterns. Data mining is also an integral part of KDD. The entire KDD process for raw data conversion into useful information is shown in Figure 1.

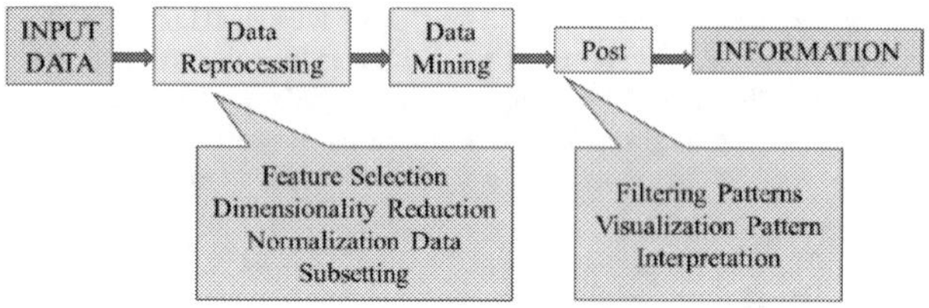

Figure 1. Process in KDD

Input data can be stored in various formats, such as flat files, spreadsheets, or relational tables, and can occupy centralized or distributed data storage in many places. The purpose of pre-processing is to transform raw input data into an appropriate format for further analysis. The steps involved in pre-processing data include combining data from multiple sources, cleansing data to remove noise and duplicate observations, and selecting records and features relevant for data mining jobs. Because there are many ways of collecting and storing data, the prepositional data stages are a time-consuming step in KDD. In addition, the data obtained from the newly deployed sensors constitute prodigious amounts of data, and the resolution desired added to this complexity.

B. Classification

Classification is the method in Data Mining that is most often used to solve real-world problems. This method examines the patterns of historical data (a collection of information - such as features, variables, features - on various characteristics of previously labeled items) with the aim of locating new objects (with previously unknown labels) into groups or classes, respectively.

The two most common steps of classification prediction are the development / training model and the testing /

deployment model. In the development model phase, a set of input data, including various actual class labels, will be trained. Once a model is "trained," the model is tested against the remaining sample data for accuracy assessment and can ultimately be implemented for real use. In the case of the presented research, the results will be used for the relevant agencies dealing with forest fire prevention. Some of the factors used to assess the model are as follows [9]:

- *Predictive accuracy*, the ability of the model to accurately predict class labels from new or never seen data;
- *Speed*, as pertains to the generation and utilization of the model as well as the computational speed of the system and its constituent components;
- *Robustness (reliability)*, the ability of the model to make predictions fairly accurately, albeit the data may be "noisy" or data may have missing values or be incorrect.
- *Scalability*, the ability to efficiently model predictions with considerable amounts of data;
- *Interpretability*, the level of understanding and insight provided by the model (e.g., how and/or whether the model makes inferences about a particular prediction).

IV. DATA PROCESSING

After obtaining the data from the sensor installation, data processing was performed. Data processing aims to facilitate the data analysis. Data analysis techniques were of two types, namely, (1) descriptive analysis, and (2) inferential analysis. The descriptive analysis of mean, median, mode, and standard deviation was operationalized by using an Access database along with Structured Query Language (SQL) queries. The inferential analysis was based upon linear regression with two or more independent variables (i.e. a statistical method to determine the relationship of a variable with other variables). In this case, the linear regression test was performed using statistical software to ascertain the relationship between the solution of a constraint of particular field with other fields.

A. *Inferential Analysis - Regression*

Inferential analysis is performed to find the relationship between the variables and then make a determination regarding these variables. The inferential analysis used was linear regression with two or more independent variables, with the calculation analysis performed via statistical software.
The linear regression test of two or more independent variables was used to predict a dependent variable Y based on two or more independent variables (X_1, X_2, and X_3) in a linear equation:

$$Y = a + b_1X_1 + b_2X_2 + b_3X_3 \quad (1)$$

Where:

Y	= dependent variable
X_1, X_2, X_3	= independent variables
a	= constants
b_1, b_2, b_3	= regression coefficients

In the regression, there are several tests that must be done which are autocorrelation test, collinearity test, coefficient test, hypothesis test, and significance test. The autocorrelation test was performed by the Durbin-Watson (DW) test as follows [10]:

- Positive Autocorrelation Detection:
  If $d < dL$, there is a positive autocorrelation,
  If $d > dU$, there is no positive autocorrelation,
  If $dL < d < dU$, the test is inconclusive or cannot be concluded.
- Negative Autocorrelation Detection:
  If $(4 - d) < dL$, there is a negative autocorrelation,
  If $(4 - d) > dU$, there is no negative autocorrelation,
  If $dL < (4 - d) < dU$, the test is inconclusive or cannot be concluded.

Medium collinearity test is a test that shows whether there is a strong correlation between the independent variables. The method of variable selection on linear regression used the stepwise method. With regards to the stepwise method, for each stage, the independent variable that has the strongest correlation with the dependent variable is included in the model first. It is followed by other variables by testing whether the first variable entered is still maintained in the model. If the first variable probability is still significant in the model, then the variable is applied. If the probability of the first variable is not significant anymore, then the variable is excluded from the analysis. This process stops when there is no longer any independent variable that must be included or excluded from the equation. Furthermore, the regression equation is tested to determine whether the regression equation is valid or not.

B. *Support Vector Machine*

Support Vector Machine (SVM) uses a linear model to find the best hyperplane as a separator of two classes on a vector input. The best hyperplane can be determined by calculating the hyperplane margin value, which is the distance between hyperplane and the nearest pattern of each class. The pattern closest to the maximum margin of hyperplane is called a support vector. Both classes -1 and +1 and hyperplane dimension d are defined as:

$$\vec{w} \cdot \vec{x} + b = 0 \quad (2)$$

Pattern $\vec{x_i}$ for negative sample (-1) and positive (+1) can then be formulated:

$$\vec{w} \cdot \vec{x} + b \leq -1 \quad (3)$$

$$\vec{w}\cdot\vec{x}+b \geq +1 \tag{4}$$

Quadratic programming is used to find the greatest margin value, i.e. $\frac{1}{\|\vec{w}\|}$ by finding the minimal point:

$$\min_{\vec{w}} \tau(w) = \frac{1}{2}\|\vec{w}\|^2 \tag{5}$$

Using the Lagrange multiplier, the primal form of quadratic programming can be transformed into a dual form with the following equation:

$$L(\vec{w},b,\alpha) = \frac{1}{2}\|\vec{w}\|^2 - \sum_{i=1}^{l} \alpha_i (y_i((\vec{x_i}\cdot\vec{w}+b)-1) \tag{6}$$

Where (i = 1,2, ..., l) and α_i are Lagrange multipliers that are either 0 or positive. The optimal value of the above equation can be calculated by minimizing L against $\vec{w}$ and maximizing L against α_i. Data correlated with a positive α_i is called a support vector.

The SVM concept can be seen in Figure 2, which uses the principle of Structural Risk Minimization (SRM) with the aim of finding the best hyperplane that separates two classes within the input space.

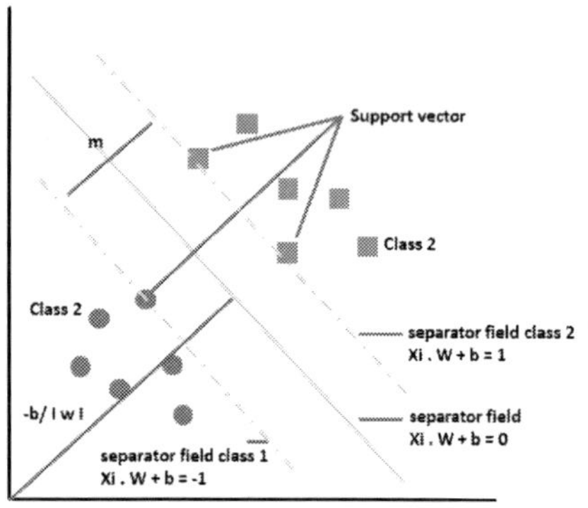

Figure 2. Support Vector Machine Concept

C. *Prediction of Underground Fire Behavior System*

Generally, the prototype system design predicts underground fire behavior by estimating the potential rate of fire explosion, fuel consumption, fire intensity, and fire description. With the help of an elliptical fire growth model, a comprehensive estimate of the fire, via fire perimeter, the growth rate of fire, the behavior of the wing of fire, as well as the rear of the fire. The flowchart is shown in Figure 3.

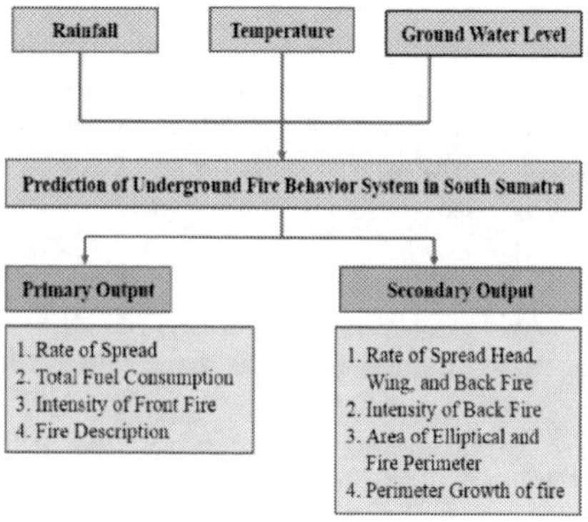

Figure 3. Research Flowchart

The system was modularized into several components, which will be described as follows: Japan International Cooperation Agency (JICA) Sensors, 3D Printed (3DP) sensors, and the the Analytics on Analytics (A2O) system.

a. *JICA Sensors*

The sensors installed by JICA are categorized as a waterlogger or "Automatic Waterlogger Telemetry" sensors with the SESAME II brand, because the main function of this particular sensor is to monitor the condition of the ground water level in the peat area, although in its use, this tool also consisted of several other devices used to collect information/other parameters besides ground water level, namely the level of drought, soil surface, rainfall, and others.

Automatic Waterlogger Telemetry JICA Sensors installed by the Regional Peat Restoration Team consisted of 2 phases. The first phase was carried out in December 2016 with 4 locations, and the second phase was carried out in June 2017 with 6 locations. Once installed, the team started data collection, but the data obtained was not optimal because of problems with telephone lines which have an unstable communication. This phenomenon of unstable communications is not only happening in South Sumatra, but also in other various regions of Indonesia and in other ASEAN countries [11].

Currently, the JICA sensors are deployed, as shown in Figure 4.

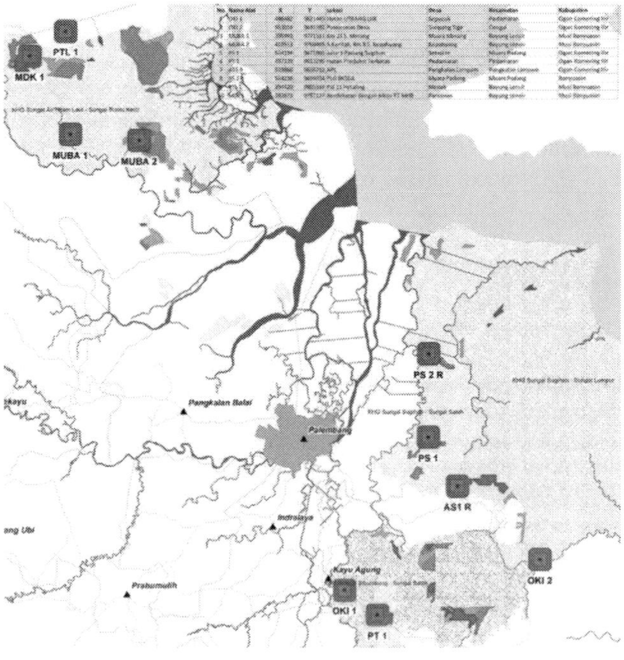

Figure 4. JICA Sensor Deployment [12]

The following locations and coordinates of several sensors are distributed in South Sumatra Province, as shown in Table 1.

TABLE 1. LOCATION AND COORDINATE POINT OF JICA SENSORS IN SOUTH SUMATRA [13]

No.	Code	Location	Coordinate Point
1	OKI-1	- Kelurahan Kedaton, Kecamatan Kayu Agung, Kab. OKI	S3°25'25.82", E104°52' 41.87"
		- KHG Sungai Sibumbung – Sungai Batok	
		- Outside of State Forest	
2	OKI-2	- Desa Simpangtiga, Kecamatan Tulung Selapan, Kab. OKI	S3°19'58.60", E105°27' 33.22"
		- KHG Sungai Sugihan – Sungai Lumpur	
		- Outside of State Forest	
3	MUBA-1	- Desa Bakung, Kecamatan Lalan, Kab. MUBA	S2°2'50.90", E104°3' 4.29"
		- KHG Sungai Air Hitam Laut-Sungai Buntu Kecil	
		- Hutan Produksi KPH Lalan Mangsang Mendis (Production Forest Non Concession)	
4	MUBA-2	- Desa Kepayang, Kecamatan Lalan, Kab. MUBA	S2°5'7.27", E104°16' 2.34"
		- KHG Sungai Air Hitam Laut-Sungai Buntu Kecil	
		- Hutan Produksi KPH Lalan Mangsang Mendis (Production Forest Non Concession)	
5	PS-1	- Desa Baru, Kecamatan Pangkalan Lampam, Kab. OKI	S2°57'49.69", E105°7' 28.19"
		KHG Sungai Sugihan – Sungai Saleh	
		Conservation Forest	
6	PS-2R	- Desa Sidomulyo, Kecamatan Muara Padang,Kab. Banyuasin	S2°43'9.06", E105°7' 45.61"
		KHG Sungai Sugihan – Sungai Saleh	
		Conservation Forest	
7	AS-1R	- Desa Riding, Kecamatan Pangakalan Lampam, Kab. OKI	S3°6'44.24", E105°12' 49.29"
		KHG Sungai Sugihan – Sungai Lumpur	
		Areal Penggunaan Lain (Head of Dusun) (Outside of State Forest	
8	PT-1	- Desa Pulau Geronggang, Kecamatan Pedamaran Timur, Kab. OKI	S3°29'41.87", E104°58' 2.04"
		- KHG Sungai Sibumbung – Sungai Batok	
		- Hutan Produksi Terbatas Pedamaran Kayu Agung, KPH Wil. V Mesuji (Production Forest Non Concession	

In June 2018, the team conducted checks and evaluations of the installed sensors. It turned out that from the ten sensors that had been installed, 2 sensors were lost/stolen. This resulted in a new destination within the data — locations that should be monitored but are not actually monitored. The form of the sensor installed can be seen in Figure 5 below. The sensor features a safety fence to avoid physical interference from the outside but was not always successful against theft.

Figure 5. JICA Sensor Deployment

From the tenth location of the sensor, data was obtained from sensors located in the Village of Cinta Jaya (Department Sepucuk), District Pedamaran, Ogan Komering Ilir and was labelled with the name of the sensor device "OKI 1." The sensor measures the three main components of the temperature, ground water level and rainfall. The collection of sample data is based on the consideration that during July 2018, there were recorded peatland fires involving 105 hectares in the area [14], which were part of the company's land. Data samples can be seen in Table 2, namely as many as 10 samples from the total number of 525 data from each component.

TABLE 2. DATA SAMPLE FROM SENSOR OKI 1
JULY 11th, 2018 – JULY 20th, 2018 [15]

No	Temperature	Rainfall	Groundwater Level
1	30.4	0.0	0.29
2	31.6	0.0	0.31
3	30.6	10.0	0.31
4	29.8	18.0	0.28
5	30.1	0.0	0.30
6	29.4	2.0	0.31
7	28.2	24.5	0.30
8	30.5	0.0	0.28
9	27.9	39.0	0.26
10	29.4	0.0	0.23

Low resolution remote sensing data has been widely used to monitor forest fires such as hotspot detection and burnt land scar mapping. In a study conducted by Indonesian National Institute of Aeronautics and Space (Lembaga Penerbangan dan Antariksa Nasional or LAPAN), the determination of the temperature threshold for hotspot detection was carried out using Landsat-8 TIRS (Thermal Infrared Sensor) data with a spatial resolution of 100 m was utilized so as to increase the accuracy of information with the objective of identifying the source of fire smoke. From these studies, obtained temperature limits that can be said to be potentially a fire are in the range of $\geq 43°$ C [16].

From the existing sample data, temperatures that exceeded the established threshold for those sensors at the Sepucuk area were not detected. At that time, peatland fires were occurring, which required serious and rapid handling by the firefighting team. However, given the sensor specifications, the sensor range was limited to 5-10 km, which was insufficient to reach the area where the fire occurred.

The other weakness of this particular sensor type is that it cannot automatically analyze. whether the area has the potential for fire or not. So, the government officers only monitor based upon existing data without being able to ascertain any fire pattern. In the case of underground fires / peatland fires, this sensor cannot be used optimally.

b. 3DP Sensors

The JICA Sensors are spread out throughout the province of South Sumatra, and the parameters collected are sparse. For this reason, 3DP Sensors, such as based upon those that were produced by South Sumatra government officials via the Joint Weather Sensor Team (JWST) for the 2018 Asian Games have great potential. After all, these sensors can collect many parameters, such as shown in Figure 6 and 7 below.

The 3DP Sensors assembled by the JWST are supported by the Center for Research on IoT, Data Science, and Resiliency (CRIDR) team; each sensor contains a cellular SIM card for the required Internet connectivity related to data collection. This avoided the JICA experienced problem of unstable telephones lines.

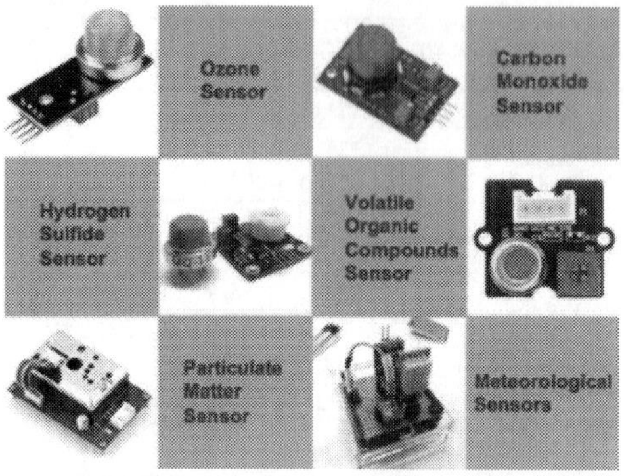

Figure 6. Exemplar Components aboard 3DP Sensors

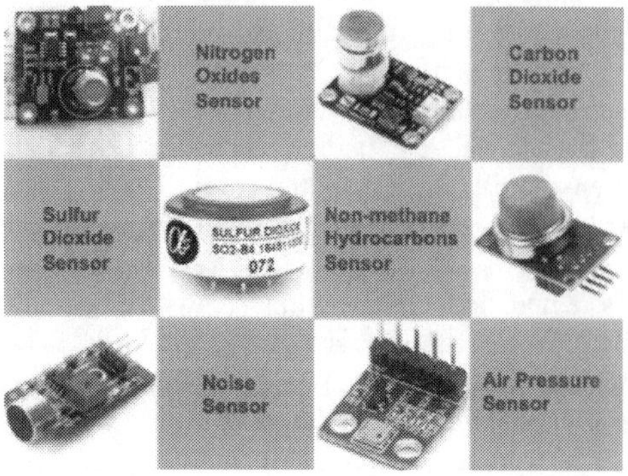

Figure 7. Exemplar Components aboard 3DP Sensors

c. Analytics on Analytics (A2O) System

Among other modules of the A2O system, there is a Deep Learning module, which is based upon a modified [Deep Convolutional] Generative Adversarial Network (GAN). Each GAN is comprised of two neural networks, which are pitted again each other. This results in the "adversarial" aspect of an unsupervised machine learning paradigm. Unsupervised machine learning refers to the task of inferring a function that describes the structure of "unlabeled" data or data that has not been classified or categorized. The generative aspect is best described by contrasting it to a discriminative aspect. Whereas discriminative models endeavor to learn the boundary between classes (given the labels y and features x, the formulation p(y|x) equates to "the probability of y given x"), generative models endeavor to model the distribution of individual classes (the focus is on "how you get x," and the formulation p(x|y) equates to "probability of x given y" or the probability of features given a class). GANs are well known for being able to, for example, find the roads on an aerial map, fill in the missing details of an image (up-sampling, given the edges), and construct an image, which postulates how a person might look when they are older. A2O utilizes a stacked GANS; hence the described paradigm is that of Stacked Generative Adversarial Network (SGAN) for the Deep Learning module of A2O.

V. CONCLUSIONS AND FUTURE WORK

The result of this research was to provide an enhanced baseline analysis for regions of the Province of South Sumatra and determine the potentiality of fire for particular areas as well as their escalation potential. This was based upon the requisite characteristics for accelerating fire spread patterns within posited predetermined limits. However, the data from the available JICA sensors was too sparse, and more sensors are needed. Currently, the sparse data does not provide macro-trends or patterns. This is related to the number of constituent components of the JICA sensors and the current resolution of the constituent components. To produce a better assessment, more sensors are needed. As one line of effort, the utilization of 3DP sensors has potential, as they can be scaled in terms of volume (as well as desired add-on components) at very low cost. The combination of both JICA and CRIDR 3DP would likely provide greater context for the analytical engines; A2O's Deep Learning module was able to glean quite interesting and discerning trends for the locales where the sensors were located, but the few sensors and the far distances among the sensors were problematic.

The location of the sensor installations greatly affected the data generated. Sensor locations play a critical role in many sensor network applications, such as environment monitoring and target tracking. Considering the cyber aspect, simplistic attack vectors, such as Denial of Service (DOS) can render the sensor inoperable. In essence, the location estimation at sensor nodes can be readily subverted and sensor networks can be readily taken off-line. For example, cyber-attackers may provide incorrect location references by replaying the beacon packets intercepted in different locations. Moreover, an attacker may compromise a beacon node and distribute malicious location references by spoofing the location or manipulating the beacon signals. In either case, non-beacon nodes will determine their locations incorrectly [17].

Based on the above, the sensors currently in South Sumatra Province have not been able to produce the requisite data so as to be able to determine an accurate pattern of fire distribution. Predictions of forest fires cannot be done precisely because of the many weaknesses pertaining to the quality of components and data, so it cannot be determined whether the monitored areas pose fire potential or not. Sensors of appropriate quantity and quality will greatly assist South Sumatera province as pertains to forest fires.

After this research, it is expected that more high-quality sensors will be installed in South Sumatra and a system that can provide outcall notification to the control room and first responder smartphones will be implemented. This is aimed at preventing and handling forest fires more effectively and efficiently.

ACKNOWLEDGMENT

This research is supported by the Center for Research on IoT, Data Science, and Resiliency (CRIDR), an initiative of Decision Engineering Analysis Laboratory (DEAL) and The International Center for Theoretical Physics (ICTP), a United Nations Educational, Scientific, and Cultural (UNESCO) Category 1 Institution.

The source of data in this research is derived from a cooperation between the Center for Research on IoT, Data Science, and Resiliency (CRIDR) and the South Sumatra Provincial Government via 3D Printed Sensors (3DP) as well as cooperation assistance between JICA (Japan International Cooperation Agency) and the South Sumatera Provincial Government, namely the installation of sensors at specific locations within South Sumatra that have the potential of forest fires.

REFERENCES

[1] H. Smith, S. Jones, and M. Farrer, "Greece Wildfires: Scores Dead as Holiday Resort Devastated," The Guardian, July 24th, 2018.

[2] Holmes, Oliver, "*Forest Fires in Indonesia Choke Much of South-East Asia*," *The Guardian*, 5th October 2015, [accessed 11th November 2018, <https://www.theguardian.com/environment/2015/oct/05/forest-fires-in-indonesia-choke-much-of-south-east-asia>.

[3] Tamara L. Sheldon and Chandini Sankaran, "Transboundary Pollution in Southeast Asia: Welfare and Avoidance Costs in Singapore from the Forest Burning in Indonesia," Department of Economics, University of South Carolina, 5th December 2016.

[4] Holmes, Oliver, "*Forest Fires in Indonesia Choke Much of South-East Asia*," *The Guardian*, 5th October 2015, [accessed 11th November 2018], <https://www.theguardian.com/environment/2015/oct/05/forest-fires-in-indonesia-choke-much-of-south-east-asia>.

[5] Nurhasim, Ahmad, "*Smoke Disaster, 612 Thousand Hectares of Forests Burn in South Sumatra*," *Tempo*, 30th November 2015, [accessed 23th October 2018], <https://nasional.tempo.co/read/723445/bencana-asap-612-ribu-hektare-hutan-terbakar-di-sumatera-selatan#DkYo0M3P4VRqUv8f.99>.

[6] Nugroho and Bagus Prihantoro, "*Review of Forest Fires, President Jokowi Attends the Land Line from Palembang*," *Detik*, 6th September 2015, [accessed 12th October 2018], <http://news.detik.com/berita/3011142/tinjau-kebakaran-hutan-presiden-jokowi-tempuh-jalur-darat-dari-palembang>.

[7] Aries, Maspril. "*US Consul Offers Cooperation to the Governor of South Sumatra*," *Republika*, 10th February 2017, [accessed 7th October 2018], <http://nasional.republika.co.id/berita/nasional/daerah/17/02/10/ol6166377-konsul-as-tawarkan-kerja-sama-ke-gubernur-sumsel.>

[8] FFPCP, "Projects's Final Workshop for Phase 1, 24-25 February 1998 in Palembang, Input Papers form Project Experts. Ministry of Forestry and European Union, European Commission. NRI, BCEOM Indonesia, CIRAD Forest and SCOT Conseil," 1998.

[9] Santosa, Budi, "Applied Data Mining with Matlab," 2007.

[10] Jean-Marie, Dufour and Marcel G. Dagenais, "Durbin_watson Tests For Serial Correlation in Regressions with Missing Observations," Journal of Econometrics no. 27, pp. 371-381. North-Holland, 1985.

[11] Japan Forest Technology Association, Nippon Koei Co.Ltd, "Data Collection Survey on Forest and Peatland Fire Control and Peatland Restoration in Indonesia Final Report," pp. 2-22-2-24, October 2007.

[12] Tarigan, Muara Laut, Peat Restoration Team, South Sumatra Provincial Government, 2018, unpublished.

[13] Tarigan, Muara Laut, Peat Restoration Team, South Sumatra Provincial Government, 2018, unpublished.

[14] Aji YK Putra and Reni Susanto, "305 hectares of land in OKI were burning badly", Kompas. 18th July 2018.

[15] Tarigan, Muara Laut, "SESAME_brg_oki_1." Peat Restoration Agency, South Sumatra Provincial Government, 2018, https://web.sesame-system.com/portal, unpublished.

[16] Kustiyo and Ratih Dewanti Dimyati, "Determination of the Temperature Threshold for the Detection of Smoke Source for Forest / Land Fires from Landsat-8 Data (Case Study of the Kalimantan P. Region in the 2015 Spring Lake)," Prosiding Seminar Nasional Penginderaan Jauh 2015. LAPAN:Bogor, pp.755-763, 2015.

[17] T. Kavitha, and D. Sridharan, "Security Vulnerabilities In Wireless Sensor Networks: A Survey," Journal of Information Assurance and Security, no. 5, pp. 31-44, 2010.

Countering an Anti-Natural Language Processing Mechanism in the Computer-Mediated Communication of "Trusted" Cyberspace Operations

Bi-Normal Separation Feature Scaling for Informing a Modified Association Matrix for Enhanced Event Correlation

Steve Chan
Decision Engineering Analysis Laboratory
San Diego, California U.S.A.
email: schan@dengineering.org

***Abstract*—There are bypass mechanisms to Natural Language Processing capabilities, such as the usage of irony, sarcasm, and satire, particularly as pertains to Computer-Mediated Communications. The problem then is that of the gradations between irony, sarcasm, and satire. Irony is used to convey, usually, the opposite meaning of the actual things said, but its purpose is not necessarily intended to hurt the target. The purpose of sarcasm, unlike irony, is to hurt the target. Satire might utilize irony, exaggeration, ridicule, and/or humor to expose and criticize shortcomings and/or vices of the target. The detection of these usages is an intriguing challenge. For example, sarcasm detection is difficult as there are several gradations; sarcasm might be comprised of real sarcasm, semi-irony, or friendly sarcasm. Determining the cognitive context, which triggered the original manifestation remains a bridge to be solidified. Also, sarcasm detection often exceeds even the concept of context, as it can be distorted by either the sender and/or receiver. This remains a herculean challenge in the domain, as others remain focused on first-order metarepresentations (e.g., analogies), while the challenges of second-order metarepresentations are more sparsely addressed. This paper presents a possible framework to address the problem by utilizing Bi-Normal Separation Feature Scaling for informing a Modified Association Matrix as contrasted to a framework utilizing Inverse Document Frequency and a prototypical Association Matrix. It is posited that the former will exhibit faster convergence and accuracy for enhanced detection of irony, sarcasm, as well as satire, and preliminary results seem to indicate this. The main output of the paper is a potential solution stack that directly contends with the second-order metarepresentation issue.**

Keywords-Satire; Natural Language Processing; Deep Learning; Dimensionality Reduction; Bi-Normal Separation Feature Scaling; Modified Association Matrix.

I. INTRODUCTION

Computer-Mediated Communication (CMC) has become prevalent (e.g., in-game text-based chat) in Massively Multiplayer Online Games (MMOGs) (e.g., World of Warcraft) and digital media entertainment services (e.g., Playstation Network). This trend is increasing as various open-source chat Software Development Kits and Application Programming Interfaces (e.g., PubNub ChatEngine) become available for the developers in a growing gaming industry. The vulnerabilities presented by CMC are discussed within literature. In an academic sense, if Natural Language Processing (NLP) were applied to this type of chat traffic, the analysis would be more challenging due to the variety of newly coined jargon words, etc. that continually emerge in this domain. However, the use of elevated language conjoined with satire constitutes an even greater challenge and a recipe for an anti-NLP (making a comparison to Anti-Face) mechanism that potentially poses a threat that impacts "trusted" cyberspace.

The remainder of this paper is organized as follows: Section II provides a primer by discussing some advantages of Inverse Document Frequency (IDF) over the simplicity of the Poisson distribution. Subsequently, Section III provides additional background information by discussing some advantages of neural embeddings (a.k.a. word embeddings) over n-grams. Then, Section IV delves into the complexities of the computational processing associated with figurative language as compared to literal language. Section V discusses some advantages of transfer learning (with bi-normal separation feature scaling) over deep learning in addressing the challenges of figurative language as well as posited improvements over IDF. Section VI discusses optimizing the [deep] transfer learning convolutional neural network inference engine, which was discussed in Section V. Section VII further discusses optimizing the inference engine with a modified association matrix. Section VIII posits a framework for the enhanced experimental inference engine, particularly as pertains to irony, sarcasm, and satire detection. Section IX presents the experimental results from the experimental inference engine solution stack, which incorporates the elements discussed in Section V, Section VI, and Section VII. Finally, the paper reviews and emphasizes key points within Section X, the conclusion.

II. FROM POISSON TO INVERSE DOCUMENT FREQUENCY

NLP pertains to the interactions between computers and human languages. In the operationalization of primordial NLP, word frequency is often practiced, as the following logic is utilized: "Low frequency words tend to be rich in content, and vice versa" [3]. This logic focuses upon "rare words," and there is an implicit assumption that words (e.g., n-grams) are distributed by a single parameter distribution, such as a Poisson process or a binomial. However, these distributions do not fit data very well; in fact, the Poisson distribution predicts that "lightning is unlikely to strike twice (or half a dozen times) in a single document" [4]. According to this logic, there should not be an expectation of seeing two or more instances of a "rare word" in a single document (unless there is some sort of hidden dependency that goes beyond the Poisson [4]; generally speaking, the utilization of Poisson for modeling the distribution of words [e.g., n-grams] fails to fit the data except in the case wherein there are almost no interesting dependencies). Yet, dependencies are indeed prevalent [8], and many NLP applications endeavor to discriminate documents on the basis of certain hidden variables, such as topic, author, genre, style, and the like [9]. The more that a keyword (e.g., n-gram) deviates from Poisson, the stronger the dependence on hidden variables, and the more useful, potentially, the n-gram is for discriminating documents on the basis of these hidden dependencies.

In the modern age of search engine optimization (which will include, among other techniques, keyword density), the likelihood of seeing a "rare word" is actually quite high. Hence, the employing of word frequency (a.k.a. raw frequency) has an inherent deficiency for the task-at-hand, as all terms are arbitrarily given equal weighting as pertains to assessing relevancy for a query. For example, a collection of documents discussing the "game" industry is likely to have the term "game" in almost every document. To mitigate this particular effect of certain "rare words" (a.k.a. "rare terms"), which occur too frequently within the collection (so as to be meaningful for relevance determination), an IDF mechanism is often utilized. Indeed, much better fits are obtained by introducing a second parameter, such as IDF, which is defined as $-\log 2df_w/D$, where D is the number of documents in the collection and df_w is the document frequency (i.e., the number of documents, which contain w); observationally speaking (e.g., as contrasted to Poisson), the IDF for a "rare term" is high, whereas the IDF of a "frequent term" is likely to be low [10]. This is consistent with the current notion that words with larger IDF tend to have more inherent content, and a good "[rare] word" should be located farther from the chance of Poisson [11].

III. FROM N-GRAMS TO NEURAL EMBEDDINGS

This paper endeavors to address a key NLP problem known as *sarcasm detection* by utilizing a combination of models based upon, among others, specifically engineered Convolutional Neural Networks (CNNs). The automated detection for an expression of sarcasm is non-trivial and, in many cases, involves a reversal of the polarity of a sentence. By way of example, "I love working eighty hours a week to be this poor" is such an expression of sarcasm. Another commonly cited example is "I love the pain of breakup" [12]. In both cases, it is difficult to extract the requisite crystalline aspects needed to determine the presence of sarcasm within the sentence. The example, "I love working eighty hours a week" provides aspects of an expressed sentiment (in this case, that of a positive nature), and "to be this poor" describes a contradicting sentiment (that of a negative nature). Hence, we dissect these amalgams.

In the realm of language, a simile compares one thing to another (similes are more likely to utilize the words "like" and "as," which a metaphor does not utilize. Verbal irony refers to the use of vocabulary to describe something in a way that is other than what it seems; indeed, verbal irony can consist of "ironic similes," which are comparisons between two items that are not alike at all [e.g., "fire and ice"]). Hao and Veale conducted various experiments over a corpus of "ironic similes" in which the authors found that most of the examined ironic comparisons utilize a precursor positive sentiment to impart a negative view (~70%) [13]. They found that sarcasm is very topic-dependent and highly contextual. Thus, sentiment and other contextual clues are vital for *sarcasm detection*, and this is at the core of anaphora resolution.

Certain features (e.g., n-grams), although somewhat useful for *sarcasm detection*, produce very sparse (often too sparse) feature vector representations or sparse vectors, and this had led to a surge of work centered upon representing words as dense feature vector representations or dense vectors. These representations, referred to as "word embeddings" or "neural embeddings," have been shown to perform well for a variety of NLP tasks. For example, in the often utilized *word2vec*, a distributed representation of a word is used in the form of a vector with many dimensions. Each word is represented by a distribution of weights across those elements. Hence, instead of a one-to-one mapping between an element in the vector and a word, the representation of a word is spread across all of the elements within the vector, and each element in the vector contributes to the definition of many words. The multi-dimensional vector comes to represent, abstractly, the "meaning" of a word. In essence, there is a word-context matrix M for which each row i corresponds to a word, each column j corresponds to a context for which the word has appeared, and each matrix entry M_{ij} corresponds to some association measure between the word and the context. Words are then represented as rows in M or in a dimensionality-reduced matrix based upon M. By examining a large corpus of text, it is possible to ascertain word vectors that are able to capture relationships between words in a surprisingly expressive way. Along this vein, these vectors can be utilized as inputs to a deep learning CNN. It is found that these CNN-learned word representations well capture meaningful syntactic and semantic regularities [14]. Along this vein, many NLP tasks benefit from word representations that do not treat individual words as unique symbols, but instead reflect similarities and dissimilarities between them.

The common paradigm for deriving such representations is based upon the distributional hypothesis of Harris [15], which asserts that words in similar contexts have similar meanings. Dingemanse et al. claim that universal words (e.g., "huh") occur in a large sample of unrelated languages and have similar contexts [16]; consequently, affirmation of context (e.g., same contexts in different languages) can be useful.

Specifically, the regularities observed are translated into constant vector offsets between pairs of words sharing a particular relationship. In fact, these vectors are very good at answering analogy questions of the form a is to b as c is to ?. However, CNNs are time-consuming to train, so other models are often utilized that might not be able to represent the data as precisely as CNNs but can often be trained efficiently on much more data. By way of example, the previously discussed *word2vec* is similar to an autoencoder. However, rather than training against the input words, via reconstruction, as a restricted Boltzmann machine does, *word2vec* trains words against other neighboring words in the input corpus, via two exemplar models: (1) Continuous Bag-of-Words (CBOW), using context to predict a target word, and (2) Skip-Gram, using a word to predict a target context. The latter model is often utilized, as it produces more accurate results on large datasets.

IV. FROM LITERAL TO FIGURATIVE LANGUAGE

In NLP, Word Sense Disambiguation (WSD) is the challenge of determining which "sense" (i.e., meaning) of a word is activated by the use of the word in a particular context. Literal language means exactly what it says. In contrast, figurative language represents one of the most difficult tasks for NLP. Several types of figurative language include personification, hyperbole, idioms, onomatopoeia, simile, and metaphor. Lakoff and Johnson assert that metaphor is a method for transferring knowledge from a concrete domain to an abstract domain (a first-order metarepresentation), and they posit that the degree of abstractness in a word's context is correlated with the likelihood that the word is used metaphorically [17]. Consider the following sentences: (L) He shot down my plane, and (M) He shot down my argument. The literal sense of "shot down" in L invokes knowledge from the domain of war [17]. The metaphorical usage of "shot down" in M transfers knowledge from the concrete domain of war to the abstract domain of debate [17]. Danesi contends that metaphor transfers associations from the source domain to the target domain [18]. Accordingly, the metaphorical usage of "shot down" in M carries associations that are not conveyed by L. To contend with the abstractness, various approaches are utilized for textual inference; one such approach is that of Recognizing Textual Entailment (RTE) [19]. To posit correct inferences, as pertains to RTE, systems must be able to distinguish between the literal and metaphorical senses of a word, and the degree of abstractness of words is one approach. For instance, the "plane" in L is rated with a lower number (i.e., relatively concrete), whereas "argument" in M is rated with a higher number (i.e., relatively abstract), which suggests that the verb "shot down" is used literally in L, whereas it is used metaphorically in M [17]. Turney and Littman rated words according to their semantic orientation, such as denotative (i.e., literal) or connotative (i.e., non-literal, metaphorical); by way of example, "deep mud" is labeled as denotative, and "deep gratitude" is labeled as connotative.

Unlike literal language, figurative language utilizes linguistic devices (e.g., simile, metaphor) to communicate indirect meanings (e.g., sarcasm) which, usually, are not readily interpreted by simply decoding syntactic or semantic information. Indeed, figurative language reflects patterns of thought that are not only challenging in their linguistic representations, but also for the involved requisite computational processing; figurative language processing can involve a variety of processes, such as sentiment analysis or opinion mining. Katz et al. posit that irony tends to be more difficult to comprehend than metaphor because irony requires the ability to recognize, at the very least, a second-order metarepresentation [20]. This same notation applies to sarcasm and satire; accordingly, irony, sarcasm, and satire constitute second-order metarepresentations.

V. FROM PROTOTYPICAL DEEP LEARNING TO TRANSFER LEARNING WITH BI-NORMAL SEPARATION FEATURE SCALING

To address the aforementioned challenges, deep learning is often utilized. Prototypical deep learning can be broken down into two parts: training and inference. When the deep learning CNN has been well trained on what to detect, the inference engine proceeds to make inferences or predictions based upon the input data. In general, deep learning requires a prodigious amount of data for training. Unfortunately, collecting this data for niche areas, where data is typically sparse, is challenging. One approach towards resolving this dilemma is known as Transfer Learning, wherein the model becomes trained on other datasets (i.e., pre-training), and weights for each layer are assigned in a "rough-tuned" fashion, iteratively. Hence, instead of initializing the weights for each layer randomly, as is typically done for models being trained from scratch, the learned weights for each layer of the pre-trained model are "fine-tuned" during the training on the sparse data. Theoretically, this TL paradigm has a better chance of converging much more quickly, and it is typically achieved, via the following pathways:

A. Continuous Back Propagation

The involved pre-trained model can be further "fine-tuned" by continuing the back propagation and updating the weights of all the layers. Alternatively, only certain layers may be "fine-tuned." Comprehensively, the "fine-tuning" can start at the highest-level layer and progress towards the lowest-level layer with a continuous assessment of the performance and determinations made accordingly along the way in terms of tuning.

B. *Hybridizing CNN with Support Vector Machine*

The involved pre-trained model can also serve as a feature extractor for the data. These features can then be fed into a linear classifier, such as a Support Vector Machine (SVM). This hybridized approach is ideal if the dataset is particularly sparse and "fine-tuning" the model is likely to result in over-fitting.

C. *Bi-Normal Separation Feature Scaling*

The described pre-trained model can, ideally, infer — by way of example — what decision is likely to be made next. Ideally, the pre-trained model can make robust inferences from new data based upon its prior training. In the realm of NLP, wherein the numerical feature value for a given word/term is often represented by its Term Frequency (TF) (within the given text) multiplied by its IDF (within the entire corpus), the "TF·IDF" combinatorial has become a prevalent representation [21]. However, IDF is oblivious to the training class labels and will, as a consequence, scale some features inappropriately. In contrast, Bi-Normal Separation (BNS) feature scaling has been shown to outperform other feature representation schemes for a wide range of text classification tasks. The superiority of BNS is especially pronounced for collections with a low proportion of positive class instances. With BNS, features are allocated a weight according to $|F^{-1}(tpr) - F^{-1}(fpr)|$, where F^{-1} is the Inverse Normal Cumulative Distribution Function (INCDF), tpr is the true positive rate (P(feature|positive class)), and fpr is the false positive rate (P(feature|negative class)). BNS produces the highest weights for features that are strongly correlated with either the negative or positive class. Features that occur fairly evenly across the training instances are given the lowest weight. Furthermore, BNS scaling has yielded better performance even without feature selection, potentially obviating the need for such [21]. This accelerates the performance of the inference engine.

VI. Optimizing the Transfer Learning CNN

There are two main approaches to modifying the TL CNN for reducing latency, particularly in the case of applications operating across other networks. The first approach is that of eliminating layers of the CNN that are not activated after training. The second approach is that of combining various layers of the CNN into a single computational step. These approaches should result in a similar accuracy of prediction, but simplified, compressed, and optimized for runtime performance (some compare this to the case of optimizing [i.e., compressing] an image for the WWW; ideally, the differences between the uncompressed and compressed image will be indistinguishable to the human eye) [22]. In essence, this further accelerates the performance of the inference engine.

VII. Modified Association Matrix

A final accelerant for the inference engine comes by way of a Modified Association Matrix (MAM). A typical Association Matrix (AM) is a 2-dimensional matrix, wherein each cell c_{ij} represents the correlation factor between the terms in the query and the terms in the documents. This matrix is used to reformulate an original query to improve its performance [23]. Each correlation factor, denoted as c_{ij} is calculated in accordance with (1):

$$c_{ij} = \sum_{d_k \in D} f_{ik} \times f_{jk} \qquad (1)$$

where c_{ij} is the correlation factor between term *i* and term *j*, and f_{ik} is the frequency of term *i* in document *k*. Additionally, these correlation values are used to calculate the normalized association matrix in accordance with (2):

$$s_{ij} = c_{ij}/(c_{ii} + c_{jj} - c_{ij}) \qquad (2)$$

where s_{ij} denotes the normalized association score, and c_{ij} represents the correlation factor between term *i* and term *j*. A higher normalized association score implies a higher degree of correspondence with the original query [23]. Words with the highest association scores are selected to be added back into the original query, and this new query (instead of the original query) is utilized to calculate cosine similarity. This new query, theoretically, should have a similar profile to the intent of the formulation of the query, and this will be reflected, via cosine similarity [24].

With regards to intent, Hancock had examined differences in verbal irony usage, via face-to-face and CMC, and found that irony (specifically, sarcasm) was more common in CMC settings and was primarily signaled through punctuation [25]. Reyes & Rosso utilized a corpus of review comments regarding products on Amazon.com, and they utilized six factors for their model: N-Grams (NG) (i.e., recurrent word combinations), Part-of-Speech (POS) N-Grams (POSNG) (i.e., recurrent POS combinations), words with semantic characteristics of sexuality or relationships (using values from WordNet), Positive and Negative Values (PNV) of words (using values from the Macquarie Semantic Orientation Lexicon [MSOL]), Pleasantness Value (PV) of words (using values from Whissel's Dictionary of Affect in Language [WDAL]), and Affective words Demonstrating Subjectivity (ADS) (using values from WordNet) [25]. The model utilized for this paper had some deletions and incorporated some modifications to the Reyes & Rosso model. For example, the MSOL was conjoined with the Yelp Restaurant Sentiment Lexicon (YRSL) and the Amazon Laptop Sentiment Lexicon (ALSL). The WDAL was complemented by the National Research Council (NRC) [Canada] Hashtag Emotion Lexicon (HEL) and the NRC Word-Emotion Association Lexicon (WEAL).

By applying specific scaling methods on an association matrix, unigrams were placed into a higher dimensional space, such that the unigrams with similar associative patterns were placed in similar regions of the dimensional space. This resultant space is referred to as the Word Association Space (WAS). The number of dimensions will vary depending on how much of the information of the free association database is compressed, but intermediate values between 200 and 500 are to be expected [26]. Typically, the dimensionality of the WAS equates to the number of features for the unigrams. Of note, with too few dimensions, the similarity structure of the resulting vectors does not capture enough granularity of the original associative structure within the free association database. With too many dimensions (e.g., the number of dimensions approaches the number of features), the information is not compressed enough, and the similarity structure of the vectors does not capture enough of the indirect relationships regarding the associations between the involved unigrams. Overall, this modified association matrix results in an enhancement of the first-order metarepresentation. In addition, the associations between the first-order metarepresentations are enhanced. Accordingly, the reversals of the polarity of sentences are better detected by the MSOL, YRSL, and ALSL-trained CNN. These lexical databases provide a more robust corpus for the sentiment of various words and are further buttressed by WDAL, HEL, and WEAL-training. By way of example, "I love working eighty hours a week to be this poor" can now be identified as an amalgam of two first-order representations that involve a reversal of polarity. Given this reversal of polarity identification, the involved first-order metarepresentations can be tagged and associated with sarcasm. This then segues to an improvement of the second-order metarepresentation for *sarcasm detection*.

VIII. POSITED FRAMEWORK FOR AN ENHANCED INFERENCE SYSTEM, PARTICULARLY FOR IRONY, SARCASM, AND SATIRE DETECTION

A prototypical Deep Learning Engine (Training Engine and Inference Engine) with the specified components for the experiment is as delineated in Figure 1. Several exemplar layers (NG, POSNG, PNV, PV, and ADS) are provided for the Training Engine. These same exemplar layers are utilized for both the Forward Propagation "Rough-Tuning" for the Training Model as well as the Continuous Back Propagation "Fine-Tuning" for the Pre-Trained Model. As discussed previously in Sections II through VII, BNS and MAM may be leveraged as accelerants for the inference engine. When combined with a specifically chosen datasets to assist in the pre-training, the Transfer Learning is enhanced. By way of explanation, the Untrained Model eventually becomes a "Rough-Tuned" Trained Model (upon ingestion of the initial Training Dataset and Forward Propagation). Further "Rough Tuning" can be achieved by training specific layers, such as PNV and PV (e.g., via MSOL and WDAL, respectively). Eventually, the Trained Model becomes a Pre-Trained Model, and "Fine-Tuning" can be achieved by Continuous Back Propagation and optimizing at certain training layers, such as PNV (e.g., via YRSL and ALSL), and PV (e.g., via HEL and WEAL). The Pre-Trained Model is then further optimized when the New Dataset is Ingested. To avoid over-fitting, the Pre-Trained Model of the CNN can also serve as a feature extractor for which the features can be fed into an SVM. Collectively, the hitherto described constituent components constitute the posited framework for an enhanced TL CNN inference engine for *sarcasm detection*.

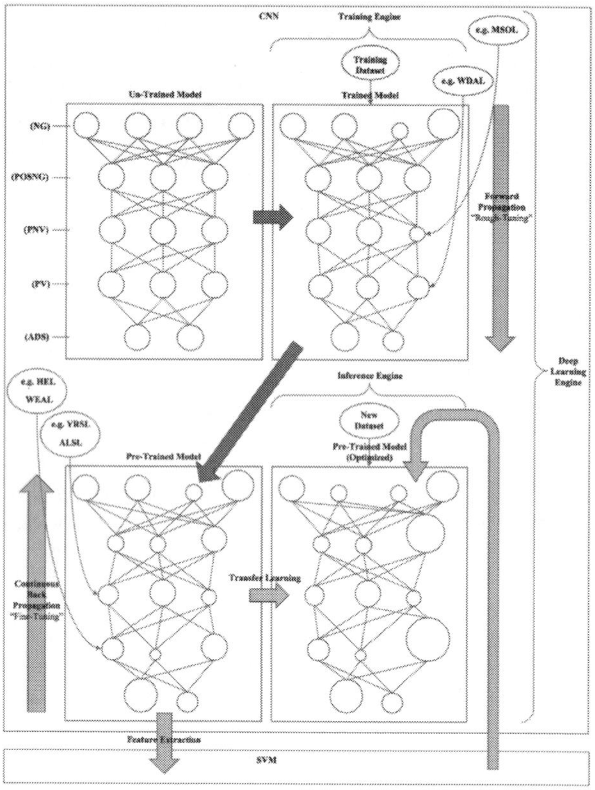

Figure 1. Posited Experimental Framework For an Enhanced Inference System, Particularly for Irony, Sarcasm, and Satire Detection.

Overall, the posited experimental framework comprised of a prototypical Deep Learning Engine (Training Engine and Inference Engine) with various enhanced layers (NG, POSNG, PNV, PV, and ADS) for the Training Engine seems to be quite useful for the Forward Propagation "Rough-Tuning" process for the Training Model as well as the Continuous Back Propagation "Fine-Tuning" process for the Pre-Trained Model.

IX. Preliminary Results from the Experimental Inference Engine Solution Stacks

The hitherto described solution stacks are as follows: (1) Solution Stack #1: IDF & AM, and (2) Solution Stack #2: BNS & MAM. This is shown in Figure 2 below as Phase 1 of the experiment for Solution Stack #1 and Phase 2 of the experiment for Solution Stack #2. The preliminary results are also shown in Figure 2 and indicate a 9% performance edge by Solution Stack #2 over Solution Stack #1 when benchmarked against the Self-Annotated Reddit Corpus (SARC), a corpus of 1.3 million sarcastic remarks. SARC was chosen as it had both sarcastic and non-sarcastic comments, thereby allowing for learning in both balanced and unbalanced label regimes [27]. However, there are also deficiencies with SARC. By way of explanation, Reddit users have adopted a common method for sarcasm annotation consisting of adding the marker "/s" to the end of sarcastic statements (this originates from the HTML usage <sarcasm>...</sarcasm>). As with Twitter hashtags, using the markers "/s" as indicators of sarcasm "is noisy, for many users do not use the marker, do not know about it, or only use it where sarcastic intent is not otherwise obvious" [27]. The experiment also has not yet treated the case of false positives and false negatives. Further investigation is needed, as these are preliminary results only, and only one "New Dataset" was utilized for testing.

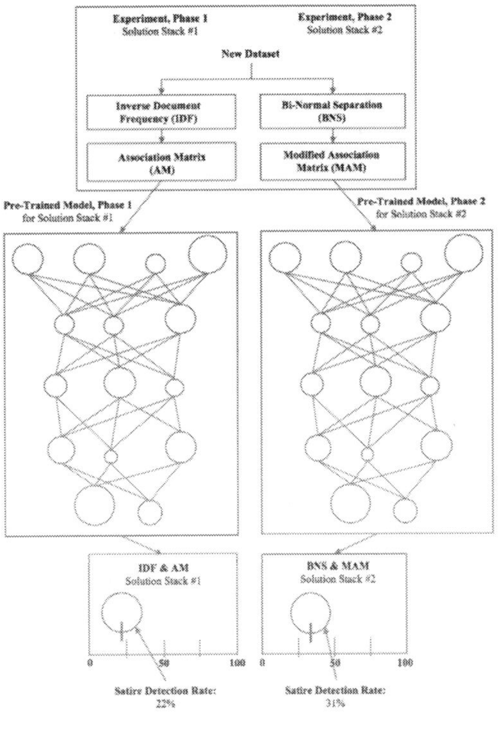

Figure 2. Solution Stack #1 (IDF & AM) versus Solution Stack #2 (BNS & MAM): Solution Stack #2 demonstrates a 9% performance edge over Solution Stack #1 (for a single test case).

Overall, Solution Stack #2 from Phase 2 of the experiment seems to have an advantage over Solution Stack #1 from Phase 1 of the experiment when benchmarked against the SARC. However, there is much more work to be done regarding false positives and false negatives.

X. Conclusion

This paper presents the benchmarked performance results of a posited framework for an enhanced inference system. The premise for devising such a system was predicated on the problems with *sarcasm detection* (i.e., detecting for a second-order metarepresentation) within the NLP arena. The described work utilized SARC as well as a variety of datasets for a Pre-Trained Model. The preliminary results of an approximately 9% performance edge by Solution Stack #2 (BNS & MAM) over Solution Stack #1 (IDF & AM) seem promising, but only one test was performed. Future work necessitates a further investigation with a much more robust performance metric and benchmarking paradigm, as well as the potential involvement of other useful viable datasets for fine-tuning of the CNN Pre-Trained Model. An updated literature review will be performed for updated techniques and methodologies.

Acknowledgment

The author would like to thank the Decision Engineering Analysis Laboratory (DEAL) for its encouragement and motivation throughout the process of pursuing and completing this research. Without their initial and continuing assistance, as well as the ideas, feedback, suggestions, guidance, resources, and contacts made available through that support, much of this research would have been delayed. The author would also like to thank VT & IE^{2}SPOMTF. This is part of a paper series on enhanced event correlation. The author would like to also thank USG leadership (e.g., the CAG). The author would further like to thank the International Academy, Research, and Industry Association (IARIA) for the constant motivation to excel as well as the opportunity to serve as a contributing IARIA Fellow within the cyber and data analytics domains, particularly in the area of mission-critical systems.

References

[1] New Jersey Fusion Center, "Bronx Bloods Members Communicating Through PlayStation Network (PSN)," Federal Bureau of Investigation New York, pp. 1-3, 28 July 2011.

[2] M. Ruskin, "Playing in the Dark: How Online Games Provide Shelter for Criminal Organizations in the Surveillance Age," Arizona Journal of International and Comparative Law, vol. 31, pp. 875-906, 2014.

[3] K. Church and W. Gale, "Inverse Document Frequency (IDF): A Measure of Deviations from Poisson," vol. 11, pp. 283-295, 1999.

[4] K. Church and W. Gale, "Poisson Mixtures," vol. 1, pp. 163-190, June 1995.

[5] D. Bahdanau et al., "Learning to Compute Word Embeddings on the Fly," ArXiv, pp. 1-12, 7 March 2018.

[6] M. Luong, I. Sutskever, Q. Le, O. Vinyals, and W. Zaremba, “Addressing the Rare Word Problem in Neural Machine Translation,” Proceedings of the 53rd Annual Meeting of the Association for Computational Linguistics (ACL) and the 7th International Joint Conference on Natural Language Processing of the Asian Federation of Natural Language Processing, vol. 1, pp. 11-19, 2015.

[7] M. Evans, “Probability and Statistics: The Science of Uncertainty,” Content Technologies, Inc., 2013.

[8] S. Khudanpur and J. Wu, “A Maximum Entropy Language Model Integrating N-grams and Topic Dependencies for Conversational Speech Recognition,” IEEE International Conference on Acoustics, Speech, and Signal Processing, pp. 553-556, 1999.

[9] S. Armstrong et al., “Natural Language Processing Using Very Large Corpora,” Springer-Science+Business Media, B.V., 1999.

[10] C. Manning, H. Schutze, and P. Raghavan, “Introduction to Information Retrieval,” Cambridge University Press, 7 July 2008.

[11] C. Manning and H. Schutze, “Foundations of Statistical Natural Language Processing,” MIT Press, 1999.

[12] S. Poria, E. Cambria, D. Hazrika, and P. Vij, “A Deeper Look into Sarcastic Tweets Using Deep Convolutional Neural Networks,” 26th International Conference on Computational Linguistics (COLING 2016), pp. 1601-1612, 2016.

[13] A. Perez, “Linguistic-based Patterns for Figurative Language Processing: The Case of Human Recognition and Irony Detection,” Universitat Politecnica De Valencia, pp. 107-109, July 2012.

[14] T. Mikolov, W. Yih, and G. Zweig, “Linguistic Regularities in Continuous Space Word Representations,” Proceedings of the 2013 Conference of the North American Chapter of the Association for Computational Linguistics (NAACL): Human Language Technologies (HLT), pp. 746-751, June 2013.

[15] M. Sahlgren, “The Distributional Hypothesis,” Italian Journal of Linguistics, vol. 20, pp. 1-18, 2008.

[16] M. Hayashi, G. Raymond, and J. Signell, “Conversational Repair and Human Understanding: Huh? What? – A First Survey in 21 Languages,” Cambridge University Press, pp. 343-380, 2013.

[17] P. Turney, Y. Neuman, D. Assaf, and Y. Cohen, “Literal and Metaphorical Sense Identification through Concrete and Abstract Context,” Proceedings of the Conference on Empirical Methods in Natural Language Processing (EMNLP), pp. 680-690, 2011.

[18] S. Mohammad, E. Shutova, and P. Turney, “Metaphor as a Medium for Emotion: An Empirical Study,” Proceedings of the Joint Conference on Lexical and Computational Semantics, pp. 23-33, 2016.

[19] I. Dagan, D. Roth, M. Sammon, and Fabio Zanzotto, “Recognizing Textual Entailment: Models and Applications,” Morgan & Claypool, pp. 157-159, 2013.

[20] L. Bobrova and J. Lantolf, “Metaphor and Pedagogy,” CALPER Working Paper Series, Center for Advanced Language Proficiency Education and Research, pp. 1-34, 2012.

[21] G. Forman, “BNS Feature Scaling: An Improved Representation over TF•IDF for SVN Text Classification,” Proceedings of the 17th Association for Computing Machinery (ACM) Conference on Information and Knowledge Management, pp. 263-270, 2008.

[22] M. Copeland, “What’s the Difference Between Deep Learning Training and Inference?” Nvidia, pp. 1-2, 22 August 2016.

[23] A. Boutari, C. Carpineto, R. Nicolussi, “Evaluating Term Concept Association Measures for Short Text Expansion Two Case Studies of Classification and Clustering,” Proceedings on Extending Database Technology (EDBT), pp. 163-174, 2010.

[24] J. Chartee, E. Cankaya, and S. Phithakkitnukoon, “Query Expansion using Association Matrix for Improved Information Retrieval Performance,” Artificial Intelligence and Hybrid Systems, iConcept Press, pp. 1-6, 2013.

[25] S. Skalicky and S. Crossley, “A Statistical Analysis of Satirical Amazon.com Product Review,” European Journal of Humour Research, vol. 2, pp. 66-85, 31 July 2018.

[26] M. Steyvers, R. Shiffrin, D. Nelson, “Word Association Spaces for Predicting Semantic Similarity Effects in Episodic Memory,” Decade of Behavior: Experimental Cognitive Psychology and its Applications, pp. 237-249, 2014.

[27] M. Khodak, N. Saunshi, and K. Vodrahalli, “A Large Self-Annotated Corpus for Sarcasm,” The International Conference on Language Resources and Evaluation (LREC), pp. 1-6, 22 March 2018.

Harnessing Machine Learning, Data Analytics, and Computer-Aided Testing for Cyber Security Applications

Achieving Sustained Cyber Resilience for Typical Attack Surface Configurations and Environments

Thomas J. Klemas
Decision Engineering Analysis Laboratory
Cambridge, USA
tklemas@alum.mit.edu

Steve Chan
Decision Engineering Analysis Laboratory
San Diego, CA
stevechan@alum.mit.edu

***Abstract*—While media reports frequently highlight the exciting aspects of the cyber security field, many cyber security tasks are quite tedious and repetitive. At the same time, however, strong pattern recognition, deductive reasoning, and inference skills are required, as well as a high degree of situational awareness. As a direct consequence, the field of cyber security is replete with potential opportunities to apply data analytics, machine learning, computer aided testing, and other advanced approaches to reduce the frustration of cyber security operators by easing key challenges. In fact, given a typical range of cyber attack surfaces, leveraging these machine-enhanced analysis and decision approaches in conjunction with a robust defense-in-depth posture is a crucial step towards achieving sustained, predictable performance across typical cyber security tasks and promotes cyber resilience. This paper will both outline details for a near-term research effort and explore a variety of key opportunities to exploit these approaches with the objective of raising awareness, providing initial guidance to aid potential adopters, and developing effective strategies to incorporate them into existing cyber security constructs.**

Keywords- artificial intelligence; expert systems, machine learning; supervised learning, unsupervised learning, pattern recognition, spectral methods, k-means, modularity, Lagrange multiplier, optimization, anomaly detection, data analytics, data science, networks, cyber security operator, cyber defensive tools, cyber resilience.

I. INTRODUCTION

It is well known that cyber security defense is a very challenging task [1]. One significant contributor to this defensive complexity is the inherently dynamic nature of the cyber environment. Client workstations, servers, other computers and devices, operating systems, and software become obsolete in a timescale of years and must be replaced with newer models or versions. Frequently, organizations will undergo transformations in size, focus, or organization that result from business mergers, growth, or decline and cause dramatic changes in the enterprise network composition. Because of any of these types of changes, organizations are constantly assembling unique new networks or modifying existing networks. Members may join, depart, shift to different sub-units, or change roles within the organization. In addition, network users themselves can be sources of great variability and can frequently frustrate cyber security operations by taking short-cuts for security measures or actively resisting inconvenient policy controls. Finally, external dynamics contribute to the defensive challenge: Criminals and other cyber attackers are perpetually scanning, searching, and finding new vulnerabilities to exploit, building new tools, developing new approaches to disguise their tracks, and refining their techniques to achieve their objectives.

Beyond the internal and external dynamic factors described above, paradigm-shifting technological changes are dramatically altering the cyber landscape, introducing innovations and improvements but potentially simultaneously increasing the attack surfaces and vulnerabilities within them [5]. The rapid evolution of new technologies, both hardware and software varieties, and increasing integration levels suggest that the challenges of cyber security will continue to grow for the foreseeable future [2]. For example, increasing Internet of Things (IoT) capabilities will incorporate new types of devices into the internet-accessible realm, thereby increasing attack surfaces and possibly exposing new types of vulnerabilities due to new Application Programming Interfaces (APIs) associated with new classes of devices. Thus, the addition of these technologies can increase the internal defensive complexity. Resourceful attackers may very well be able to find ways to exploit the increasing connectivity to access these new devices for their purposes.

While there are efforts to build in security into designs and even standards [3], frequently, security lags novel capabilities, sometimes to a significant degree. The dynamics, persistent advancement of malicious actors, and revolutionary technological change combine to elevate defensive complexities facing cyber security operators. As many defensive tasks are tedious and repetitive in nature, such fertile grounds will incubate the growth of errors. To counter this state of affairs, many cyber security innovators are leveraging data analytics, computer-aided testing, and machine learning to enhance or even replace human operator activities.

The remainder of this paper is organized as follows: Section II discusses the role of machine learning and other automated decision support tools in cyber security and presents applications. Subsequently, Section III explores how data analytics encompasses a crucial part for both supporting the function of these techniques and the decisions of cyber security operators. Then, Section IV delves into the benefits of leveraging computer-aided testing for the benefit of a wide variety of cyber security activities. Finally, the paper reviews and emphasizes key points in Section V, the conclusion.

II. ROLE OF MACHINE LEARNING

Numerous cyber security tasks can be eased and accelerated by incorporation of pattern recognition and machine learning approaches. In particular, many modern cyber monitoring tools already incorporate machine learning and enhanced visualization to provide insights that guide and accelerate decision-making [1] [2]. Pattern recognition is important capability for cyber security monitoring support tools. For example, signature-based detection of malicious activity often involves scrutinizing specific attributes of packets, email, or other data for values of identifying features that may match the corresponding values of previously known feature set entry in a pre-loaded data set captured from previous attacks of malicious actors. Thus, signature-based methods are quite effective against previously seen attacks but typically ineffective against first-time attacks for which the feature set entries would not yet be included in threat profiles. However, these technologies play a vital role in a layered, defense-in-depth system [11] [12].

To deal with first time events, other anomaly detection tools would normally be utilized that learn about the "normal," non-anomalous patterns of behavior. Once the defensive systems can recognize the patterns of activities that comprise normal behaviors, then the leap is not so great to be able to distinguish when a new event is an anomaly. As an example, time is the feature dimension that would be used to analyze user login behavior relative to employee work patterns. Thus, once login data is captured in logs, it would be straightforward to detect anomalous login times for users that work regular business hours. Anomaly detection can be challenging because there are many feature dimensions across which an event could be deemed anomalous, and there are many conditions and states of the enterprise, network, and associated devices required to properly characterize the normal activity patterns for each.

Another dimension for anomalous events might include login Internet Protocol (IP) addresses. In companies with brick and mortar work sites, login entries will be dominated by internal IP addresses, perhaps followed by laptops used at home, such that IP addresses associated with foreign origins would easily fall outside the normal login entry patterns enough that they would be detected as anomalies. Certain dimensions (or categories of log or traffic data) should be flagged high priority due to high risk associated with malicious activities across the dimension; for example, events that include downloads and uploads should be scrutinized particularly carefully.

The reason that machine learning, which can fall a bit short amidst many human dominated chores, can fit the bill within a layered defense in that each component of a defense-in-depth approach is only responsible to achieve subset of goals. It is the integrated combination of layers and components, each supplying their specific contributions to the sum, that comprises the ultimate level of defensive strength of the system. This includes machine learning decision support subsystems and machine-aided tools, as well as human operators. Hybrid tools that incorporate pattern recognition, signature-based, and machine learning, can dramatically enhance the performance of humans in many of the tedious defensive tasks.

TABLE I. MACHINE-AIDED APROACHES TO ENHANCE CYBERSECURITY OPERATOR AND SYSTEM PERFORMANCE

Approach	Alternative uses and cybersecurity considerations
Machine-learning	Signature matching and anomalous event detection. Classification of log entries and packet traffic data. Acceleration of asset management tasks. Semi-intelligent adversary attack agents for automated-testing activities.
Data analytics	Pre-processing and ingestion of event data records. Meta-data tagging of event entries for rapid filter searches
Automated-testing	Randomized agents capturing insider and external threat actor behaviors, pen-testing aids, and fuzz-type testing tools for software and systems

Machine learning has a strong role to play in anomaly detection. Pattern recognition techniques utilized for cyber security applications may involve identification of patterns that exist within a data set and then classifying both old and new data items into those categories or classes of patterns. Characterizing classes of normal traffic and classifying new traffic into existing patterns are well within the capabilities of machine learning algorithms, such that recognizing anomalies that do not fit into any of the existing patterns is possible.

For this classification and anomalous data detection task, a combination of signature-based systems, expert systems, supervised, unsupervised, and semi-supervised learning approaches may be advantageous to address the various challenges posed by different components of the data [7]. One of the objectives of this research was to examine the efficacy of applying a combination of classification approaches to categorize packet traffic data and log data. Previous work with clustering [13] [15] demonstrated some success in community detection. For these methods, feature set selection and determination of the number of classes are key steps to develop a successful classification tool. If feature sets are well chosen, clustering methods may be able to learn the numbers of basic types and the feature-based characteristics of the basic types of data with minimal human assistance, and then collect traffic or log entry statistics based upon those groupings.

Then, once group statistics are accumulated, it becomes possible to consider detection of anomalous data points that do not fit into any of the previously learned groupings. In this manner, anomaly detection systems can be constructed that classify data or messages into normal categories if they fit, and items that fall outside of the regular categories may be deemed anomalous or suspicious, potentially triggering some sort of alert, perhaps even associating a concern level for the degree of anomaly. Thus, these sorts of machine learning tools can support identification of traffic types, detection of anomalies and alerting for monitoring.

III. DATA ANALYTICS

Data analytics are crucial to the success of most machine learning approaches as well as human-led cyber security defensive operations. Data analytics includes pre-processing to clean and prepare the data, capturing essential auxiliary data that maximize the usefulness of data, ingesting the data into an extensible infrastructure, and analysis to squeeze the most insight possible from the data.

One of the often-overlooked aspects is the post-data-collection labeling or metadata tagging, which may involve detailed parsing of the data element. Using a network packet as an example, some typical fields that might require parsing include the time field, the protocol type, the source and destination IP addresses (if any), packet length, status fields, among other fields. This labeling step is vitally important to maximize the usefulness and efficacy of subsequent analysis stages. For packet traffic data, this step may require some special guidance to provide network subnet structure to group packet traffic by subnet since the detailed subnet structure would not necessarily be clear from the traffic itself, either implicitly or explicitly. Creating and populating a database with the dataset and the metadata tags of interest to facilitate further analysis, ensures the correct fields and values are available for rapidly searching data sets for samples of interest and associating data points that match in specified metadata attributes.

Another key objective of data analytics is computation of critical statistics that aid in preliminary decision-making and assist in selection of optimal approaches. A wide variety of statistics might be computed for network traffic that could include the relative composition of network traffic by protocol, subnet distribution of traffic across the enterprise network, IP addresses statistics, activity timing statistics, and many more. Once these statistics are computed, they can be utilized as additional dimensions for machine learning activities or for human decision-making.

IV. COMPUTER AIDED TESTING

The value of computer- assisted testing cannot be overstated in cyber security. While poor testing approaches can lead to outcomes that are worse than no testing, many testing efforts do not require a tremendous amount of intelligence to be successful but require thoroughness and are necessarily quite tedious, stretching the boundaries of human patience. By its very nature, computer-aided testing is comprehensive, methodical, and yet, can also incorporate randomness, and so this one of the key reasons why computers can fill this testing niche remarkably well.

Computer-assisted testing that includes randomized parameters is crucial because engineers frequently make assumptions during the development process, and, as these assumptions accumulate, the aggregative effect can be very hard to track and lead to inconsistencies. Thus, randomized testing approaches will occasionally violate these assumptions, causing tests to fail, by selecting test vectors within the engineers' "blind spot".

An obvious application for computer-aided testing that is used in software engineering and also applicable to cyber security defense is fuzzing or fuzz testing of software applications [8]. This sort of testing can help find website errors, database issues, and other application bugs. Similarly, a hybrid of fuzz and Monte Carlo testing can be used to aid validation of tools [9]. Recently, we developed an algorithm for calculating network complexity of virtual cyber ranges [10], but one key remaining task was validation of the algorithm. Using guided random-parameter point testing and by comparing the network complexity scores to subject matter expert expectations, we were able to make rapid improvements because the random value-generated models frequently represented attribute value permutations that fell outside our design assumptions.

One critical application area that could benefit from computer assistance is penetration testing. Some areas require human leadership, but computer-aided capabilities can assist other areas, such as tools to scan the surrounding network to enumerate devices and discern network structure and services, as well as tools to help find and infiltrate user accounts with weak passwords.

Like penetration testing, but with more requirements for stealth, automated attack tools can be used in war-gaming to challenge defensive teams or test tools. By measuring and observing the characteristics of the normal usage patterns, these tools could automatically enforce limits to ensure that communication and control traffic remains below the standard thresholding to avoid triggering cyber defensive tools. These tools could learn by passively observing and/or actively scanning its environment for vulnerabilities, potential pathways, defensive activities of concern or interest, and other exploitable opportunities that could yield the desired access or information.

V. APPROACH DETAILS

The goal of this research effort is to gain insight into the efficacy of utilizing elements from each of the sections above to enhance and simplify the process of potentially determining anomalous events, traffic composition, groupings of interest, structure, and other attributes from passive analysis of collected packet traffic data. It is our hope that these results would enable operators to gain an understanding of both the full scope of the possibilities and limitations of this approach to accelerate detection of anomalies, identification, asset management, and other important cybersecurity functions. This multi-layer decision support system will incorporate machine aided learning to derive insights from higher level data produced by a data analytics platform that includes a variety of pattern recognition capabilities and other automation support. The remainder of this section will describe the experiment design and the technical approach details underlying the machine learning decision support methods.

TABLE II. PROPOSED ALTERNATIVES FOR EXPERIMENT DESIGNS

Candidate Independent Variables	Candidate Dependent Variables	Candidate Control Variables
Number of clusters	Cluster sets	Network size
Packet traffic data set	Packet time clusters	Network structure
Source IP addresses	IP clusters	Feature weightings
Target IP addresses	Traffic composition statistics	Feature vector
Protocols	Host associations	Data set size
Packet lengths		
Packet times		
Log entry data sets		
Initial cluster centroids		

Multiple alternatives for the higher-level experiment design, required to achieve desired end goals to include traffic characterization, anomaly detection, identification/asset management, and related cybersecurity objectives are outlined in table 2. Clearly, once the exact details are specified, using this approach, a similar (subset) table would be created for each desired experiment to enable determination of the number of repetitions required for statistics that satisfy desired hypotheses acceptance/rejection thresholds and support determination of confidence levels.

Although there are some crucial pre-processing steps to clean up and label data appropriately, in the interest of focusing on the technical challenges, we will omit details here and directly skip ahead to posit that clustering may serve well as initial approach to achieve rudimentary classification of the preprocessed data. First, we will share the fundamentals of various clustering approaches. We will represent packet traffic data or log entries by a graph, H, consisting of vertices or nodes, X, that represent items of interest and edges, F, that represent the connections between the items of interest.

$$H = (X, F)$$

The edges that connect node pairs capture specific associations of interest between the items, discerned in the data. The graph could potentially be multi-partite because the packet traffic or log data might identify the source and target IP addresses. Devices are typically distributed throughout the various subnets of the network, so there could be an additional layer of mapping required between the IP addresses and subnet nodes. A grouping C_m is comprised of a cluster of nodes, orthogonal to every other grouping, because no vertex exists in more than one grouping.

$$X = \cup C_m,\ C_m \cap C_n = \{\}$$

Each item, x, can be assigned a feature vector, g_x. Figure 1 depicts an example of a multi-dimensional feature vector. Our objective is to use the feature vectors with a metric to facilitate grouping of vertices into k clusters, although, for some applications, the feature vector could be as basic a notion as connectivity. Each element of the adjacency matrix, **B**, represents a measure of the events that relate a pair of IP addresses, forming connections between the corresponding nodes in the graph formed by the interconnections (or perhaps distance in the feature space) between the devices in the network [14]. If the IP pairing vectors that arise from the columns of the adjacency matrix are compared with a proximity measure (for example: a similarity measure) then connectivity patterns can be compared between nodes with straightforward operations, such as inner products.

Also, the similarity matrix, **S**, formed by computing inner products of the adjacency matrix column vectors is another useful concept:

$$\boldsymbol{S} = \boldsymbol{B}^T \boldsymbol{B}$$

Thus, the higher valued elements of the similarity matrix will reveal node pairs, represented by the adjacency matrix column vectors, that have common patterns of connectivity.

For binary classification decisions, graph partitioning approaches may be employed that leverage spectral methods. To achieve larger numbers of classes, k-means, modularity-informed spectral methods, or hybrid k-means approaches [4][13]-[15] can be employed to compute clustering. Lagrange multipliers may be used in conjunction with these approaches to capture constraints for cluster memberships as part of standard optimization procedures.

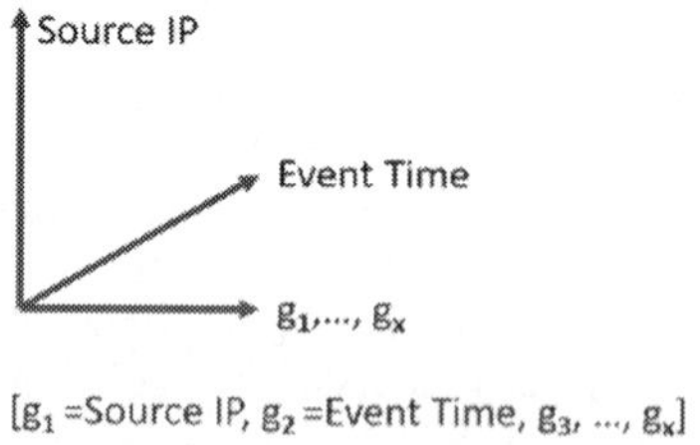

Figure 1. Example of a feature vector, g_x, which could potentially include other elements like target IP, protocol, and many more features.

We have obtained positive results with these methods [13] [15] to improve performance of the clustering algorithms for social community structure in cell phone data, so this study will explore its utility revealing insights that arise from potential groupings of traffic data or log entry items. As in our previous research, we may adopt the silhouette metric [13] [15] [16] to assess the degree of grouping structure in a proposed clustering, in which the silhouette value of one item or vertex, m, is specified

$$\text{silhouette}(m)=(p(m)-r(m))/\max\{r(m), p(m)\}$$

and r(m) represents an average dissimilarity between m and the remaining items or nodes within that cluster and p(m) is the minimum of the dissimilarities computed between m and all other clusters. Node or item dissimilarity is computed as the "distance" (e.g. Euclidean distance) between their respective feature vectors.

Accumulating the insights from multiple classification engines based on the outputs of the clustering processes, as well as outputs (e.g. alerts) of the other defensive tools, a multidimensional vector can be directed as an input to a multi-layered neural network that will form the basis for operator decision support. This research can explore the efficacy of alternative neural network methods [7], such as artificial neural networks, deep neural network, convolutional neural networks, and others to provide decision support in conjunction with the prior clustering/anomaly detection subsystem. One potential benefit of such an arrangement is that by working simultaneously, along-side the operators, essentially under continuous supervision, the neural net subsystems can improve performance with each detection decision, even as it offers suggestions to aid the operators in making their final determination. In large enterprise systems with multiple operators, this feedback loop may prove to accelerate performance improvement.

VI. Conclusion and Future Work

In this paper, we shared some cyber applications that can benefit from computer aided enhancements, such as machine learning, data analytics, and computer-aided testing. Numerous tools are entering the market, which incorporate these techniques, but it is challenging to leverage these novel tool capabilities effectively without a firm understanding of the underlying methods and the assumptions upon which they are based. Furthermore, many tools are ascribed far better performance in marketing literature than is achievable in a typical environment. As a result, there is rationale to develop internal tools and conduct thorough testing and tuning optimization for both internal and external tools of this kind. The testing and tuning iterations should measure success and accumulate statistics against common threat scenarios to ascertain overall performance.

We hope to employ the approach described in Section V to conduct a series of experiments to characterize the statistics associated with test networks as a baseline and then to study performance of enhanced systems that employ selected tools in conjunction with machine learning approaches outlined. The results should help shape new approaches to provide decision-aids and other support to cyber security operators that will help in providing insights and countering the rising challenges associated with enlarging attack surfaces that accompany the rapid evolving cyber environment and dynamics of typical enterprise networks.

Acknowledgment

The authors would like to thank the Design Engineering Analysis Laboratory (DEAL) and its affiliates for their encouragement throughout the process of completing this research. Without the assistance of the DEAL, as well as the ideas, guidance, and resources made available through that support, much of this research would have been delayed with unpredictable consequences. The authors would also like to thank the International Academy, Research, and Industry Association (IARIA) for the constant motivation to excel as well as the opportunity to serve as a contributing member within the cyber and data analytics domains.

References

[1] D. Schatz, R. Bashroush, and J. Wall. "Towards a More Representative Definition of Cyber Security". Journal of Digital Forensics, Security and Law, vol. 12, iss. 12, art. 8, 2018.

[2] https://www.telegraph.co.uk/connect/better-business/cyber-security/cyber-security-challenges-threats-in-2018/

[3] https://www.etsi.org/images/files/ETSIWhitePapers/etsi_wp18_Cyber Security_Ed1_FINAL.pdf

[4] R. Lleti, M. Ortiz, L. Sarabia, and M. Sanchez, "Selecting variable for k-means Cluster Analysis by using a Genetic Algorithm that optimizes Silhouettes", Analytica Chimica Acta, vol. 515, iss. 1, pp. 87-100, 2004.

[5] T. Klemas, R. Lively, and N. Choucri, "Cyber Acquisition Policy Changes to Drive Innovation in Response to Accelerating Threats in Cyberspace", Proceedings CYCON 2018, press.

[6] https://www.trendmicro.com/vinfo/us/security/news/security-technology/is-big-data-big-enough-for-machine-learning-in-cybersecurity

[7] S. Theodoridis and K. Koutroumbas, "Pattern Recognition", Elsevier Inc, 2009.

[8] https://searchsecurity.techtarget.com/definition/fuzz-testing

[9] D.P. Kroese, T. Brereton, T. Taimre, and Z. I. Botev,"Why the Monte Carlo method is so important today". WIREs Comput Stat., vol. 6, no. 6, pp. 386–392, 2014.

[10] T. Klemas and L. Rossey, "Network Complexity Models for Automated Cyber Range Security Capability Evaluations", ThinkMind, The First International Conference on Cyber-Technologies and Cyber-Systems, pp. 1-6, 2016.

[11] https://www.techrepublic.com/blog/it-security/understanding-layered-security-and-defense-in-depth/

[12] https://searchnetworking.techtarget.com/answer/What-is-layered-defense-approach-to-network-security

[13] T. Klemas and D. Rajchwald, "Evolutionary clustering analysis of multiple edge set networks used for modeling Ivory Coast mobile phone data and sensemaking", ThinkMind, The Third International Conference on Data Analytics, pp. 100-104, 2014

[14] M. Newman, Networks, An Introduction. Oxford : Oxford University Press, 2010.

[15] T. Klemas and S. Chan, "Automating Clustering Analysis of Ivory Coast Mobile Phone Data, Deriving Decision Support Models for Community Detection and Sensemaking", ThinkMind, The Fourth International Conference on Data Analytics, pp. 25-30, 2015.

[16] P. Rousseeuw, "Silhouettes: a graphical aid to the interpretation and validation of cluster analysis," Computational and Applied Mathematics , vol. 20, pp. 53-65, 1987.

A Multi-Agent System Blockchain for a Smart City

André Diogo, Bruno Fernandes, António Silva, José Carlos Faria, José Neves, and Cesar Analide

Department of Informatics
Centro ALGORITMI, University of Minho
Braga, Portugal

Email: a75505@alunos.uminho.pt, bruno.fmf.8@gmail.com, a73827@alunos.uminho.pt, a67638@alunos.uminho.pt, jneves@di.uminho.pt, analide@di.uminho.pt

***Abstract*—In a Smart City context, and specifically targeting public collection of sensor data from arbitrary sources by arbitrary actors, accuracy, reliability and frequency of data may be highly variable. The Blockchain technology allows the management of public immutable ledgers that track the activities of these actors closely and, as such, provides a possible solution to incentivize and empower good actors (those who supply accurate, reliable and frequent data). This paper focuses on mechanisms to provide such incentives, what we call a Proof-of-Confidence (POC), using a view of these actors as intelligent agents, capable of autonomous interaction with the Blockchain. While it is concluded that full security guarantees can not be provided without additional restrictions at the agents' behavior level, our model is used to prove the feasibility of supplying a gamified environment for such agents, with optimizable metrics which favor accurate, reliable and frequent data.**

***Keywords*-blockchain; smart city; sensor data; multi-agent systems.**

I. Introduction

Smart Cities introduce novel problems related to the management of inordinate amounts of sensor data of various types and origins. From local temperature data to road traffic, the data may be originated from a multitude of data sources, distributed through numerous autonomous and communicating devices, usually referred to as the Internet of Things (IoT). Such data must be stored adequately as it is fundamental for the analysis and development of real physical models.

The distributed management of data originated from the IoT requires a network capable of dealing with changes in the environment. An architecture comprised of regular microservices would be a valid solution to this problem, adapting to changes reactively. It lacks, however, a contextual view of these changes, meaning that the network will act on them based directly on differences in data values, and not on what these differences might mean for the analyzed environment. Intelligent agents add this contextual awareness, as well as autonomy and intelligence in the form of problem solving to achieve greater rewards as result of contributing to the network's maintenance. In fact, these agents are capable of learning, adjusting and optimizing their behaviors in the presence of incentives. The ecosystem of agents, known as a Multi-Agent System (MAS), allows further flexibility in communication and use of established Multi-Agent development platforms [1].

In regard to the network itself, Blockchains enjoy desirable characteristics to organize the collected data due to their immutable and referential nature. They effectively track all identities that inscribe data into the Blockchain using units called as transactions, which couple each identity to the data it published. A public edited ledger keeps its integrity over time, as each block in the chain references its previous, allowing blocks to become increasingly tamper-resistant. However, Blockchains by themselves do not provide incentives to produce accurate, reliable and frequent data that can be used, for example, to produce/optimize machine learning models. This situation deteriorates even further with the huge amount of distributed devices with unknown origins and data sources.

This paper aims to describe a new Blockchain model, whose goal is to enable a gamified environment for a system comprised of a multitude of agents. A system where agents that work towards its intended goal provide good data and allow the potential to identify malicious ones. Hence, this paper is structured as follows, viz. Section II will go over the unique characteristics of the conceived Blockchain, such as how interactions guarantee no data is lost and how data is stored in the Blockchain. Section III will describe how this MAS may interact with the Blockchain, followed by Section IV which describes the developed scoring system: how scores are attributed to the data, how this scoring is calculated and how this scoring achieves the desired goal of providing an optimized metric for accurate, reliable and frequent data. Section V will present a case study for this system in a more restricted environment, denominated Smart-Hub. Finally, Section VI will present a summarized conclusion of our findings, and outline future work on the proposed system, with special focus on security.

II. The Blockchain

The proposed Blockchain is very similar, in structure, to existing cryptocurrency-based public Blockchains. Indeed, it is based on a Proof-of-Work (POW) scheme [2], with some key differences (Figure 1):

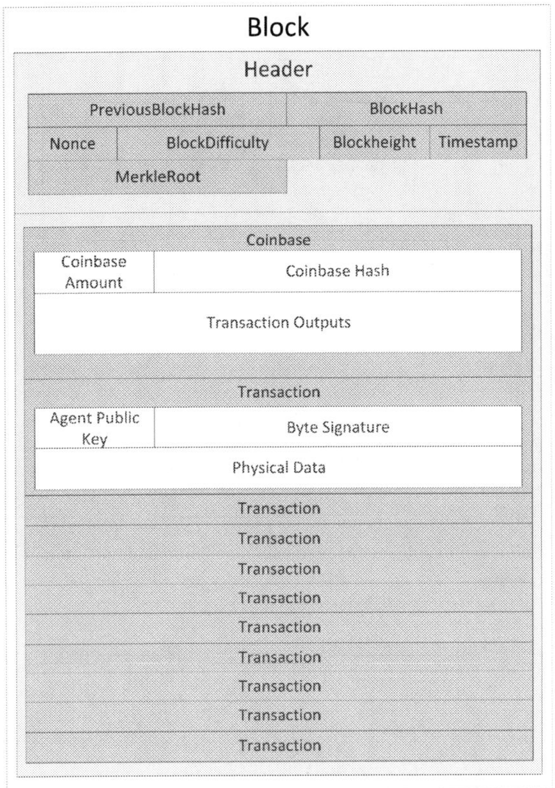

Figure 1. The block structure.

- The unit of transaction is the data collected by an agent from a specific source, tagged with a time-stamp and the agent's identity;
- There is no complex conditional scripting over these transaction;
- The value of a transaction is translated into a score, which makes up the transaction outputs, as opposed to a coin-based system;
- The cumulative score of an agent is monotonically increasing;
- This cumulative score provides a way to gauge the importance of an agent to the system, as frequently participating agents accrue higher scoring;
- Extracting a median score per transaction provides a way to gauge the accuracy of an agent, as accurate agents accrue higher score per transaction.

In the developed Blockchain, a POW schema was chosen in detriment of other schemes for ensuring investment in the Blockchain mainly for its simplicity, the adequacy to potentially resource constrained devices, as well as to avoid different tiers of agents and further implementation complexity. To interact with the Blockchain, the intelligent agents are required to have a cryptographically secure identity based on an asymmetric public and private key-pair. The public identity is the one which is referenced and tracked by the Blockchain, with the data supplied by an agent being signed with its private key, effectively rendering it tamper-proof, as well as establishing irrevocable authorship. The Blockchain is made available to these agents and any other application as a completely stand-alone library.

Advocating for open-source artifacts, all the produced software was published, in GitHub, under a MIT License [3].

A. Architecture

The developed Blockchain (Figure 2) considers three main entities: the agents that participate in building and maintaining the ledger, identified as ledger agents; the agents responsible for supplying ledger agents with processed data, known as slave agents; and data generating devices, like sensors, which may supply data to slave agents or directly to ledger ones. A group of the referred entities, connected between themselves, constitute what is denominated a Smart-Hub (Figure 2a). On the other hand, the MAS Blockchain consists of several hubs and ledger agents that opted to live outside specific hubs (Figure 2b). Each hub may be applied to distinct domains such as government management, road safety and weather forecast, among many others.

B. Data Integrity

To ensure that transactions are not lost, the agent that generates them must keep track of which transactions it issued and are not yet present in a committed block. To ensure that such transactions will populate a block, there must be a periodic diffusion of the transactions that are not yet committed. No restrictions are applied as to the time that transactions are issued, and score is not deducted at any point from a given identified agent. Due to this lack of restrictions over the validity of gathered data, and in contrast to cryptocurrency-based schemes [2] [4], a transaction is never invalidated (as would be the case for insufficient funds or cancellation). As long as the agent stores its transactions, data gathered is guaranteed to never be lost and will eventually be recorded in the Blockchain later in time.

C. Data Storage

Only the ledger agents are required to keep a copy of the ledger, with slave ones being just responsible for gathering data. The data representation is left completely configurable, provided that there is a clear distinction between each type of data. The size of such data must be calculable, as the block size is fixed (as in [2]).

Two basic assumptions are key for data storage: the first is that data exists at a point in time and the second is that it may be tied to a geographical location. As such, all data is required to be tagged by the agent through a hardware clock with the time at which that data was gathered, either by the sensor or the agent's clock. For geographically significant data, geographic coordinates can be supplied to increase data accuracy, which will impact later calculations.

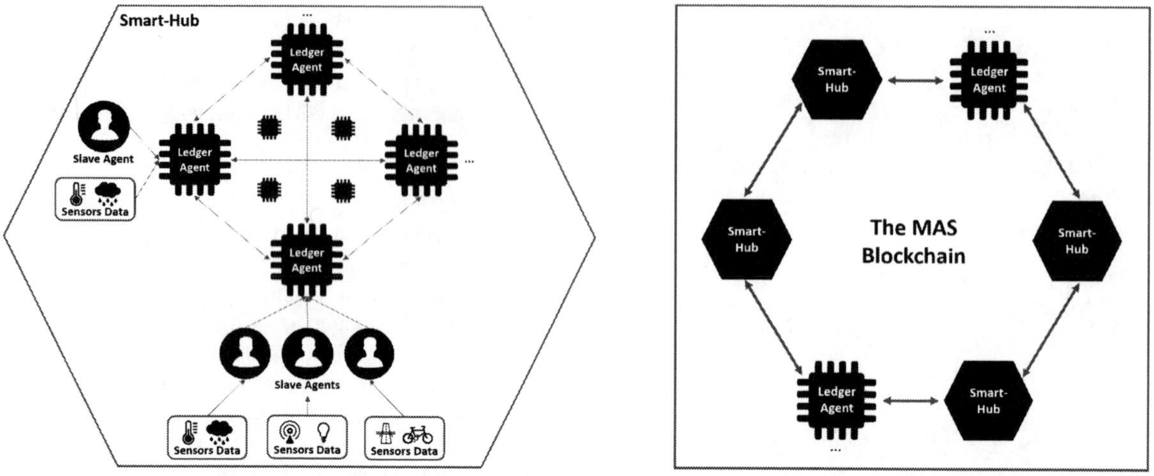

Figure 2. The Blockchain Architecture: (a) a Smart-Hub comprising Ledger and Slave agents; and (b) the MAS Blockchain comprising multi Smart-Hubs and Ledger Agents.

III. Agent Interaction

This section describes the agents' main interactions with the Blockchain (Figure 3), which are synthesized by two main behaviors: block mining and data capture. Two additional behaviors, related to data synchronization, are briefly described. It is worth noting that the Blockchain is completely independent and unaware of the agent's platform.

A. Start-up

Initially, synchronization with other running agents of the Blockchain is made through sequential transfer starting from the latest committed block of the starting agent. The mechanism for peer exchange is left up to the implementation. The agent then begins executing the succeeding behaviors.

B. Mining

To reduce computational load, agents will mine a block only once one is full interleaved with data capture into subsequent blocks. Stricter synchronization must be enforced to avoid long temporary forks, which would result in both large overhead in computation, for block validation, as well as network overhead, transmitting full blocks. Blocks are considered full only when they are populated with enough transactions as to achieve either a fixed amount of ceiling or fill the maximum allocated block size. A fixed amount of transactions help avoid extended delays in generating blocks when only very small transactions are added.

C. Data Capture

Each agent manages its own sources of data, originating in its slave devices, such as electronic sensors or other agents, as well as timings and priorities given to these sources in order to maximize their score. For this main behaviour, through which transactions are generated, an agent chooses one of these pre-configured sources to extract data and generate a transaction. This transaction is inserted to the latest block in construction and must be propagated to other agents with support from its underlying agent platform. These sources of data may be any known Application Programming Interface (API) which allows its masters to poll and extract this data.

D. Synchronization

The inherent problem of consensus in such a distributed system is still present. Therefore, mechanisms similar to those in established cryptocurrencies must be performed by the agents. These are generalized in a synchronization behavior where agents compare and exchange transactions to record in the Blockchain, as well as block headers and full blocks when necessary. This behavior has to be executed concurrently with data capture, as synchronization of known transactions is important to reduce overall computational load. Moreover, block headers are propagated between agents when mining results in a nonce that fulfills the difficulty requirements of the block. When tight synchronization of transactions is ensured, only the block header needs to be propagated, as the same already validated transactions will be present in each individual agent's current block and only the nonce and timestamp differ in the header.

IV. Scoring - A Proof-of-Confidence Metric

Work has been done in the context of public Blockchains to establish trust between cooperating peers which hold wallets and ledgers in more traditional cryptocurrency-based Blockchains. Such is the case of the NEM Blockchain [4] which relies on a Proof-of-Importance scheme (POI) and maintains peer reputations through the use of the Eigentrust++ [5] algorithm. This approach, however, focuses more on trust between peers based on their interactions than the values they supply in the form of transactions. The scoring approach taken for this paper is thus similar to the POI scheme, as it attributes

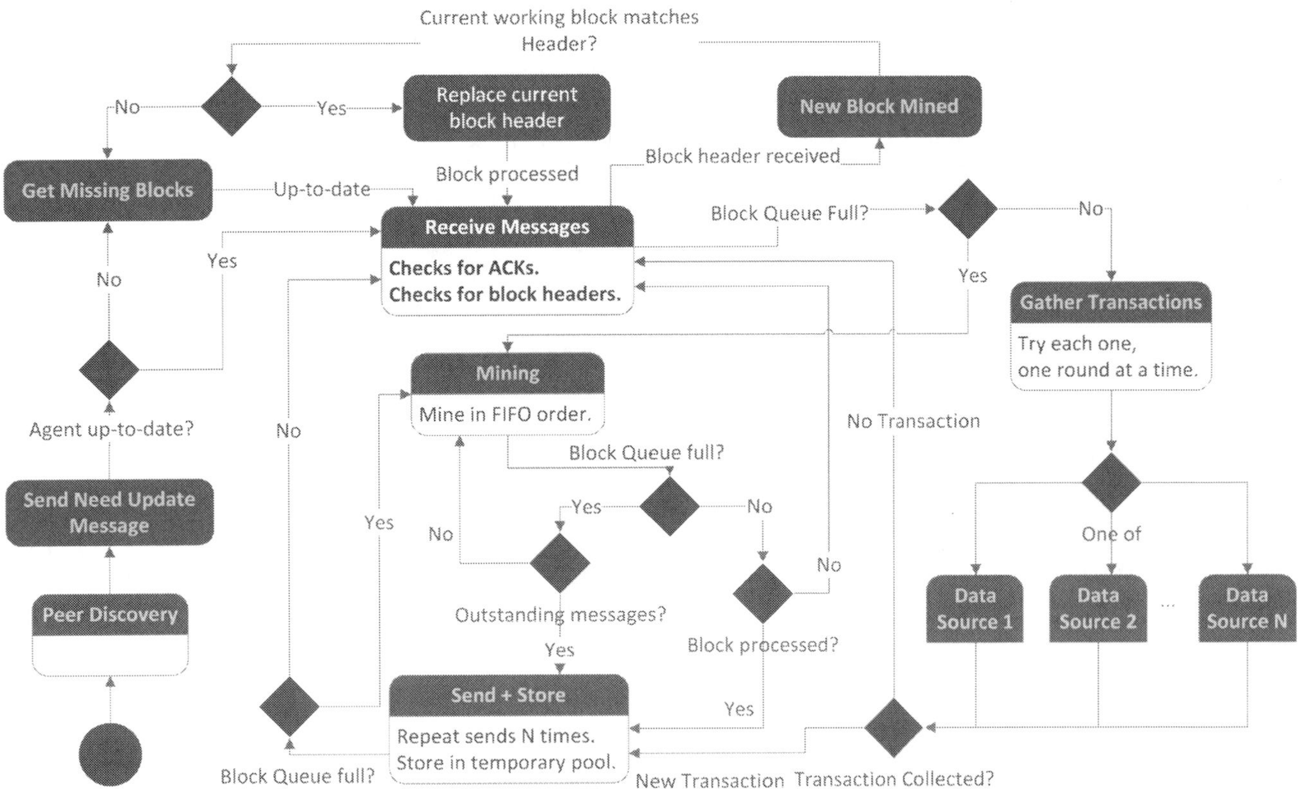

Figure 3. Activity diagram describing the agents' life cycle.

increasing importance to certain agents, but also distributing block mining equitably to all participating agents.

Scoring is the aforementioned optimizable metric and it is calculated by taking into consideration relative measurements. An agent's goal is to maximize this score, enabling a gamified environment where agents compete for the highest score. These scores are attributed to the agents that supply the transactions through the block's special coinbase transaction, and summed to its aggregated total. As usual in cryptocurrency-based Blockchains [2], each transaction is recorded such that it references which transactions were taken into account to produce the addition to the agent's outstanding score and the latest known total score for such agent prior to the new block. Thus, the main difference between scoring and traditional mined cryptocurrency comes from the fact that there is no reliance on a fixed lump-sum [2], but instead the coinbase is incrementally constructed, adding scores to each agent that adds transactions to the block.

A. Scoring Formula

The scoring is calculated via relative measurements, namely ratios between data values and time-stamps, possibly restricted to a configurable geographic radius (for geographically tagged data). In order to ascribe higher scores to data displaying desirable traits such as accuracy, reliability and frequency, a contract was established.

1) Contract:

- Any data that populates the Blockchain must, at least, allow for comparison against a previous transaction of the same type. As such, data must be identifiable by type or category (such as temperature, humidity or traffic data) and this category must allow some type of partial ordering;
- The comparison must result in a ratio of the previous value and the current value. These values depend on the type of data being measured.

2) Relative Calculations: Due to the nature of a POW metric, and the fact we consider arbitrary agents, the presence of monotonic clocks across all possible agents can not be guaranteed and, so, it is possible to commit data that is older than one would expect. As such, the insertion of data that is older than some existing data of the same category in a small geographical radius is likely to happen. The approach taken in this paper to rank data is one that is simple, although requiring complex querying over the Blockchain. Indeed, it comes from the observation that physical data tends toward homogeneity for reduced time-frames: taking, for example, temperature readings, it is highly probable that within a small region and considering a time-frame of a few seconds, temperature readings will not differ significantly. This assumption allows the protocol used for synchronization between peers to avoid additional resource usage and complexity accrued by employing time synchronization approaches, such as NEM's Blockchain [4] time synchronization protocol, based on [6] a more classic approach taking from [7]. In addition, instead of maintaining a complex scoring system, such as PageRank-based algorithms [8]), a simple short-term memory formula was developed to ease resource usage in score attribution.

3) Formula: The formula to calculate the score of a given transaction is broken into three different components, and is predicated on a comparison between the transaction to be added, noted with subscript a and the transaction closest in time to it (as measured by the time-stamp) present in the Blockchain or in the currently constructed block, of the same type, noted with subscript c:

- The first component extracts a relative measurement between the two time-stamps, noted as δ_t:

$$\delta_t = \frac{|t_c - t_a|}{t_c} \tag{1}$$

- The second component extracts a relative measurement between the values present in the data, noted δ_v, for each value i or j in the set of V_c and V_a values present in each:

$$\delta_v = \frac{|\sum v_{ci} - \sum v_{aj}|}{\sum v_{ci}}, i \in V_c, j \in V_a \tag{2}$$

- The final component is a small additive base component, which guarantees a base incentive to provide data, noted as $base$.

It must be noted that for geographically tagged data, a configurable and reasonable radius must also be defined, in which the transaction closest in time must be restricted to, in relation to the transaction to be added. These three components are then composed in order to emphasize and prioritize either the δ_t, such that frequency and reliability of the data is valued more highly; the δ_v, such that stricter homogeneity of values are valued more highly; and the base component, which incentives data collection regardless of quality and which, as to not overshadow the previous components, should be strictly smaller, preferably by, at least, one order of magnitude.

B. Data Guarantees

It should be stressed out that although no guarantees are given that malicious agents are barred from cluttering the Blockchain with arbitrary data, such agents would be easily flagged due to their naturally low scoring, either through their cumulative score or their median score per transaction. Since this scoring system effectively maintains a short term memory, as it always compares transaction data to that which is closest in time to it, although abnormal events (considering for example a fire close to a temperature sensor) result in initially poorly scored readings, subsequent readings will score higher by being compared to the previous low scoring reading.

These four key properties provide what we call a Proof-of-Confidence (POC) since this Blockchain allows for both data and agents to be ranked according to some measure of confidence, in low resource environments.

V. SMART-HUB

A simplified model of a smart city was used to develop a prototype implementation of the described system, as well as develop the main scoring formula, in which five fixed different categories of data where considered, all geographically tagged:

- Temperature data;
- Humidity data;
- Luminosity data;
- Noise data;
- Other data.

A strict categorization approach was followed in which this data not only follows the previously defined hierarchy, but is divided into classes according to its type, and in conformance with the established scoring contract.

A composition formula, developed and used in this case study, is one that values δ_t over δ_v with a very small base component, effectively prioritizing a dense timeline of data.

$$\frac{(\delta_t \cdot base_t)^2 \cdot \frac{\delta_v \cdot base_v}{2} + base}{divisor} \tag{3}$$

where,

$$base_t = 5,\ base_v = 2,\ base = \frac{1}{3},\ divisor = 50000 \tag{4}$$

The restriction radius of geographically tagged data considered for this case study is based on a percentage deviation lower than 0.1% of the transactions geographical coordinates, as it centers around a very small scoped region, of the scale of a factory or warehouse.

The entire system was developed from the ground up to be able to run on a single Java Virtual Machine (JVM) instance, enforcing the previously referred separation of the Blockchain as a library and implementing an agent as an application which uses this library using the JADE development framework [9]. This agent is designed to integrate with other agents of its kind to form a MAS and allow for easy configuration of data sources (configured via a documented file whose structure is not yet stabilized). The inclusion of other data was added for additional flexibility of the Blockchain, allowing arbitrary data to be inserted, albeit this data being an order of magnitude less valuable, by increasing its divisor (4) and bypassing the delta calculations and contract entirely, effectively supplying the maximum ratio of one for both deltas. There were no restrictions to geographical coordinates of the data for increased simplicity, though very tight bounds were assumed for the radius considered for calculations, as previously referred.

A block size of two megabytes was considered, as it was found that this particular Blockchain requires both tighter synchronization than the classical ones and a big increase in computational load in verifying block integrity. This considerably large block size allows for a big bulk of transactions to be supplied into the Blockchain at a time to compensate for the extra resource usage due to these characteristics. To provide long-term storage support, as well as complex querying capabilities, use of an embedded database management system was planned.

Throughout the development process, certain characteristics of the Blockchain were observed and conclusions extrapolated over certain key aspects, two of them, already mentioned above:

A. Computational Load

It was observed that the use of the POW scheme, coupled with the restrictions of these IoT devices, lead towards potentially undesirable computational loads, via uninterrupted mining and validation of network transmitted blocks, thus the restriction of mining only to completely full blocks.

Of note as well is the high cost in validating blocks transmitted through the network, due to the need for comparisons between potentially distant transactions in the chain, in order to recalculate scores and ensure they are correct. In order to do so, a multitude of costly queries may have to be run against the Blockchain, and as such, tighter synchronization is a must. However, in data scarcity environments, this can prove to slow down block throughput considerably. The trade-off was made to ensure less computational load, as such a general purpose Blockchain lends itself more naturally to long-term analysis, leaving more urgent applications to be solved by more local context solutions.

B. Memory Footprint

Having a considerably large block size, as well as having very few restrictions on the types of data that can potentially be supported, leaves a memory footprint potentially unacceptable for the more embedded devices, making the ledger maintaining agents more adequate to devices in a management role, such as data aggregating devices.

C. Network Bandwidth

Due to aforementioned large block size, it might be unfeasible for very restricted devices in terms of network bandwidth to participate in the Blockchain.

VI. Conclusion and Future Work

From the recorded observations, we can concluded that the conceived Blockchain model is best suited for applications that are non time-critical, but, instead, favor data management, storage and long-term analysis. It is also concluded from the conceived scoring system that the developed Blockchain is able to provide incentives for agents to supply data that tends towards accuracy, reliability and frequency. However, no strong guarantees can be provided in such a public context, due to the potential presence of malicious agents. We note an interesting property of our system, which motivates the focus of future work: as we value frequent and reliable data, agents and data sources which fail to produce such data can be identified and, if necessary, discarded. These thresholds require more definition and tests. Future work will also focus on identifying malicious agents, signaling abnormal data, as well as identifying classes of composition formulas, such as (3), best suited for prioritization of each desired characteristic of the data. Thus, the task to ensure truly accurate, trustworthy data, if so required, is left to the implementation of data gathering mechanisms used by each agent.

Three further extensions to this Blockchain model are also proposed in an attempt to close the gap between accuracy malicious activity:

- We propose either the integration of a configurable alert system directly in the Blockchain on block committal or on the agent level, themselves monitoring Blockchain activity;
- A special temporary blacklist transaction could be included that references a fixed number of irregular instances of transactions supplied by a given agent, effectively disallowing these agents to contribute to the Blockchain for a fixed number of blocks;
- A system of captive scoring could also be implemented, in which transactions by new identities are only committed to a block after ones' identity has been recognized to have produced sufficient scoring.

Acknowledgment

This work has been supported by COMPETE: POCI-01-0145-FEDER-007043 and FCT – Fundação para a Ciência e Tecnologia within the Project Scope: UID/CEC/00319/2013, being partially supported by a Portuguese doctoral grant, SFRH/BD/130125/2017, issued by FCT in Portugal.

References

[1] W. Li, T. Logenthiran, and W. Woo, "Intelligent multi-agent system for smart home energy management," in *IEEE Innovative Smart Grid Technologies - Asia (ISGT ASIA) Bangkok, Thailand*, 2015, pp. 1–6, doi: 10.1109/ISGT-Asia.2015.7386985.

[2] "Bitcoin: A Peer-to-Peer Electronic Cash System," 2008, URL: https://bitcoin.org/bitcoin.pdf [retrieved: October, 2018].

[3] "Prototype Implementation Repository," 2018, URL: https://github.com/Seriyin/mas-blockchain-main [retrieved: October, 2018].

[4] "NEM: Technical Reference," 2018, URL: https://www.nem.io/wp-content/themes/nem/files/NEM_techRef.pdf [retrieved: October, 2018].

[5] X. Fany, L. Liu, M. Li, and Z. Su, "Eigentrust++: Attack resilient trust management." 2012, URL: https://www.cc.gatech.edu/~lingliu/papers/2012/XinxinFan-EigenTrust++.pdf [retrieved: October, 2018].

[6] S. Scipioni, "Algorithms and Services for Peer-to-Peer Internal Clock Synchronization," 2009, phD Thesis URL: https://www.dis.uniroma1.it/~dottoratoii/media/students/documents/thesis_scipioni.pdf [retrieved: October, 2018].

[7] L. Lamport and P. M. Melliar-Smith, "Byzantine clock synchronization." in *Third Annual ACM Symposium on Principles of Distributed Computing*, 1984, pp. 68–74, URL: http://lass.cs.umass.edu/~shenoy/courses/summer04/readings/Lamport_52_byz_clock.pdf.

[8] L. Page, S. Brin, R. Motwani, and T. Winograd, "The PageRank citation ranking: Bringing order to the web." 1998, technical report, Stanford Digital Library, Technologies Project URL: http://ilpubs.stanford.edu:8090/422/1/1999-66.pdf [retrieved: October, 2018].

[9] K. Chmiel, D. Tomiak, M. Gawinecki, P. Karczmarek, M. Szymczak, and M. Paprzycki, "Testing the efficiency of JADE agent platform," in *Third International Symposium on Parallel and Distributed Computing/Third International Workshop on Algorithms, Models and Tools for Parallel Computing on Heterogeneous Networks*, 2004, pp. 49–66, doi: 10.1109/ISPDC.2004.49.

Threat Analysis using Vulnerability Databases
– Matching Attack Cases to Vulnerability Database by Topic Model Analysis –

Katsuyuki Umezawa
Department of Information Science
Shonan Institute of Technology
Fujisawa, Kanagawa 251–8511, Japan
e-mail: umezawa@info.shonan-it.ac.jp

Yusuke Mishina
Information Technology Research Institute (ITRI)
Advanced Industrial Science and Technology (AIST)
Koto-ku, Tokyo 135–0064, Japan
e-mail: yusuke.mishina@aist.go.jp

Sven Wohlgemuth
Research & Development Group
Hitachi, Ltd.
Yokohama, Kanagawa 244–0817, Japan
e-mail: sven.wohlgemuth.kd@hitachi.com

Kazuo Takaragi
Information Technology Research Institute (ITRI)
Advanced Industrial Science and Technology (AIST)
Koto-ku, Tokyo 135–0064, Japan
e-mail: kazuo.takaragi@aist.go.jp

***Abstract*—In this paper, we propose a threat analysis method utilizing vulnerability databases and system design information. The method is based on attack tree analysis. We created an attack tree on a evaluation target system and some attack trees on a known vulnerability, and combined the two types of attack trees to create more concrete attack trees. This enables us to calculate the probability of occurrence of a safety accident and to utilize attack trees in future analysis. Since any document has a latent topic and keywords can be generated from that topic, our vulnerability analysis algorithms use topic model analysis for natural language processing to create and analyze attack trees. The National Institute of Advanced Industrial Science and Technology (AIST) has developed a security requirement analysis support tool using topic model analysis technology. Specifically, we performed matching of attack case papers to vulnerability databases and could find about 20 items, including exact matches, from 500 items of a vulnerability database on the basis of an attack method description.**

Keywords–Threat Analysis; Vulnerability Information; Attack Tree.

I. INTRODUCTION

Interference and interruption to safety due to security incidents are recognized as a big problem in safety critical systems, such as those for electric power, information communication, automobile, aviation, railway, and medical care. Regarding the security of in-vehicle communication in the EVITA project [1], risk analysis, security requirement setting, architecture design, and prototyping, as well as a demonstration of a Hardware Security Module (HSM) by using Field Programmable Gate Arrays (FPGAs), were conducted. An attack tree was used for risk analysis in the EVITA project. One way to analyze the causal relationship between safety (hazard) and security (threat) is to express that relationship with a combination of a Fault Tree (FT) and Attack Tree (AT) [2].

The US-based MITRE Corporation provides several tools for vulnerability reporting and aggregation in a vulnerability database (DB). In Common Vulnerabilities and Exposures (CVE) [3], individual software vulnerabilities are stored in a DB. In Common Weakness Enumeration (CWE) [4], common vulnerabilities are cataloged with a focus on the cause of the vulnerability. Furthermore, Common Attack Pattern Enumeration and Classification (CAPEC) [5] is a DB classified by attack pattern.

Scientific literature related to safety analysis using FTs is, nowadays, mature [2]. However, the complexity of the problem has significantly increased in security analysis. Elaborate attacks occur with multiple combinations of those vulnerabilities. It is not easy to create an AT that comprehensively captures such possibilities.

We have focused on such problems and proposed a threat analysis method using a vulnerability DB as a practical approach [6][7]. First, we assumed that many attacks were imitations or minor changes of known attacks. Therefore, we believed that expressing attack cases that occurred in the past by using an AT could enable a designer (defender) to become aware of related attacks (recognize the danger). By gradually and continuously applying this approach, it can be useful for reducing vulnerability.

We proposed an algorithm that includes a process for matching each node of an AT described in natural language [6][7]. However, the matching method utilized was not specified. In this paper, we evaluate the feasibility of this unspecified matching process using a topic model analysis method.

In Section II, we summarize the threat analysis method we proposed in [6] and [7]. In Section III, we introduce topic model analysis. In Section IV, we verify the feasibility of matching attack cases to vulnerability DBs and show the result. Section V concludes this paper by summarizing the key points and give an outlook on future activity.

II. THREAT ANALYSIS USING VULNERABILITY DATABASES

This section presents a summary of our proposed method [7]. An overview of the threat analysis method using the vulnerability DB is shown in Figure 1. The proposed threat analysis method conducts the following three procedures:

- Create vulnerability model information.
- Create lower-level component information embedded in software.
- Perform threat analysis on the basis of design information of analysis target system.

A. *Creating vulnerability model information*

The MITRE Corporation has published several forms of vulnerability DBs [3]–[5]. However, it is difficult to create an AT for a concrete target (for example, a connected car) simply by referring to these DBs. We will create an AT with a reference to existing attack case literature, reports, etc.

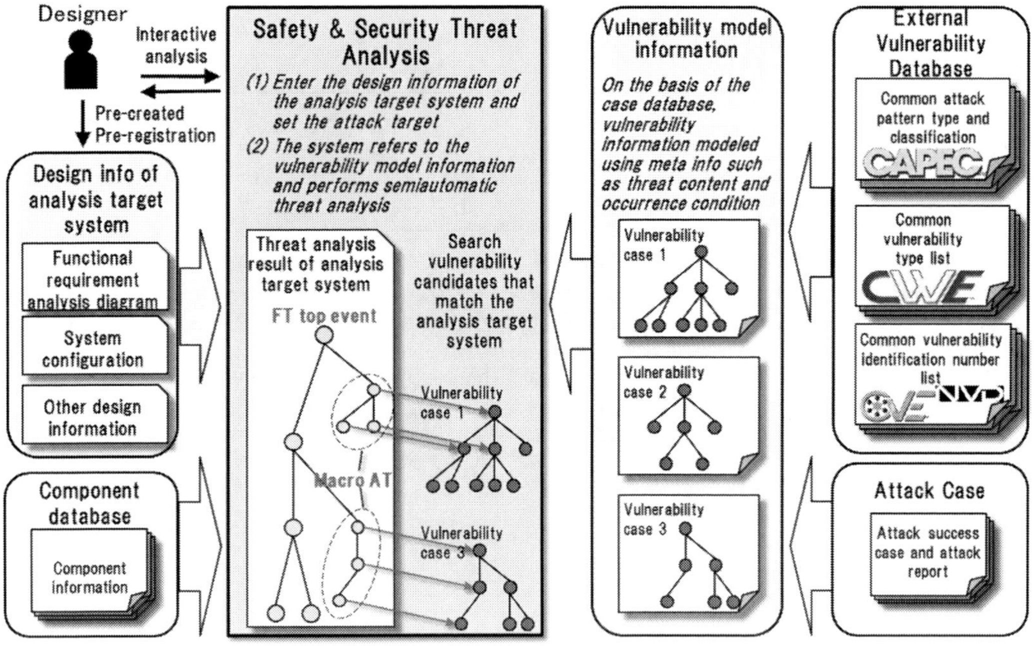

Figure 1. Overview of proposed threat analysis method

Thus, let the AT be obtained from the existing vulnerability DB and existing attack report be called the first_AT. This first_AT is hierarchically drawn into a top node, a collection of intermediate nodes and bottom nodes. A single first_AT is created for each vulnerability. A vulnerability DB such as CVE monotonically increases, so it is not necessary to recreate the first_AT once it has been generated. As will be described later, second_AT can be used as a first_AT in subsequent analysis, so that each time an analysis is performed, the quantity of first_ATs will increase.

B. Proposal of component database

In embedded systems, such as those for automobiles and general Internet of Things (IoT) devices, required lower-level components embedded within the software, not the software itself, are incorporated. However, a vulnerability DB such as CVE only includes vulnerability information for software as a whole and does not describe information on the lower-level components embedded within the software. Therefore, a correspondence table between the software version and the version for its lower-level components would be beneficial. This makes it easy to check vulnerability information at the manufacturing stage of embedded systems such as those in IoT devices. The method to create a component DB is outside the scope of this proposal.

C. Threat analysis algorithm

This section describes the threat analysis algorithm. It corresponds to the "Safety & Security Threat Analysis" section in Figure 1. The algorithm, which is based on the vulnerability model shown in Section II-A, the component DB shown in Section II-B, and the design information of the analysis target system, is as follows:

(1) Create a second_AT with the top node as a safety accident related to the evaluation target system. At this time, even if the component is not directly included in the evaluation target system, a component judged to be related by referring to the component DB is included in the second_AT (the black circle node in Figure 2 (2)). The second_AT is hierarchically depicted using the top node, the multiple intermediate nodes, and the lowest nodes. Thus, a second_AT is created (Figure 2 (2)).

(2) One of the top nodes or intermediate nodes of the second_AT is selected and Natural Language Processing (NLP) is used to mechanically determine whether there is a first_AT having a natural language expression similar to nodes of the second_AT (Figure 2 (3)). If this is the case, the first_AT is temporarily added to the second_AT (Figure 2 (4)). OR gate is attached to the node of the second_AT as a temporary cause, and the first_AT is pasted below it. This is done for all nodes of the second_AT. As a result, the second_AT is expanded more after considering the existing vulnerability database, that is, the entire set of the first_AT.

(3) The focus is now on the temporary added nodes in the expanded second_AT. We check whether the added node is necessary. Specifically, we define a node unrelated to the component of the second_AT (different components or different versions) as FALSE nodes, and the FALSE node and the AND gate that is just above the FALSE node are deleted (Figure 2 (5)).

(4) Repeat steps 1–3 for all the first_ATs that are related to the second_AT as described above. After the modification, we evaluate the occurrence probability of the top node by using the modified second_AT.

In addition, [7] describes the mathematical formulation of this proposed algorithm, calculation of attack probability, and application of actual cases of car attacks [8][9].

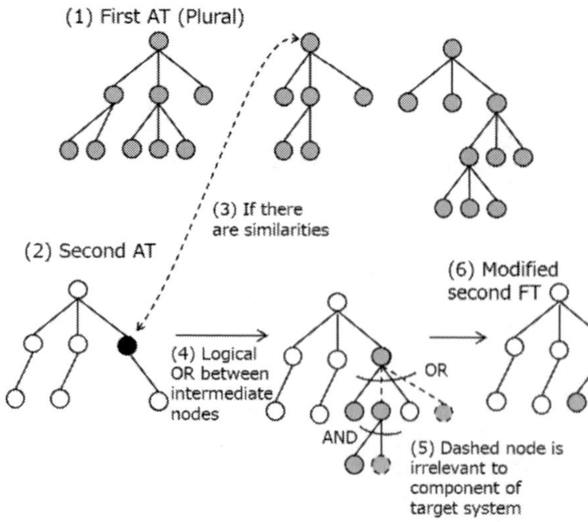

Figure 2. Threat analysis algorithm (cited from [7])

III. Topic Model Analysis

A. Latent Dirichlet Allocation (LDA)

A topic model formalized a document's properties in having a latent topic and each keyword of the document is regarded to be generated from that topic. In topic model analysis, we estimate latent topics from keywords. One of the analysis methods of topic models is Latent Dirichlet Allocation (LDA) [10]. This is a language model that assumes the probability distribution of the topic (parameter θ of the multinomial distribution) follows the Dirichlet distribution. In LDA, topics are selected in accordance with the Dirichlet distribution and words are selected in accordance with the probability distribution of words for that topic.

B. Topic model analysis tool

The National Institute of Advanced Industrial Science and Technology (AIST) has developed a security requirement analysis support tool using topic model analysis technology including LDA [11]. We preliminarily used this tool to verify whether the vast number of vulnerabilities CVE [3] listed in the order of discovery can be organized into a hierarchical structure by topic model analysis. Figure 3 shows the result of using 1500 cases from CVE-2011-3001 to CVE-2011-4500 after translating it to Japanese using Google Translate [12]. As shown in Figure 3, we see that similar vulnerabilities are classified near the hierarchical structure.

IV. Matching Attack Cases to Vulnerability Database

A. Outline explanation

As mentioned in Section II-C(2), we used NLP when matching and connecting the first_AT and the second_AT nodes. We verified the feasibility of this matching process.

We searched various reports to find vulnerabilities that should be related in the second_AT of the target system. However, depending on the report, the procedure of attack is shown but the concrete CVE number is not specified. Even in such a case, we can extract the corresponding CVE number from the attack description described in natural language.

To achieve this, we must find a node of the second_AT that conceivably matches the description in CVE. However, a mechanical word matching process will probably not lead to a correct result as it is dependent on the words used to describe sentences. The context or meaning of the known attack description in each report should be thoroughly examined. Therefore, we targeted the sentences of existing papers. Specifically, we targeted the actual case of a car attack [8]. The process flow is as follows.

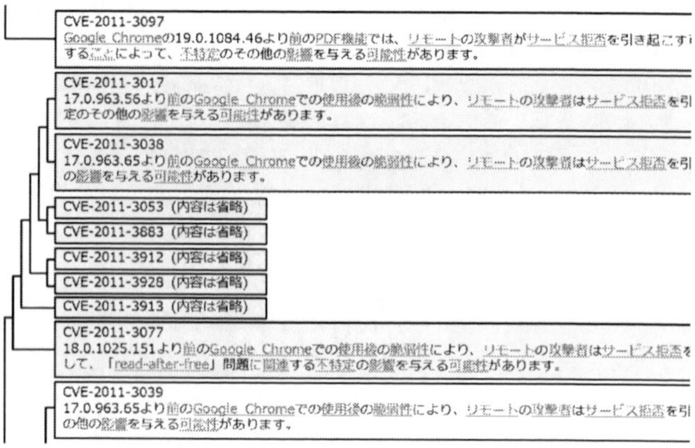

Figure 3. (Part of) Hierarchy of vulnerability DB CVE

We translated the paper [8] into Japanese by using Google Translate because the tool we used only corresponded to Japanese. An advantage of utilizing such a translation is that it can prevent notation fluctuation of terms. However, since the section on BROWSER HACKING is long and its content is related to two vulnerabilities, it was divided into two. The vulnerabilities in question were CVE-2011-3928 and CVE-2013-6282. CVE-2011-3928 is described in the section on BROWSER HACKING, and CVE-2013-6282 is described in the section on LOCAL PRIVILEGE ESCALATION. If "CVE-2011-3928" or "CVE-2013-6282" is included as a keyword, it may be detected by keyword matching, so the keywords "CVE-2011-3928" and "CVE-2013-6282" were deleted from BROWSER HACKING and LOCAL PRIVILEGE ESCALATION, respectively.

However, regarding BROWSER HACKING, there is a problem of component inclusion relationship stated in the section II-B, and the keyword "Google Chrome" is added to the sentences in which WebKit is described. This is considered to be equivalent to referring to the component DB of the proposed method. Since the topic analysis tool used has an upper limit on the number of items to be handled, it was not possible to cover all CVEs, so we targeted 500 items before and after including the target vulnerability. The limitation of 500 items is not a constraint of the topic model analysis, but an implementation limitation of the tools we used.

We specifically targeted CVEs from CVE-2011-3501 to CVE-2011-4000 including CVE-2011-3928 and those from CVE-2013-6001 to CVE-2013-6500 including CVE-2013-6282. For each section of the paper and each CVE vulnerability, similar sentences were evaluated by topic model analysis. The keyword extraction method was known as "noun and Kana", the feature quantity extraction method was "LDA", and the sentence similarity "Cosine" option was used.

B. Analysis result

The result of matching each section of the paper to each CVE vulnerability is shown in Figure 4. When we click on

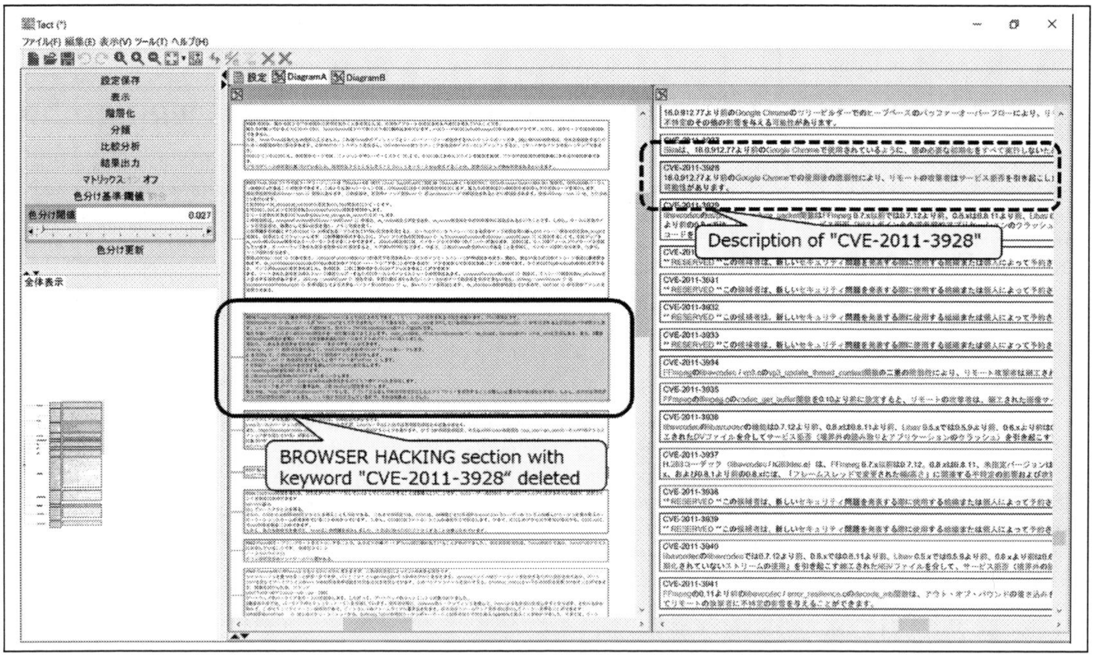

Figure 4. Matching attack cases to vulnerability DBs

a sentence in the left pane, this tool will highlight similar sentences in the right pane. The solid lined area in the left pane is the BROWSER HACKING section with the keyword "CVE-2011-3928" deleted. When clicking on this area, the dashed lined area, which is the description of CVE-2011-3928 in the right pane, is highlighted and is judged to be similar. The number of items that included the appropriate CVE from the original 500 was filtered down to 22. It can be said that the smaller the number, the better. Regarding CVE-2013-6282, a similar result was obtained by matching the information of LOCAL PRIVILEGE ESCALATION with that of CVE, in this case 23 out of the 500.

V. Conclusion

In this paper, we performed matching of attack case paper with vulnerability DBs instead of matching nodes of ATs created from design information and attack cases with those created from vulnerability DBs. We confirmed the feasibility of matching known attack cases to vulnerability DBs using a topic model analysis tool. However, this approach does not guarantee the discovery and prevention of new sophisticated attacks that are completely different from those that occurred in the past. We believe that it is necessary to apply this method to threat analysis that utilize vulnerability DBs and system design information [6][7] and evaluate it in actual cases.

Acknowledgment

Sven Wohlgemuth's contribution to this work is based on his research at Albert-Ludwig University, Freiburg, Germany, and other organizations before he joined Hitachi, Ltd. in February 2017. This work was supported by the Council for Science, Technology and Innovation (CSTI), Cross-ministerial Strategic Innovation Promotion Program (SIP), "Cyber-Security for Critical Infrastructure" (funding agency: NEDO).

References

[1] A. Ruddle et al., "Deliverable D2.3: Security requirements for automotive on-board networks based on dark-side scenarios," Seventh Research Framework Programme of the European Community, July 2008, pp. 1–138.

[2] I. N. Fovino, M. Masera, and A. D. Cian, "Integrating cyber attacks within fault trees," Reliability Engineering and System Safety 94, 2009, pp.1394–1402.

[3] MITRE Corporation, "CVE - Common Vulnerability and Exposure," https://cve.mitre.org/ [retrieved: September, 2018]

[4] MITRE Corporation, "CWE List - Common Weakness Enumeration," https://cwe.mitre.org/data/ [retrieved: September, 2018]

[5] MITRE Corporation, "CAPEC - Common Attack Pattern Enumeration and Classification," https://capec.mitre.org/ [retrieved: September, 2018]

[6] K. Umezawa, Y. Mishina, K. Taguchi, and K. Takaragi, "A Proposal of Threat Analyses using Vulnerability Databases," Proceeding of the Symposium on Cryptography and Information Security (SCIS2018), 1C2-6, January 2018, pp. 1–8.

[7] Y. Mishina, K. Takaragi, and K. Umezawa "A Proposal of Threat Analyses for Cyber-Physical System using Vulnerability Databases", 2018 IEEE International Symposium on Technologies for Homeland Security (IEEE HST), October 2018.

[8] S. Nie, L. Liu, and Y. Du, "Free-Fall: Hacking Tesla from Wireless to Can Bus," Briefing, Black Hat USA 2017, July 2017. pp. 1–16.

[9] C. Miller and C. Valasek, "Remote Exploitation of an Unaltered Passenger Vehicle," Briefing, Black Hat USA 2015, pp. 1–91.

[10] D. Blei, A. Ng, and M. Jordan, "Latent Dirichlet Allocation", in Journal of Machine Learning Research, 2003, pp. 1107–1135.

[11] K. Handa, H. Ohsaki, and I. Takeuti, "Security Requirements Analysis Supporting Tool: TACT," Information Processing Society of Japan (IPSJ) SIG Software Engineering (SIGSE), Proceeding of the Winter Workshop 2017. pp. 5–6.

[12] Y. Wu et al. "Google's Neural Machine Translation System: Bridging the Gap between Human and Machine Translation," arXiv:1609.08144, 2016. pp. 1–23.

Reviewing National Cybersecurity Awareness in Africa: An Empirical Study

Maria Bada
Department of Computer Science, Global Cyber Security Capacity Centre, University of Oxford
Oxford, UK / Academy for Computer Science and Software Engineering University of Johannesburg, Johannesburg, South Africa
e-mail: maria.bada@cs.ox.ac.uk

Basie Von Solms
Academy for Computer Science and Software Engineering University of Johannesburg, Johannesburg, South Africa
e-mail: basievs@uj.ac.za

Ioannis Agrafiotis
Department of Computer Science, Global Cyber Security Capacity Centre, University of Oxford
Oxford, UK
e-mail: ioannis.agrafiotis@cs.ox.ac.uk

***Abstract*—Over the last years, there has been an unprecedented increase in cybercrime globally. Africa is a region with one of the highest rates of cybercrime and significant financial losses. Yet, awareness of risks in cyberspace amongst citizens of African countries is in its infancy and capacity building initiatives focusing on designing and implementing such campaigns are lacking. As part of the Global Cybersecurity Capacity Centre (GCSCC) programme, we visited six countries and assessed their cybersecurity posture based on the Cybersecurity Capacity Maturity Model for Nations (CMM) developed by the GCSCC. In this paper, we analyse qualitative data collected by conducting focus groups with experts in awareness campaigns during our visits. We reflect on best practice approaches for developing campaigns and draw conclusions on what the current state of African countries is regarding awareness in risks from cybercrime, what are the main obstacles in combating cybercrime and how countries should identify and prioritise their actions. We believe that our paper contributes in research concerned with how to mitigate cybercrime.**

Keywords-cybersecurity national strategies; cyber threat awareness; risk.

I. Introduction

Over the last years, there has been an unprecedented increase in cybercrime globally [1] [2]. Africa is a region with one of the highest rates of cybercrime affecting the strategic, economic and social growth development of the region [3]. Reports suggest that, inter alia, estimated costs have soared up to \$550 million for Nigeria, \$175 million for Kenya and \$85 for Tanzania [3]. One of the factors creating a permissive environment for cybercrime is the lack of awareness in the African public regarding risks when using cyberspace [3]. Additionally, the level of development of digital infrastructure in African countries directly influences their security posture. Reports suggest that cyber criminals rely on the very poor security habits of the general population [4] and urge policy makers to engage in awareness campaigns [3] since there is strong evidence that such initiatives can efficiently lower the success rate of cybercrime [5]. More specifically, there are white papers estimating that an investment in security awareness and training can potentially change user's behavior and reduce cyber-related risks by 45% to 70% [5]. It is evident that Cybersecurity Awareness is a very important step in the fight against cybercrime in Africa. For that reason, it is essential for any African country that intends to implement interventions in this area to have a holistic understanding of the level of Cybersecurity Awareness in that country. Towards this direction, there have been efforts to capture the status of Cybersecurity Awareness (understanding on cyber threats and risk, cyber hygiene, and appropriate response options) in Africa [6], and in general, the findings suggest that the absence of awareness campaigns regarding cybersecurity and Internet safety create a lax environment for information security [6]. In this paper, we analyse qualitative data from six African countries that was collected when applying the Cybersecurity Capacity Maturity Model for Nations (CMM) developed by the Global Cybersecurity Capacity Centre (GCSCC) at the University of Oxford [7]. We reflect on best practice approaches for developing campaigns and draw conclusions on what the current state of African countries is regarding awareness in risks from cybercrime, what are the main obstacles in combating cybercrime and what actions countries should prioritise in order to increase awareness of risks from cybercrime in their population. In what follows, Section 2 provides a literature and best practice review on developing cybersecurity awareness campaigns and existing efforts in Africa. Section 3 provides a brief overview of the CMM and the CMM methodology when deployed in a country. Section 4 describes the results from the CMM reviews in six African countries and our analysis of the qualitative data obtained from focus groups during these reviews. As this paper concentrates on Cybersecurity Awareness, which is one component of the CMM, only the results of this component will be discussed. No countries will be referenced, but a general overview of the outcome will be described. Section 5 discusses the results of our analysis and Section 6 concludes the paper.

II. Cybersecurity Awareness Raising Campaigns

According to the UK Her Majesty's Government (HMG) Security Policy Framework [8], it is government's role to raise cybersecurity awareness within a country. '*People and behaviours are fundamental to good security. The right security culture, proper expectations and effective training are essential. Everyday actions and the management of people, at all levels in the organisation, contribute to good security*'. Awareness is used to stimulate, motivate, and remind the audience what is expected of them [9]. This is an important aspect of cybersecurity policy or strategy because it enhances the knowledge of users about security, changes their attitude towards cybersecurity, and their behaviour patterns.

A. *Developing Cybersecurity Awareness Raising Campaigns*

There is an abundance of best practice approaches describing principles in designing and implementing an awareness-raising campaign. Little emphasis, however, was put on how to strategically decide the areas where awareness campaigns should focus. NIST [10] is one of the pioneers in this field. Their framework provides three alternatives on how organisations should be structured, detailing for each category the processes for an effective and efficient campaign. For all three approaches, namely centralised, partially decentralised and fully decentralized, NIST provides information on how a 'needs assessment' should be conducted; a strategy should be developed; an awareness training program be designed; and an awareness program be implemented.

Focusing on the design and implementation of awareness-raising campaigns, literature suggests that successful awareness campaigns need to be a 'learning continuum' [10], commencing from awareness, evolving to training and resulting in education. According to OAS [11], it is of paramount importance that stakeholders from the public and private sector, Non-profit Government Organisations (NGOs), and technology and finance corporations must be involved. Once stakeholders are identified, the next steps in the OAS model provide instructions on how to define the goals of the campaign, the audience it targets and the strategy via which the campaign will be implemented.

Even by following best practise, several difficulties exist when it comes to creating a successful campaign: a) not understanding what security awareness really is; b) a compliance awareness program does not necessarily equate to creating the desired behaviours; c) usually there is lack of engaging and appropriate materials; d) usually there is no illustration that awareness is a unique discipline; e) there is no assessment of the awareness programmes [12]; f) not arranging multiple training exercises but instead focusing on a specific topic or threat does not offer the overall training needed [13].

Perceived control and personal handling ability, the sense one has that he/she can drive specific behaviour, has also been found to affect the intention of behaviour but also the real behaviour [14]. Culture is another important factor for consideration when designing education and awareness messages [15] as it can have a positive security influence to the persuasion process. Moreover, even when people are willing to change their behaviour, the process of learning a new behaviour needs to be supported [15].

B. *Cybersecurity Awarness Rasising Campaigns in Africa*

A review in cybersecurity policies in African countries [16] shows that awareness raising is key issue either as a separate factor or as part of the role of the proposed National CSIRT. A cybersecurity policy and strategy may not be in place yet for all countries in Africa. However, there are already a number of organisations that have identified the need for continental coordination and increased cybersecurity awareness including the African Information Society Initiative (UNECA/AISI) [17], The Internet Numbers Registry for Africa (AfriNIC) [18], ITU/GCA [19], Interpol, The Southern African Development Community (SADC) [20] and ISG-Africa [21].

There are existing efforts in Africa such as the ISC Africa [22]. This is a coordinated, industry and community-wide effort to inform and educate Africa's citizens on safe and responsible use of computers and the Internet, so that the inherent risks can be minimised and consumer trust can be increased. Also, Parents' Corner Campaign [23] is intended to co-ordinate the work done by government, industry and civil society. Recently Facebook has also announced partnerships with over 20 non-governmental organisations and official agencies from the DRC, Ghana, Kenya, Nigeria and South Africa in support of Safer Internet Day (SID) marked on 6 February [24]. SID advocates making the internet safer, particularly for the youth, and is organised by the joint Insafe-INHOPE network with the support of the European Commission and funded by the Connecting Europe Facility programme (CEF).

Usually, most of official awareness-campaign sites include advice, which usually comes from security experts and service providers, who monotonically repeat suggestions such as use strong passwords. One of the main reasons why users do not behave optimally is that security systems and policies are often poorly designed [25]. There is a need to move from awareness to tangible behaviours.

III. THE CYBER SECURITY CAPACITY MATURITY MODEL FOR NATIONS (CMM)

The CMM of the Global Cybersecurity Capacity Centre (GCSCC) at the University of Oxford is a comprehensive framework which assesses the cybersecurity capacity maturity of capabilities which are foundational to building resilience of a country over 5 different dimensions: 1) Cybersecurity Policy and Strategy; 2) Cyber Culture and Society; 3) Cybersecurity Education, Training and Skills; 4) Legal and Regulatory Frameworks; 5) Standards, Organisations, and Technologies.

Every Dimension consists of a number of Factors which describe what it means to possess cybersecurity capacity. Each Factor is composed of a number of Aspects that structure the Factor's content. Each Aspect is composed of a series of indicators within five stages of maturity. These indicators describe the steps and actions that must be taken to achieve or maintain a given stage of maturity in the aspect/factor/dimension hierarchy. These 5 maturity stages are: 1) Start up; 2) Formative; 3) Established; 4) Strategic; 5) Dynamic. The progressive nature of the model assumes that lower stages have been achieved before moving to the next.

In this paper, we focus on the factor '*Cybersecurity Awareness Raising*'. The Aspects, within this factor are '*Awareness Raising Programmes*' and '*Executive Awareness Raising*' with various Indicator specifications for every Maturity Stage. The Aspect '*Awareness Raising Programmes*' examines the existence of a national coordinated programme for cybersecurity awareness raising, covering a wide range of demographics and issues, while the Aspect '*Executive Awareness Raising*' examines efforts raising executives' awareness of cybersecurity issues in the public, private, academic and civil society sectors, as well as how cybersecurity risks might be addressed. The CMM model was developed by conducting systematic reviews on best practice approaches which are publicly available, as well as consulting experts from various disciplines.

So far, the CMM has been deployed at the national level (rather than at the company/enterprise level), and 54 countries have been evaluated through engagement and collaboration with international organisations and the host country.

The CMM employs a focus group methodology since it has been acknowledged to offer a rich set of data compared to other qualitative approaches [26]-[28]. Stakeholders are identified based on their expertise in each one of the components of every Dimension of the CMM. Focus groups sessions are led by the CMM Review Team.

IV. CMM RESULTS FOR AWARENESS RAISING IN AFRICA

In Africa, a team from the GCSCC has reviewed and evaluated 6 countries based on the CMM and following the methodology described in Section 3. These countries were selected for a review at the time because they were in the process of drafting a cybersecurity strategy. Therefore, the review would assist this process. These reviews have been conducted during the period June 2015 to January 2018.

Regarding the Aspect 'Awareness Raising Programs' and 'Executive Awareness Raising', 12 focus groups have been conducted in total. The stakeholders who participated in the focus groups are from the following sectors: Public Sector Entities; Legislators/Policy Makers; Criminal Justice and Law Enforcement; Armed Forces; Academia; Civil Society; Private Sector; CSIRT and IT Leaders from Government and the Private Sector; Critical national infrastructure; Telecommunications Companies; and Finance Sector. Each focus group session had approximately 10-15 stakeholders and lasted on average 2 hours.

In order for the stakeholders to provide evidence on how many indicators have been implemented by a nation and to determine the maturity level of every aspect of the model, a consensus method is used to drive the discussions within sessions. During focus groups, researchers use semi-structured questions to guide discussions around indicators. During these discussions, stakeholders should be able to provide or indicate evidence regarding the implementation of indicators, so that subjective responses are minimised.

A. Analysis of maturity level data

Three countries have been identified to be at a start-up stage of maturity, two countries have been identified at a formative stage and one at a start-up stage with few of the indicators from the formative stage of maturity being present.

The results clearly indicate that the majority of examined countries in Africa are identified at a start-up stage of maturity. This translates into lack of a national programme for cybersecurity awareness raising. The need for awareness of cybersecurity threats and vulnerabilities across all sectors is not recognised, or is only at initial stages of discussion. Furthermore, awareness raising programmes (if existing) may be informed by international initiatives but are not linked to a national strategy.

Finally, it was identified that awareness raising programmes, courses, seminars and online resources might be available for target demographics from public, private, academic, and/or civil sources, but no coordination or scaling efforts have been conducted. In the next Section, we provide further details, based on our qualitative analysis, on these initial findings.

B. Qualitative analysis of results

We have transcribed all the recordings from focus groups and conducted a thematic analysis on the qualitative data for each country. We adopted a blended approach (a mix of deductive and inductive approach) to analyse focus group data and used the indicators of the CMM as our criteria for a deductive analysis. The inductive approach is based on 'open coding' meaning that the categories or themes are freely created by the researcher, while the deductive content analysis requires the prior existence of a theory to underpin the classification process.

Excerpts that did not fit into themes were further analysed to highlight additional issues that stakeholders might have raised during the focus groups or to inform our understanding on what the next steps should be for a country.

Overall, we identified eight themes in our qualitative analysis for every country. Four themes were based on the aspects described in the CMM model and four themes emerged from the inductive approach. The themes from the inductive approach pertained information on what actions African countries should implement next. Since these eight themes were common for all six countries, we merged the excerpts for each theme from every country. We further examined these excerpts to identify common areas which hindered progress in cybersecurity awareness raising as well as key actions which countries should implement next to improve their cybersecurity posture in awareness raising.

More specifically, the four main themes that emerged from the deductive approach are: a) the lack of national level programmes; b) the existence of ad-hoc initiatives; c) the relationship between ICT literacy (the ability to use digital technology and tools) and awareness and d) executive awareness. In a similar vein, the inductive approach identified four themes which revolved around the same concepts described in the deductive analysis; the difference being that excerpts in the inductive themes pertained information about recommendations and next steps.

1) Deductive Theme Analysis: For all countries, it is evident that a national programme for cybersecurity awareness raising is absent. In many cases, stakeholders mentioned that '*lack of awareness is an institutional problem, not a user problem*' and also that '*a proper cyber awareness programme is needed*'. The importance for such a programme was acknowledged across the various stakeholders in all countries reviewed in Africa. A main hindrance for the implementation of a national programme is the general lack of cybersecurity awareness outside the technical communities, which stakeholders pointed that its origin is the low ICT literacy in the population of these countries.

It was further emphasised that awareness-raising programmes need to be developed alongside other capacity enhancements, such as incident response, training for cybersecurity educators, national and organisational cybersecurity policies, etc.

Regarding the initiatives theme, there are ad-hoc initiatives in cybersecurity awareness raising that are supported by various institutions. These are being offered from various organisations such as Facebook while the financial sector, civil society and academia organise programmes for schools to raise awareness. According to a stakeholder, '*some telecommunication companies and banks are engaged in awareness activities which includes messages via the media, directed to end-users, e.g. password security*'.

These initiatives, however, are not yet coordinated at the national level. Therefore, it was widely recognised that a more centralised awareness-raising programme would greatly expand a fundamental understanding of cybersecurity capacity.

Often, civil society actors initiate efforts into targeted cybersecurity awareness-raising. Different stakeholders agree that a '*common ground*' between government, private sector and civil society could enable the proliferation of awareness raising to the broader society. Moreover, often it was mentioned that the government needs to work alongside existing efforts in academia to ensure that new initiatives capitalise from the academic experience. Such synergy is critical to ensure that awareness-raising efforts are efficient and effective.

As often mentioned by stakeholders '*people trust social media and do not expect that someone will harm them, we are brothers!*'. A stakeholder also noted that '*It is common in African countries that mobile phones are used to access the Internet, use social media, for e-banking services etc. but people who use online services are not aware of risks*'. Often, lack of awareness leads to a sense of '*blind trust online. A stakeholder noted that 'users trust social media and think that their information is secure, although often websites are still insecure*'.

Another interesting theme that emerged from the analysis of data is the low ICT literacy rate in Africa. Stakeholders indicated that awareness of the effective use of ICT is still only gaining initial traction and that security is seen as only relevant once ICT and Internet literacy is sufficient.

Regarding the theme revolving around awareness among executives, both in public and private sectors, cybersecurity awareness is very limited, which is one reason why cybersecurity awareness raising is not yet perceived as a priority. This has been identified as an important gap, as executives are usually the final arbiters on investment into security.

Some major telecommunications companies conduct internal awareness raising trainings across all levels, but there is not a publicly available initiative which targets executives. As mentioned by a stakeholder, '*the reason for that is that there is limited awareness for cybersecurity threats and risks in the private sector overall, unless in major international organisations, in particular in the banking and telecommunications sectors which face strategic implications of cybersecurity*'.

It was commonly stated that there is a sharp disconnect between the terminology and priorities of the engineers working in IT systems and security, and those at the higher level seeking to make sound business decisions based on risk.

2) Inductive Theme Analysis: Stakeholders mentioned during focus group sessions that '*aspects of cybersecurity need to be introduced in the school curricula and improve ICT literacy*'. It was also noted that '*even in universities, people are not aware of the possible risks and procure without following standards*'. Integrating cybersecurity awareness efforts into ICT literacy courses could provide an established vehicle for cybersecurity awareness campaigns.

Culture is another factor that can impact the effectiveness of cybersecurity awareness programmes. As seen above, the collectivist cultural aspect that characterises offline behaviour in Africa, is also pertained in online behaviour [29].

Currently, due to the lack of national level awareness programmes, '*being hacked brings awareness usually*' as a stakeholder noted. Therefore, the development of such a programme with specified target groups focusing on most vulnerable users is identified as necessary [30]. Also, appointing a designated organisation (from any sector) to lead the cybersecurity awareness raising programme and engaging relevant stakeholders from public and private sectors in the development and delivery of the awareness raising programme is crucial. As stakeholders mentioned in one of the reviews in Africa '*The government realises that lack of awareness is crucial and recognises the importance of a multi-stakeholder approach towards this goal*'. Moreover, it was noted that '*People access social media through their smart phones and security is the last thing on their mind and that convenience is usually coming first*'.

Regarding the executive awareness raising aspect, developing a dedicated awareness raising programme for executives within the public and private sectors is essential. A stakeholder noted that '*different levels of authority need different kind of awareness in order to promote collaboration as well*'. Currently, executives and management are being called upon to address cyber risk alongside other risks that businesses face.

V. DISCUSSION

Reflecting on the results presented in Section 4, the lack of a central authority, which is crucial in all modes of operation as presented by NIST model [31], is evident. The absence of such authority prohibits the execution of holistic 'needs assessments', amplifies the difficulties in prioritising the areas in which campaigns should be implemented and renders the design of ad-hoc campaigns by a limited number of stakeholders the only alternative. It is imperative that African countries allocate an authority to conduct a national needs assessment, identify the areas where campaigns should focus first, develop a strategy for how these campaigns will be designed and implemented, and coordinate the ad-hoc efforts of different stakeholders.

Focusing on the design and implementation of awareness-raising campaigns, literature suggests that successful awareness campaigns need to be a 'learning continuum' [31], commencing from awareness, evolving to training and resulting in education. Our results highlight the need of African countries to involve stakeholders which are established in all the aforementioned sectors. Our analysis suggests that the audience of the campaigns should prioritise smartphone users, employees of SMEs and board members. The goals should be to communicate the risks from cybercrime, illustrate the need for better security controls and practices, and the need to establish a chief information security officer (CISO), respectively.

This means that businesses and government agencies should start to take steps to increase their awareness and understanding of cybersecurity with a view of the potential impact on overall business performance. Lack of boardroom expertise makes it challenging for directors and councilors to effectively oversee management's cybersecurity activities.

Cybersecurity awareness should reach all levels and inform all users of the internet – from vulnerable, school-going children to families, industry, critical national infrastructures, governments and the African continent with its unique needs [31]-[34]. This will enhance resilience against cybercrimes and attacks and inform African policy development.

If a country has already developed a national cybersecurity strategy, or is working towards that goal, then linking the development of the programme to that Strategy will facilitate the coordination of different capacities towards the development of the programme and its effective implementation.

Regarding the implementation of these campaigns, there are several organisations with ad-hoc initiatives that could facilitate the design and implementation of cybersecurity campaigns, such as ISC Africa [22] and Parents corner [23]. To conclude, it is worth mentioning that the timing for the development of these campaigns coincides with efforts in African countries to increase ICT literacy. As our findings underline, it is a unique opportunity for all African countries to combine ICT development with cybersecurity awareness. In contrast to western societies, where cybersecurity campaigns endeavour to change the norms on how users currently behave online (behaviour shaped since the inception of the Internet), campaigns in Africa can reflect on best practice and create new norms which will encompass cybersecurity requirements.

Moreover, enacting evaluation measurements to study effectiveness of the awareness programme will not only lead to the assessment of the programme but also identify possible gaps that need to be addressed [10] [30].

VI. CONCLUSIONS AND FUTURE WORK

Several reports are depicting a bleak picture regarding the unprecedented increase of cybercrime in Africa. Yet, efforts to raise cybersecurity awareness in the general public are in an embryonic stage. In this paper, we conducted twelve focus groups in six different African countries to shed light into the current situation and identify critical actions which can significantly decrease the success rate of cybercriminals.

Our results suggest that all six African countries do not possess a national programme for raising awareness, there are extremely low ICT literacy levels which hinder any design of cybersecurity campaigns and that executive members in organisations myopically underestimate the problem. To better defend against cybercrime, African countries need to establish a central authority which will coordinate the existing ad-hoc efforts in awareness campaigns and identify the target groups of these campaigns with particular focus on SMEs, mobile-phone users and executive board members. We believe that African countries have a unique opportunity to combine ICT literacy campaigns with cybersecurity principals and shape the norms of the society towards best practice.

As part of our future work, we intend to explore the effectiveness of a national coordinated cybersecurity awareness programme and how it relates to the actual security posture of a country. Our future work will be based on data from developed countries where the CMM has already been applied, as well as on data collected by other international organisations such as the ITU - GCI [35], Australian Strategic Policy Institute - ASPI [36], The Potomac Institute for Policy Studies (PIPS) - CRI [37], WEF - Global Competitive Index [38] and others.

ACKNOWLEDGMENTS

The authors would like to thank Ms. Eva Ignatuschtschenko, Ms. Eva Nagyfejeo, Mr. Taylor Roberts and Ms. Carolin Weisser from the GCSCC for conducting field work and data collection. We are also immensely grateful to Prof. Sadie Creese and Prof. Michael Goldsmith for their comments on an earlier version of the manuscript.

REFERENCES

[1] Trend Micro: "Is there a budding west african underground market?" https://www.trendmicro.com/vinfo/us/security/news/cybercrime-and-digital-threats/westafrican-underground, 2017. [retrieved: July 2018].

[2] O. Tomi: "Cyber-crime is africa's 'next big threat', experts warn". http://www.bbc.co.uk/news/world-africa-34830724, 2015. [retrieved: July 2018].

[3] Serianu: "Africa cyber security report". http://www.serianu.com/downloads/AfricaCyberSecurity Report2016.pdf, 2016. [retrieved: June 2018].

[4] Symantec: "Cyber crime and cyber security trends in africa". https://www.thehaguesecuritydelta.com/media/com hsd/report/135/document/Cybersecurity-trends-report-Africa-en.pdf, 2016. [retrieved: June 2018].

[5] Wombat Security Technologies (Wombat) and the Aberdeen Group: "African union cybersecurity profile: Seeking a common continental policy". https://jsis.washington.edu/news/africanunion-cybersecurity-profile-seeking-common-continental-policy/, 2016. [retrieved:June 2018].

[6] T. Skye: "The last mile in it security: Changing user behaviors". https://www.sbs.ox.ac.uk/cybersecuritycapacity/system/files/ CMM%20revised%20edition 09022017 1.pdf, 2016. [retrieved: May 2018].

[7] Global Cyber Security Capacity Centre: "Cybersecurity capacity maturity model for nations (cmm): Revised edition". https://www.wombatsecurity.com/press-releases/research-confirmssecurity-awareness-and-training-reduces-cyber-security-risk, 2016. [retrieved: June 2018].

[8] HMG: "Security policy framework". https://www.gov.uk/government/uploads/system/uploads/ attachment data/file/316182/Security Policy Framework - web - April 2014.pdf, 2016. [retrieved: June 2018].

[9] T. R. Peltier, "Implementing an information security awareness program", Information Systems Security, vol. 14(2): pp. 37–49, 2005.

[10] National Institute of Standards and Technology: "Framework for improving critical infrastructure cybersecurity". https://www.nist.gov/sites/default/files/documents/cyberframe work/cybersecurityframework-021214.pdf, 2014. [retrieved: June 2018].

[11] Organization of American States: "Cybersecurity awareness toolkit". https://www.sbs.ox.ac.uk/cybersecuritycapacity/system/files/2015%20OAS%20%20Cyber %20Security%20Awareness%20Campaign%20Toolkit%20%28English%29.pdf, 2015. [retrieved: June2018].

[12] B. Khan, K. S. Alghathbar, S. I. Nabi, and M. K. Khan, "Effectiveness of information security awareness methods based on psychological theories", African Journal of Business Management, vol 5(26), pp. 10862, 2011.

[13] I. Winkler and S. Manke, "Reasons for security awareness failure", CSO Security and Risk, 7.

[14] I. Ajzen, "Perceived behavioral control, self-efficacy, locus of control, and the theory of planned behavior", Journal of applied social psychology, vol 32(4), pp. 665–683, 2002.

[15] M. W. Kreuter and S. M. McClure, "The role of culture in health communication", Annu. Rev. Public Health, vol. 25, pp. 439–455, 2004.

[16] I. Dlamini, B. Taute, and J. Radebe, "Framework for an African policy towards creating cyber security awareness", The Southern African Cyber Security Awareness Workshop (SACSAW) 2011, pp. 15-31.

[17] United Nations: Economic Commission for Africa, "The african information society initiative (aisi) - a decades perspective". https://www.uneca.org/publications/african-informationsociety-initiative-aisi-decade2015. [retrieved: June 2018].

[18] AfriNIC: "The internet numbers registry for africa". https://www.afrinic.net/, 2018. [retrieved: June 2018].

[19] International Telecommunication Union: "Towards a common future". https://www.itu.int/en/action/cybersecurity/Pages/gca.aspx, 2018. [retrieved: June 2018].

[20] The Southern African Development Community: Global cybersecurity agenda (gca). http://www.sadc.int/, 2018. [retrieved: June 2018].

[21] Information Security Group of Africa: Profile. http://pressoffice.itweb.co.za/isgafrica/ profile.html, 2018. [retrieved: June 2018].

[22] ISC: "Internet safety campaign". http://iscafrica.net/, 2018. [retrieved: June 2018].

[23] Parents Corner: "Digital curfews — what are they & do your kids need one? " https://parentscorner.org.za, 2017. [retrieved: June 2018].

[24] L. Masibulele: "Africa rallies in support of safer internet day". http://www.itwebafrica.com/ict-and-governance/523-africa/242730-africa-rallies-in-supportof-safer-internet-day, 2018. [retrieved: June 2018].

[25] J.R.C. Nurse, S. Creese, M. Goldsmith, and K. Lamberts, "Guidelines for usable cybersecurity: Past and present". In Cyberspace Safety and Security (CSS), 2011 Third International Workshop pp. 21–26, IEEE..

[26] M. Williams, "Making sense of social research. Sage, 2002.

[27] J. Knodel, "The design and analysis of focus group studies: A practical approach", Successful focus groups: Advancing the state of the art, vol. 1, pp. 35–50, 1993.

[28] R. A. Krueger and M. A. Casey, "Focus groups: A practical guide for applied research". Sage publications, 2014.

[29] H. C. Triandis, Cultures and organizations: Software of the mind", 1993.

[30] M. Bada and A. Sasse, "Cyber Security Awareness Campaigns: Why do they fail to change behaviour?", in proceedings of the International Conference on Cyber Security for Sustainable Society (CSSS, 2015) Coventry, UK, pp. 118-131.

[31] E. Kritzinger, M. Bada, and J.R.C. Nurse, "A study into the cybersecurity awareness initiatives for school learners in south africa and the uk", in IFIP World Conference on Information Security Education, Springer, 2017, pp. 110–120.

[32] H. Twinomurinz, A. Schofield, L. Hagen, S. Ditsoane-Molefe, and N. A. Tshidzumba, "Towards a shared worldview on e-skills: A discourse between government, industry and academia on the ict skills paradox", South African Computer Journal, vol. 29(3), pp. 215–237, 2017.

[33] E. Kritzinger, "Growing a cyber-safety culture amongst school learners in south africa through gaming", South African Computer Journal, 29(2), 2017.

[34] E. Kritzinger, "Short-term initiatives for enhancing cyber-safety within south african schools". South African Computer Journal, vol. 28(1), pp. 1–17, 2016.

[35] International Telecommunication Union: "Global cybersecurity index". https://www.itu.int/en/ITU-D/Cybersecurity/Pages/GCI.aspx, 2018. [retrieved: June 2018].

[36] Australian Strategic Policy Institute: "Cyber maturity in the asia pacific region". https://www.aspi.org.au/, 2017. [retrieved: June 2018].

[37] The Potomac Institute for Policy Studies: "Cyber readiness index 2.0". http://www.potomacinstitute.org/images/CRIndex2.0.pdf, 2015. [retrieved: June 2018].

[38] The Global Competitiveness Report: https://www.weforum.org/reports/the-global-competitiveness-report-2017-2018 [retrieved: June 2018].

Building A Collection of Labs for Teaching IoT Courses

Xing Liu
Dept. of Computer Science and Information Technology
Kwantlen Polytechnic University
Surrey, Canada
xing.liu@kpu.ca

***Abstract*—This paper introduces a collection of labs that can be used for teaching Internet of Things (IoT) courses. An IoT system consists of physical devices, the Internet, and the cloud. The labs are designed to give students opportunity to experiment with these three aspects of IoT. On the physical devices side, the labs use a Raspberry Pi single board computer, selected sensors and actuators. On the software side, Python libraries are used for coding device interfaces and IoT applications. Amazon Web Services (AWS) IoT is the cloud platform used by the labs. A laptop computer with a Virtual Network Computing (VNC) client installed serves as the development platform which connects to the Raspberry Pi computer via a local WiFi network. The Raspberry Pi computer interacts with sensors and actuators and communicates with the AWS IoT cloud service through the Internet. The paper provides details on how the labs are developed. Test results are presented to illustrate how the labs work.**

Keywords-Internet of Things; IoT; teaching; courses; labs.

I. INTRODUCTION

The Internet of Things (IoT) has gone through rapid development in past few years. Numerous commercial products have been developed. The technology is being applied to many aspects of our life. In order to provide the much needed workforce for both development and applications of IoT technology, universities and technical institutions have started teaching IoT courses in their computer science, computer engineering, or information technology curriculum [1]-[4].

In order to help students understand the technical concepts of IoT, hands-on training is essential. Ideally, IoT courses should be taught along with a series of labs.

Although IoT course samples are not difficult to find on the Internet, detailed hands-on labs used in the courses are rarely available. Therefore, it is the author's intention to share such information in this paper.

The paper summarizes the author's experience in developing labs for an IoT course. Detailed descriptions are provided regarding setting up the lab platform, the use of sensors and actuators and the AWS IoT cloud platform, together with computer code snippets for the labs.

The paper is organized as follows. Section II gives an introduction to the Internet of Things. Section III describes the architecture of the system for the labs. Section IV explains the details of the selected labs. Test results are provided in Section V.

II. INTERNET OF THINGS

According IEEE [5], IoT is "a network that connects uniquely identifiable things to the Internet. The things have sensing/actuation and potential programmability capabilities. Through the exploitation of unique identification and sensing, information about the thing can be collected and the state of the thing can be changed from anywhere, anytime, by anything".

Essentially, an IoT system has three components: physical devices, which are also called the *things*, the Internet, and the cloud. The simplified IoT model can be represented using Figure 1.

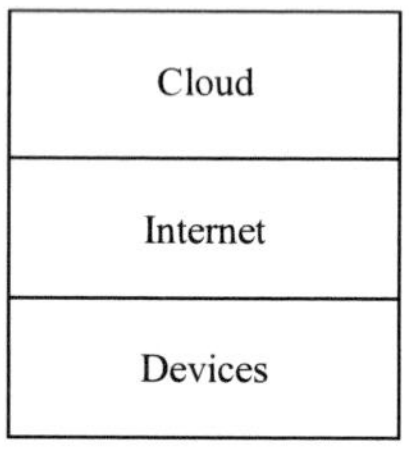

Figure 1. Simplified model of an IoT system

In order to provide students opportunities to understand various aspects of IoT, properly designed labs of an IoT course should cover these three components.

The learning objectives include having students understand IoT operations from a system perspective and gain hands-on skills in constructing IoT systems and developing related software. After completing the labs, students should understand what sensors and actuators are and what they can do. Students should also be able to design and build basic electronic interface circuits for sensors and actuators. Students will understand the concepts of data sampling, data collection and data transfer. Students will also understand how physical devices should identify themselves to cloud services and communicate with the services securely. Students are expected to be able to set up AWS IoT services to collect data from sensors and store the data in the cloud. The labs should enable students to use other cloud services to process data as well.

Preparing students for employment in the region is the rationale of selecting AWS and AWS IoT as the cloud platform for the labs.

III. SYSTEM DESCRIPTION

All labs are designed based on the system architecture as shown in Figure 2. The system has a Raspberry Pi single board computer, sensors, actuators, Internet connection, and the cloud. The Raspberry Pi computer, sensors, and actuators make a *thing* which is a physical device with computing power. The thing can send its data to the cloud via the Internet. A service in the cloud can interact with the thing via the Internet as well. The laptop computer connected to the Raspberry Pi serves as the development platform.

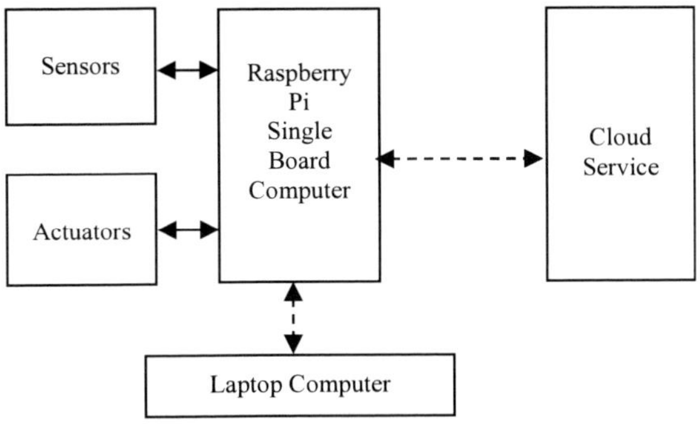

Figure 2. System architecture for running the labs

A. *The Raspberry Pi Single Board Computer*

The single board computer for the labs is a Raspberry Pi 3 model B with a 1.2GHz 64-bit quad-core ARMv8 CPU and 1 GB of RAM. It has both wired and wireless network interfaces. The wireless network interfaces include 802.11n Wireless LAN and Bluetooth. The Raspberry Pi has a powerful Input/Output interface called GPIO which stands for "general purpose input output", as well as a camera interface. The "hard disk" of the Raspberry Pi is a SD card which can have tens of gigabytes of memory. Although the Raspberry Pi can have different types of operating systems, its "official" operating system is called Raspbian, which is of a Linux type. The Raspberry Pi can be programmed using popular programming languages such as C, JavaScript, Java, and Python. The collection of labs in this paper are based on Python.

B. *Sensors*

Sensors make the main component of an IoT system. They are used to measure environment parameters such as temperature, humidity, motion, light intensity etc, just to name a few. The labs of this paper use sensors that are readily available on the market and are of low cost, such as the DHT11 temperature/humidity sensor. Students are encouraged to obtain sensor kits designed for IoT applications as well. These kits not only have a variety of sensors, but also electronic components for building circuits, such as breadboards, wires, and resistors.

C. *Actuators*

Actuators in IoT systems generate movements, rotations, or other actions. The actuator used by the labs of this paper is a DC servo motor. The servo motor generates movements so that students understand what "actuation" means. The labs of this paper use a micro servo motor called SG90.

D. *Camera*

The camera used in the selected labs is a Raspberry Pi Camera with a Sony Exmor IMX219 Sensor and a resolution of 8 mega pixels. It has a fixed focus lens. The camera connects to the Raspberry Pi via an interface called Mobile Industry Processor Interface Camera Serial Interface Type 2 (MIPI CSI-2). The camera can be used to take still pictures or record video.

E. *The Cloud*

The labs use AWS IoT as its cloud service. AWS IoT is a popular Amazon web service for IoT applications. Physical devices connected with AWS IoT can interact with each other and with other AWS cloud services. Sensor data can be stored in the AWS cloud and can be analyzed there.

The main components of AWS IoT are: 1). A device gateway which enables physical devices to securely communicate with AWS IoT; 2). A message broker that helps devices and AWS IoT applications to publish and receive messages using the Message Queuing Telemetry Transport (MQTT) protocol; 3). A Rules Engine that provides message processing and integration capabilities, as well as to republish messages to other subscribers; 4). A Registry that allows users to register devices and their attributes; 5). A Device Shadow that is used to store and retrieve device state information; 6). A Device Provisioning Service that maintains device entries in the registry, certificates which devices use to authenticate with AWS IoT, and policies which determine what operations a device can perform in AWS IoT. The reason for choosing AWS IoT is to have students learn a popular industrial cloud service which is particularly useful for industry in the region.

IV. DETAILS OF SELECTED LABS AND TEST RESULTS

The labs are designed in such a way that students will learn the practical skills of the thing side first. These are the labs for driving sensors and actuators locally through the Raspberry Pi without an Internet connection. The students learn the basics of sensors and actuators, I/O interfaces, and how to interact with them through the Raspberry Pi. After the students have become familiar with the local thing side, additional labs will give them the opportunity to connect the thing to the cloud, experiment with sending data to the cloud and receiving instructions from the cloud. Further labs will enable students to learn data processing using other AWS cloud services such as machine learning.

A. *Set Up the Raspberry Pi*

Assembling a newly purchased Raspberry Pi is straightforward. One caution is that heat sinks should be installed to avoid overheat so students should not omit this step. Usually a new Raspberry Pi comes with the operating system Raspbian pre-installed. If not, Raspbian can be downloaded from the official Raspberry Pi website [6] and can be installed using software tools that work with SD cards.

It is recommended to install the Raspbian OS with a desktop-type GUI so that the user can connect to AWS IoT later via the web browser of Raspbian.

However, Raspberry Pi is "headless", meaning there is no monitor or even a LCD screen connected initially. The most convenient way to use a Raspberry Pi is for it to share the monitor, keyboard and mouse with a laptop computer. However, separate keyboard and mouse are still needed to set up the Raspberry Pi the first time in order to enter initialization information, such as the SSID and password of a wireless network and to enable VNC on the Raspberry Pi.

Installing the software applications PuTTY, Angry IP Scanner, RealVNC, SDFormatter on the laptop computer before setting up the Raspberry Pi is very useful. The laptop computer only has to be on the same WiFi network as the Raspberry Pi in order to use RealVNC to connect to the Raspberry Pi.

In order to run Python programs on a Raspberry Pi, the Python engine has to be available. The way to verify that Python is installed properly on the Raspberry Pi is by typing the command "python" on a Raspbian command terminal and run a line of Python code such as `print "Hello, World!"`.

It is necessary to run all of the following commands to install or upgrade Python drivers on the Raspberry Pi before developing and running programs written in Python:

```
sudo apt-get update
sudo apt-get install python-dev python-pip
sudo pip install --upgrade distribute
sudo pip install ipython
sudo pip install --upgrade RPi.GPIO
```

Among the list of commands above, `python-pip` is a package management system used to install and manage software packages written in Python. `ipython` (Interactive Python) is a command shell. `RPi.GPIO` is the GPIO pin driver API, which is usually already included in Raspbian.

B. *Drive A LED*

Being able to light up a LED is essential for the labs because LEDs can be used conveniently as indicators of various activities in the IoT system. A LED can help detect if a circuit or a pin of an output port on the Raspberry Pi is working or if a sensor is triggered.

The circuit diagram for the LED lab is shown in Figure 3 where GPIO Pin 17 is used to drive the LED.

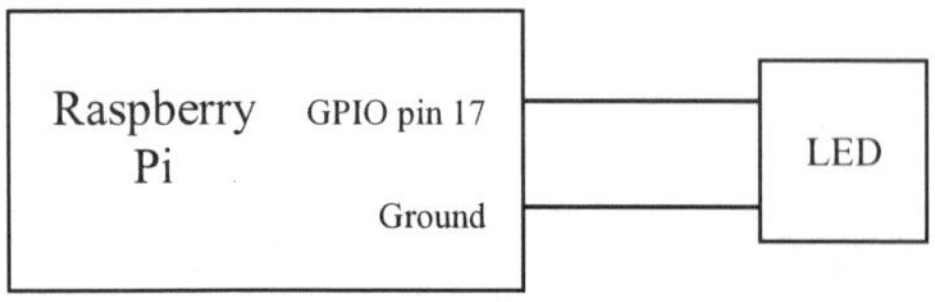

Figure 3. Circuit for driving a LED

Key Python code snippets for the LED lab is shown in Figure 4.

```
import RPi.GPIO as GPIO
GPIO.setmode(GPIO.BCM)
led_pin=17
GPIO.setup(led_pin, GPIO.OUT)
GPIO.output(led_pin, GPIO.HIGH)
GPIO.output(led_pin, GPIO.LOW)
```

Figure 4. Python code for the LED lab

In Figure 4, Line 1 imports the Python GPIO driver. Line 2 specifies the GPIO pin mode because there are two options for numbering the GPIO pins. The `GPIO.BCM` option above means that the pins are referenced by the "Broadcom SOC Channel" numbering system. In this option, the pin numbers have the prefix "GPIO". The other option is `GPIO.BOARD` which specifies the pin numbers based on the numbers printed on the circuit board such as "01", "02", and "40". Line 4 sets up the `led_pin` for output. Line 5 turns the LED on and Line 6 turns the LED off. Students can write their own code to have the LED on for certain amount of time and at different intervals to create interesting display patterns.

C. *Read A Pushbutton*

Reading a pushbutton as shown in Figure 5 can be useful when a user wants to interact with the IoT system via a "real button" instead of a virtual button displayed on a graphical user interface. The circuit program is shown in the Figure 5.

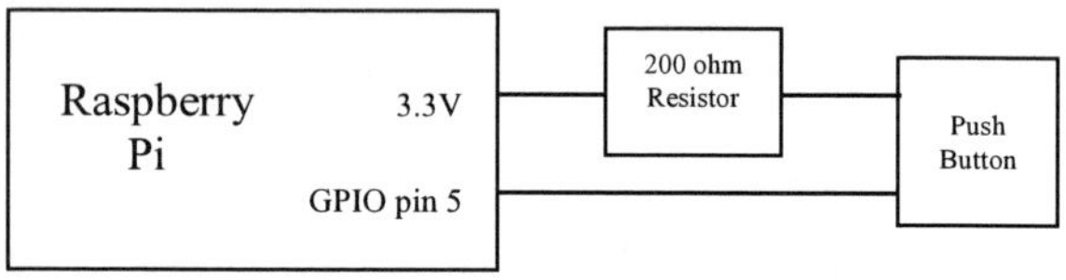

Figure 5. Circuit for reading a pushbutton

Key Python code snippets for the pushbutton lab is shown in Figure 6.

```
import RPi.GPIO as GPIO

push_pin=5
GPIO.setmode(GPIO.BCM)
GPIO.setup(push_pin, GPIO.IN,
           pull_up_down=GPIO.PUD_DOWN)

GPIO.add_event_detect(push_pin,
           GPIO.RISING, bouncetime=200)

def on_push_down(channel):
    print("Pushbutton is pressed.")

GPIO.add_event_callback(push_pin,
                  callback=on_push_down)
```

Figure 6. Python code for the pushbutton lab

In Figure 6, similar to the LED lab, the Python GPIO driver is imported and the pin mode is set to `GPIO.BCM`. In

Line 6, `pull_up_down=GPIO.PUD_DOWN` means that a value of `GPIO.HIGH` will be read by Python code when the button is pressed (because the circuit between the +3.3V pin and the GPIO pin 5 is closed). Line 8 means that the `push_pin` is set for rising edge detection and it will ignore further edges for 200ms to compensate for switch bounces. The last line registers the Python function `on_push_down` as a callback function, which means function `on_push_button` will execute after the pushbutton is pressed. A pushbutton press can be used to simulate any action that will trigger an event.

D. *Read A Temperature Sensor and A Humidity Sensor*

Measuring environmental parameters such as temperature and humidity is common for IoT applications. There are many types of temperature and humidity sensors available on the market. A popular sensor named DHT11 can measure both temperature and humidity. The circuit for using the DHT11 sensor is shown in Figure 7.

The DHT11 temperature/humidity sensor has three wires. The wire in the middle of the connector is the data wire. The other two wires are for power and the ground.

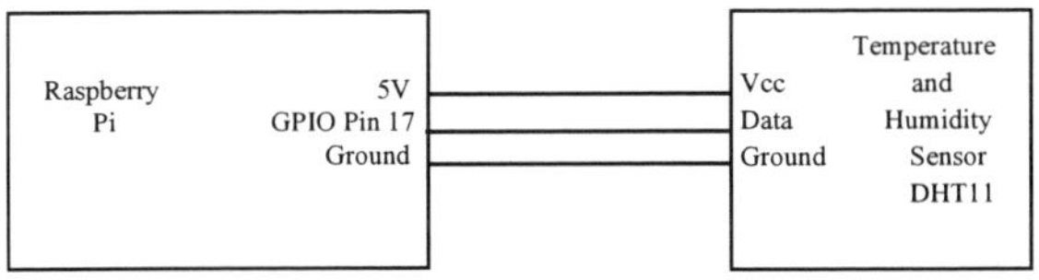

Figure 7. Circuit for the temperature/humidity measurement lab

Writing the Python code from the ground up to talk to the DHT11 sensor is complex because the code has to handle digital pulses and their encodings. However, a Python driver that makes application development much easier has been written and is available for download [7].

Two files should be downloaded from the above site: `dht11.py` and `dht11_example.py`. With the help of the `dht11.py` driver module, the key Python code for reading data from the DHT11 sensor can be made very simple and is shown in Figure 8.

```
import RPi.GPIO as GPIO
import dht11

GPIO.setmode(GPIO.BCM)

instance = dht11.DHT11(pin=26)
result = instance.read()
if result.is_valid():
  print("Temperature: %d" % result.temperature)
  print("Humidity: %d %%" % result.humidity)
```

Figure 8. Python code for the temperature and humidity sensor lab

Some tests were performed in a residential home. Temperature and humidity data from the DHT11 sensor were recorded by taking a screenshot of a Raspbian terminal window in which the Python program prints its output. Test run results are shown in Figure 9.

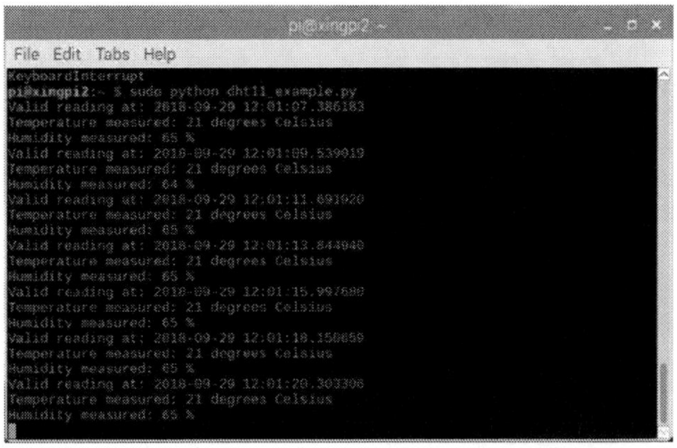

Figure 9. Test results for the DHT11 temperature and humidity sensor

E. *Control A Servo Motor*

The labs of this paper use the micro servo motor SG90. Although Raspberry Pi has pin GPIO18 designated for producing pulse width modulation (PWM) pulses, other pins can be used to drive the servo motor SG90 as well.

It takes 20ms of the pulse width for the SG90 to travel through its full rotational range. By design, when the pulse width of the PWM signal is 1 millisecond (ms), the position of the servo motor is at its very LEFT side. The duty cycle of this position is (1ms/20ms) x 100 = 5%. For pulse widths of 1.5ms and 2ms, the servo motor is at its MIDDLE position with a duty cycle of 7.5% and at its far RIGHT position with a duty cycle of 10%.

The circuit for the servo motor lab is shown in Figure 10.

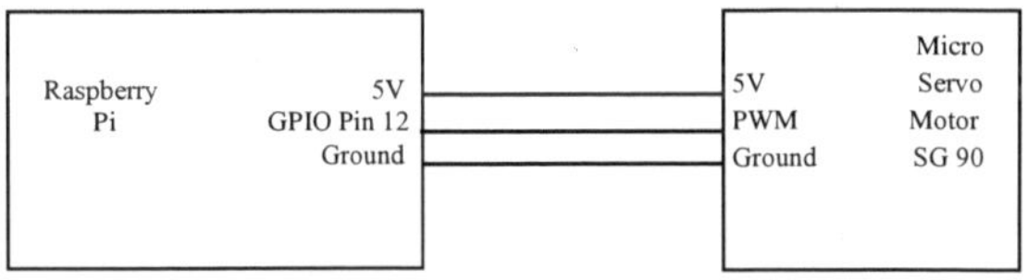

Figure 10. Servo motor control circuit

Key Python code for driving the servo motor is shown in Figure 11.

```
import RPi.GPIO as GPIO

GPIO.setmode(GPIO.BCM)
GPIO.setup(18, GPIO.OUT)

pwm = GPIO.PWM(18,50)

pwm.start(5) #Start at 0 degrees
time.sleep(1)

pwm.ChangeDutyCycle(7.5) #turn to 90 degrees
time.sleep(1)

pwm.ChangeDutyCycle(10) # turn to 180 degrees
```

Figure 11. Key Python code for servo motor control

In Figure 11, `GPIO.PWM(18,50)` sets GPIO Pin 18 to output square wave pulses with 50 Hz of frequency. The two key Python functions are `start` and `ChangeDutyCycle`, which are used to position and rotate the shaft of the servo motor.

F. Control A Camera

The camera named Raspberry Pi Camera is the "official" camera to be used with Raspberry Pi. With this camera users can take still pictures, apply image effects and record video. Caution has to be exercised when installing the camera on the Raspberry Pi. Users have to make sure that the blue side of the ribbon cable face the Ethernet port and the silver side face the HDMI port. The camera has to be enabled under the configuration of Raspberry Pi as well. Another important set-up step is to enable VNC streaming of live images from the camera to the laptop computer. Otherwise no image displays can be seen on the screen of the laptop computer. This can be done by opening a terminal window on the Raspberry Pi, type command "`vncserver`", navigate to "Menu" then "Options" followed by "Troubleshooting", and select "Enable experimental direct capture mode". Figure 12 shows what a streamed image looks like on the screen of a laptop computer.

Figure 12. Pi camera captured image streamed to a laptop computer

In order to run Python code to control the camera, the Python module PiCamera has to be imported. Important functions are `start_preview`, `stop_preview`, and `capture` which is used to capture an image and `start_recording` which is used to record a video. Code samples are shown in Figure 13. Videos recorded can be viewed by running the command "`omxplayer`" followed by the name of the video file.

```
from picamera import PiCamera
camera = PiCamera()
camera.start_preview()
camera.capture('/home/pi/Desktop/image.jpg')
camera.stop_preview()
camera.start_preview()
camera.start_recording('/home/pi/video.h264')
sleep(10)
camera.stop_recording()
camera.stop_preview()
```

Figure 13. Sample Python code for using the Pi camera

G. Communicate with the Cloud

The cloud service used in the labs is Amazon's AWS IoT. In order to develop Python code running on the Raspberry Pi that can communicate with AWS IoT, a software development kit (SDK) has to be downloaded and installed on the Raspberry Pi. The SDK file can be downloaded from Amazon's website [8].

The SDK file should be unzipped and the user has to run the command "`sudo python setup.py install`" to install the SDK to a proper folder in the Raspberry Pi.

The SDK comes with several sample files which can be used as the starting point for development.

In order for the Raspberry Pi to communicate with AWS IoT, an identity of it named a "Thing" has to be created in AWS IoT. A set of security certificates have to be created and associated with the "Thing". These certificates have to be downloaded onto the Raspberry Pi which will use them to identify itself to AWS IoT when connecting. Policies have to be created to specify what the "Thing" is allowed to do in AWS IoT as well.

In the Python code running on the Raspberry Pi, an AWSIoTMQTTClient has to be created. This client will be used to publish messages to the AWS IoT cloud service and receive messages back from the AWS IoT cloud service via a "Topic" set up in the AWS Simple Notification Service (SNS).

Figure 14 shows the essential AWS IoT SDK functions needed for the Raspberry Pi to connect to AWS IoT and publish data to a topic in AWS SNS.

```
from AWSIoTPythonSDK.MQTTLib import
AWSIoTMQTTClient

myMQTTClient = AWSIoTMQTTClient("My Pi")

myMQTTClient.configureEndpoint("A3XXX.iot.e
u-west-1.amazonaws.com", 8883)

myMQTTClient.configureCredentials("/home/pi
/cert/RootCA.pem", "/home/pi/cert/xxxx-
private.pem.key", "/home/pi/cert/xxxxx-
certificate.pem.crt")

myMQTTClient.connect()
myMQTTClient.publish("my_topic",
"connected", 0)

payload = "sensor data"

myMQTTClient.publish("my_topic",payload,0)
```

Figure 14. Key Python code for communicating with AWS IoT

Sensor data can be used to build a "payload" which is published to AWS IoT. The AWS SNS service needs to subscribe to the topic which the MQTT client running on the Raspberry Pi publishes sensor data (payload) to. When data is being published, AWS SNS will receive and display them almost instantly. Users have the option to suspend the reception of data as well.

Figure 15 is a screenshot that shows a Thing in AWS IoT. This Thing is essentially a virtual representation of the

Raspberry Pi and its associated sensors in the AWS IoT cloud.

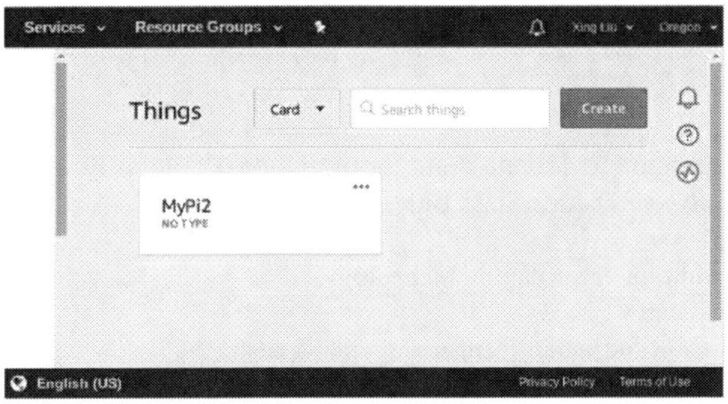

Figure 15. Screenshot that shows a "Thing" in AWS IoT

The AWS SNS service provides controls for publishing and subscribing to topics and a window for showing live topic data. Figure 16 is a screenshot that shows sensor data published by the DHT11 sensor via the Raspberry Pi and received by AWS SNS on a topic named "MyPi2Topic".

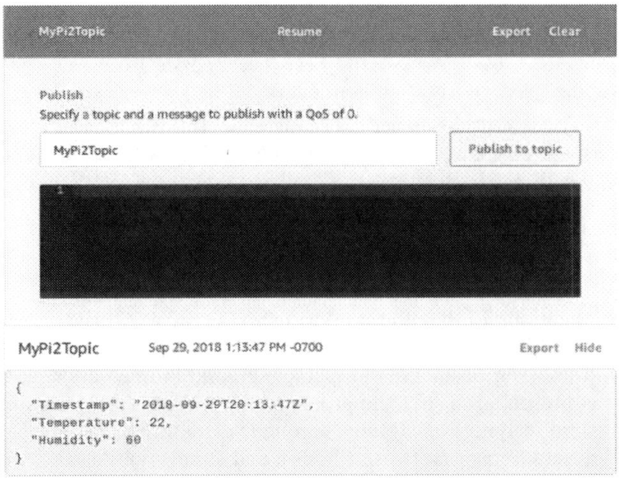

Figure 16. Screenshot showing sensor data received by AWS SNS

H. Labs under Development

Although the above set of labs have covered the three aspects of IoT, i.e., physical devices, the Internet and the cloud, some labs still need to be developed. For example, labs for generating email notifications and text messages; labs for controlling physical devices from the cloud; labs that allow one device to control another device via the cloud. Labs are also needed to teach students how to transfer large amount of data such as images and videos to the AWS cloud and store them there. These labs are still under development.

V. CONCLUSION

This paper has introduced a collection of labs that can be used in teaching IoT courses. The labs give students opportunities to learn different aspects of IoT ranging from physical devices to the cloud. Details of the labs and key Python code snippets are provided.

ACKNOWLEDGMENT

The author would like to express his gratitude for the support provided by the Provost's office of Kwantlen Polytechnic University.

REFERENCES

[1] X. Liu and O. Baiocchi, "An IoT Course for A Computer Science Graduate Program", International Conference on: Communication, Management and Information Technology (ICCMIT'16), Cosenza, Italy, April 26-29, 2016.

[2] Ryerson University, "Course Series in The Internet of Things (IoT)", https://ce-online.ryerson.ca/ce/calendar/default.aspx?id=5&section=program&mode=program&sub=atd&cert=CSTIOT00. Accessed on October 13, 2018.

[3] Northern Alberta Institute of Technology, "IOT/IOE Certificate", http://www.nait.ca/program_home_101497.htm. Accessed on October 13, 2018.

[4] Kwantlen Polytechnic University, "INFO 4381: Internet of Things and Applications", http://www.kpu.ca/calendar/2018-19/courses/info/index.html. Accessed on October 20, 2018.

[5] R. Minerva, A. Biru, and D. Rotondi, "Towards a definition of the Internet of Things (IoT)", 27 May 2015, IEEE Internet Initiative. https://iot.ieee.org/images/files/pdf/IEEE_IoT_Towards_Definition_Internet_of_Things_Revision1_27MAY15.pdf. Accessed on September 29, 2018.

[6] Raspberrypi.org, https://www.raspberrypi.org/downloads/. Accessed on October 13, 2018.

[7] DHT11 Python library, https://github.com/szazo/DHT11_Python. Accessed on October 13, 2018. Accessed on October 13, 2018.

[8] AWS SDK, https://s3.amazonaws.com/aws-iot-device-sdk-python/aws-iot-device-sdk-python-latest.zip. Accessed on October 13, 2018.

IoT-Based Secure Embedded Scheme for Insulin Pump Data Acquisition and Monitoring

Zeyad A. Al-Odat*, Sudarshan K. Srinivasan*, Eman Al-qtiemat*, Mohana Asha Latha Dubasi*, Sana Shuja†
*Electrical and Computer Engineering, North Dakota State University
Fargo, ND, USA
†Electrical Engineering, COMSATS Institute of Information Technology,
Islambad, Pakistan
Emails: *zeyad.alodat@ndsu.edu, *sudarshan.srinivasan@ndsu.edu, *eman.alqtiemat@ndsu.edu,
*MohanaAshaLatha.Duba@ndsu.edu, †SanaShuja@comsats.edu.pk

***Abstract*—This paper introduces an Internet of Things (IoT)-based data acquisition and monitoring scheme for insulin pumps. The proposed work employs embedded system hardware (Keil LPC1768-board) for data acquisition and monitoring. The hardware is used as an abstract layer between the insulin pump and the cloud. Diabetes data are secured before they are sent to the cloud for storage. Each patient's record is digitally signed using a secure hash algorithm mechanism. The proposed work will protect the patient's records from being breached from unauthorized entities, and authenticates them from improper modifications. The design is tested and verified using μVision studio, the Keil board mentioned above, and an ALARIS 8100 infusion pump. Moreover, a test case for a real cloud example is presented with the help of the Center of Computationally Assisted System and Technology. This center provided the infrastructure service to test our work.**

Keywords–IoT; Security; Embedded system.

I. Introduction

The physical devices that are linked as Internet of Things (IoT) are continuously increasing [1]. These devices are allowed to mimic human being's senses. For example, the use of a smart home as an IoT-based application can turn on the air conditioning system when sensing residents are close [2][3]. The industrial world has moved toward the use of IoT by adding Internet connection to small electronic boards [4]. Moreover, the connections between different primitives are made possible through mobile communications [5].

Recent improvements in IoT design helps with the support of some health care systems. An example is tracking patient's records and biomedical devices using the Internet [6]. Medical devices for diabetic care have also joined the world of IoT through supporting versatile design options. However, security issues need to be addressed to ensure device security and the patient's privacy. A system with an authentic security mechanism is required to guarantee the security of patient's records. One of the existing methods that can be easily implemented in hardware is the Secure Hash Algorithm (SHA) [7]. The SHA is an official hash algorithm standard that was standardized by the National Institute of Standards and Technology (NIST). SHA is compatible with hardware-level implementation, and this makes it one of the more desirable methods for hardware designers to use to secure and authenticate their designs [8].

The implementation of IoT technology in hardware has become crucial for high performance. The benefit of using hardware to manipulate the increased size of patient's records is that the hardware allows for high-speed computation to manipulate and retrieve records. Therefore, hardware designers have moved toward the use of IoT hardware units in their designs, these units support high-speed computation power for IoT related functions [9]. This paper introduces an IoT-based embedded system for insulin pump data acquisition and monitoring. Data related to a patient's diabetes disease along with other health records are stored on the cloud. All these data need to be secured and authenticated when they are retrieved from the cloud. We use the SHA mechanism in our design to support security and authentication.

The rest of the paper is organized as follows. Section II describes related work. The proposed methodology is presented in Section III. Results are detailed in Section IV. Section V concludes the paper.

II. Related Work

There is a lot of recent work in the employment of IoT applications for health monitoring and control [6][7][10]–[12]. A novel IoT-aware smart architecture for automatic monitoring and tracking of the patient, personnel, and biomedical devices, was presented in [6]. The proposed work built a smart hospital system relying on Radio Frequency Identification (RFID), Wireless Sensor Network (WSN), and smart mobile. The three hardware components were incorporated together through a local network, to collect surrounding environment and patient's physiology related parameters. The collected data is sent to a control center in real-time, which makes all the data available for monitoring and management by the specialist through the Internet.

A smart E-health care system for ubiquitous health monitoring is proposed in [10]. The proposed work exploits ubiquitous health care gateways to provide a higher-level of services. The Gateways are the bridging point between IoT and applications (software or hardware). This work studied significant ever-growing demands that have an important influence on health care systems. The proposed work suggests an enhanced health care environment where control center burdens are transferred to the gateways. The security of this scheme is taken into consideration as the system deals with substantial health care data.

A personalized health care scheme for the next generation wellness technology has been proposed in [11]. The security of patient's records was addressed in case of data storage and retrieval over the cloud. The proposed work established a patient-based infrastructure allowing multiple service providers including the patient, service providers, specialists, and researchers to access the stored data. Their work was implemented on a cloud-based platform for testing and verification. Liu *et al.* [12] have presented a scheme for secure sharing of personal health records in the cloud. The health records are ciphered before they are stored in the cloud. The proposed work uses Cipher-Text Attribute-Based Signcryption Scheme (CP-ABSC) as an access control mechanism. Using this scheme, they are able to get fine-grained data access over the cloud.

The use of embedded micro-controllers for data monitoring and acquisition has also been previously explored. The Keil LPC1768 micro-controller has been used in two different schemes for medical device control [7][9]. In [7], an online design of patient's data monitoring system was presented. The proposed work employed an Advanced RISC Machine (ARM) Cortex M3 microprocessor embedded on the Keil LPC1768 board. Pulse, temperature, and gas sensors were used to collect the patient's medical parameters. The LPC1768 board was used as the hardware layer between the Internet and the medical sensors. A data acquisition and control system using the ARM Cortex M3 microprocessor was also presented in [9]. Monitored sensor data are sent to the Internet using an Ethernet-controlled interface. The interface was built using an Keil LPC1768 board. The proposed work employed two sensing devices (temperature and accelerator-meter) to collect data from the surrounding environment. The collected readings are sent to the Internet through the Ethernet interface. According to the uploaded readings, a specialist can change the behavior of the device through an Internet browser.

In the next section, we will present our proposed IoT-based secure data acquisition and monitoring scheme. The integration between the embedded architecture and the cloud-computing based storage will be discussed in detail.

III. PROPOSED METHODOLOGY

We provide some background information before getting into the details of the proposed methodology. In the subsequent text, we provide a brief description of the secure hash standard.

A. Background: Secure Hash Algorithm

SHA takes a message with an arbitrary size and produces a message hash through some calculations. The process is defined in equation (1).

$$h = H(M) \tag{1}$$

where, M is the input message and h is the digest generated using the hash algorithm H.

In our scheme, the SHA2/256 standard is employed for securing the patient's records. Data are signed with the SHA2/256 before they are stored in the cloud. The stored records are made available for research centers and medical institutions. Figure 1 depicts the general procedure that is used to compute the hash for any given message. The input message of size less than 2^{64} is padded first to make its size a multiple of 512. The full message is divided into equal size blocks of 512-bits. The blocks are then processed sequentially using compression function F, and Initial Hash Value (IHV_0) that are defined in [8].

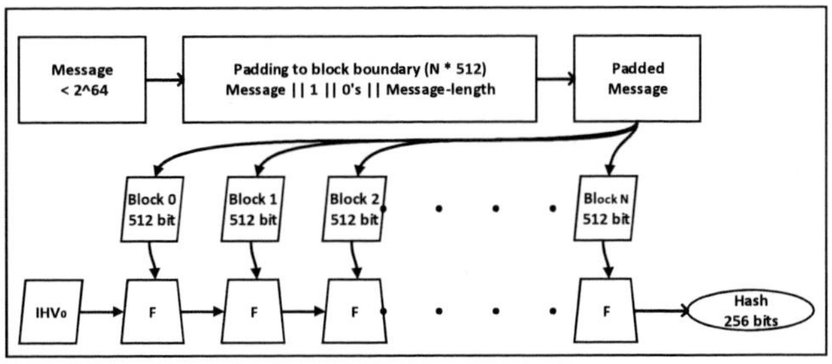

Figure 1. SHA general architecture: Padding, dividing, compression, and computation of SHA-256.

At the end of the process, the hash value that is generated from the last block produces the final 256 bits hash. A detailed description of the secure hash algorithm can be found in [8].

B. General Architecture of the Proposed Scheme

The proposed design for the secure IoT-based embedded system is depicted in Figure 2. A patient using the Alaris 8100 infusion pump will take preset insulin doses regularly. The Alaris infusion pump is controlled and monitored by the Keil Cortex M3 board through a serial connection. All dosage related records that are given to the patient are sent to the cloud through the Keil board using an Ethernet connection. To secure and authenticate the recorded data, they are digitally signed using the SHA compression function. The signature and patient's records are then stored in the cloud.

In the cloud, a Secure Socket Shell (SSH) is provided to entities authorized to access the data. For instance, a physician can follow up with a patient's case using a mobile application or a web browser. Furthermore, research institutions are given the authorization to access health records upon agreements made between patient, medical centers, and research institutions.

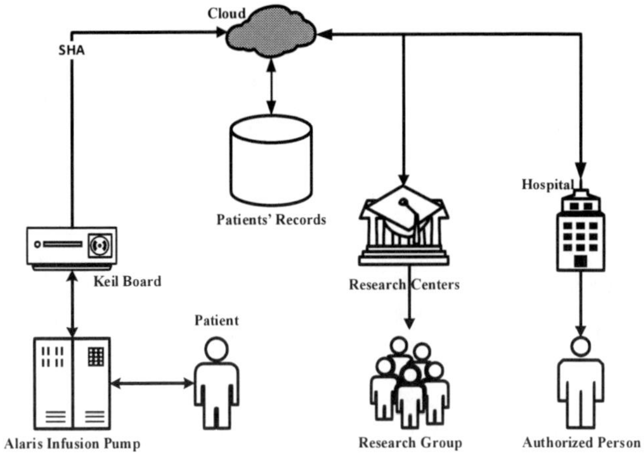

Figure 2. General architecture of the proposed scheme.

The security and authenticity of the health care records are verified using the SHA signature. The SHA value is computed after the health records or prescription commands are generated. Then the generated SHA is appended to the corresponding data (health record or preset control command). The health record and its signature are remained correlated in all places (cloud, hospital, and patient's side). For instance, the physician in the hospital confirms that the record is received without altering using SHA signature. When the health record is received at the hospital, SHA computation will be carried out. The resultant SHA will be compared with the appended SHA value. Once both SHA values are equal, the record will be affirmed to its corresponding patient. Otherwise, the health record will be discarded as is does not belong to the patient.

In the case of the preset control command, this command is generated from the hospital and appended with its corresponding hash value. The preset control command and the SHA signature are sent through the cloud to the infusion pump. At the patient's end, the hardware takes the responsibility to check the genuineness of the received control command by SHA computation and comparison. The Keil micro-controller computes the SHA value for the received preset control command and then compares the result with the appended SHA value. Once authorized, the preset control command is passed to the infusion pump for a new schedule. Figure 3 shows the connection between the Keil LPC1768 board and the Alaris 8100 infusion pump.

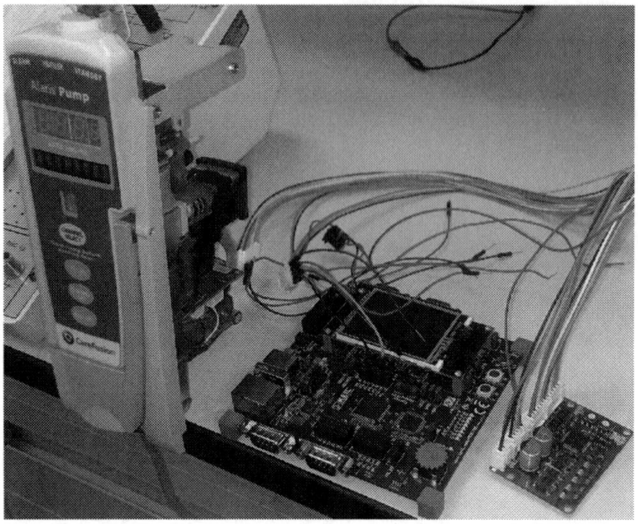

Figure 3. Connection of Alaris Infusion Pump 8100 with Keil 1768 PCB board

In the case of a fault exception, all Cortex-M processors (including Keil LPC1768) have a fault exception mechanism embedded inside the processor. If any fault is detected, the corresponding exception handler will be executed [13]. The hardware setup was done at the NDSU-Electrical and Computer Engineering laboratories. The infusion pump was first disassembled, interfaced with the Keil micro-controller, and then programmed using a serial cable and the Keil μVision studio 5.

IV. Results and Discussion

The proposed design has been tested and verified using data from [14]. The sample data includes glucose levels in the patient's body during a 24 hour period, a patient's profile information, and the patient's medical information. A snipped portion of the sample data is shown in Figures 4. Figure 5 shows the modified sample data. The data are stored in the cloud regularly, where each copy has its designated SHA value.

```
Impression: Sub optimal sugar, control with retinopathy

Home Glucose Monitoring:
AC breakfast 110 to 220
AC breakfast mean 142
AC dinner 100 to 250
AC dinner mean 120

Plan
Medications:
HUMULIN INJ 70/30 20 u ac breakfast

PRINIVIL TABS 20 MG 1 qd
```

Figure 4. Snipped health record from the original sample

```
Impression: Sub optimal sugar, control with retinopathy

Home Glucose Monitoring:
AC breakfast 110 to 220
AC breakfast mean 144
AC dinner 100 to 250
AC dinner mean 120

Plan
Medications:
HUMULIN INJ 70/30 20 u ac breakfast

PRINIVIL TABS 20 MG 1 qd
```

Figure 5. Snipped health record from the modified sample

To ensure the integrity of data, SHA-256 is applied to both sides (cloud and patient) after any query from either side.

The record is valid if its generated hash value on the patient's side is the same as the hash value on the cloud side. Table I shows a valid record hash. However, two different hash values are depicted for the same record in Table II, because the received record on the patient's side has been altered. Accordingly, the corresponding hash value has also been altered. The micro-controller will detect the alteration and discard the received record.

TABLE I. SHA-256 HASH VALUES OF THE SAMPLE DATA ON BOTH SIDES.

Cloud side:	14b93acf-ccdcbe40-ea3795be-c1073498-51a96c90-6cedfc9c-49d8e2cf-a141befb
Patient side:	14b93acf-ccdcbe40-ea3795be-c1073498-51a96c90-6cedfc9c-49d8e2cf-a141befb

TABLE II. SHA-256 HASH VALUES OF THE ORIGINAL AND MODIFIED SAMPLE DATA ON BOTH SIDES.

Cloud side:	14b93acf-ccdcbe40-ea3795be-c1073498-51a96c90-6cedfc9c-49d8e2cf-a141befb
Patient side:	358c4f29-f0e2bb60-8efa35d4-a88a6b3b-58939ffd-deebf824-8065c195-b834b8cd

The patient's intervention for the proposed design is limited to turn on and off the infusion pump. However, the future work of our design will upgrade the patient's privileges, e.g., change the infusion pump schedule according to predefined levels.

V. Conclusion and Future work

We have presented a secure IoT-based embedded data acquisition and control scheme. The work employed three modules: Keil micro-controller, LPC1768 board, and Alaris 8100 infusion pump. Secure Hash Algorithm standard SHA-256 is used to ensure the authenticity of the system. The authenticity of the proposed work was verified with a cloud storage utility using a real sample record. The results show that any altering in the health record is going to be identified immediately, thus the patient remains safe from false prescriptions. In future, we plan to apply the proposed scheme to hand-held glucose devices.

Acknowledgment

This publication was funded by a grant from the United States Government and the generous support of the American people through the United States Department of State and the United States Agency for International Development (USAID) under the Pakistan - U.S. Science & Technology Cooperation Program. The contents do not necessarily reflect the views of the United States Government.

References

[1] A. Al-Fuqaha, M. Guizani, M. Mohammadi, M. Aledhari, and M. Ayyash, "Internet of things: A survey on enabling technologies, protocols, and applications," IEEE Communications Surveys & Tutorials, vol. 17, no. 4, 2015, pp. 2347–2376.

[2] L. Atzori, A. Iera, and G. Morabito, "The internet of things: A survey," Computer networks, vol. 54, no. 15, 2010, pp. 2787–2805.

[3] R. Kazi and G. Tiwari, "Iot based interactive industrial home wireless system, energy management system and embedded data acquisition system to display on web page using gprs, sms & e-mail alert," in Energy Systems and Applications, 2015 International Conference on. IEEE, 2015, pp. 290–295.

[4] I. Ungurean, N.-C. Gaitan, and V. G. Gaitan, "An iot architecture for things from industrial environment," in Communications (COMM), 2014 10th International Conference on. IEEE, 2014, pp. 1–4.

[5] D. Hinge and S. Sawarkar, "Mobile to mobile data transfer through human area network," IJRCCT, vol. 2, no. 11, 2013, pp. 1181–1184.

[6] L. Catarinucci et al., "An iot-aware architecture for smart healthcare systems," IEEE Internet of Things Journal, vol. 2, no. 6, 2015, pp. 515–526.

[7] G. Harsha, "Design and implementation of online patient monitoring system," International Journal of Advances in Engineering & Technology, vol. 7, no. 3, 2014, p. 1075.

[8] F. PUB, "Secure hash standard (shs)," FIPS PUB 180, vol. 4, 2012, pp. 1–27.

[9] L. P. Boppudi and R. Krishnaiah, "Data acquisition and controlling system using cortex m3 core," International Journal of Innovative Research and Development, vol. 3, no. 1, 2014, pp. 29–33.

[10] A.-M. Rahmani et al., "Smart e-health gateway: Bringing intelligence to internet-of-things based ubiquitous healthcare systems," in Consumer Communications and Networking Conference (CCNC), 2015 12th Annual IEEE. IEEE, 2015, pp. 826–834.

[11] P.-Y. S. Hsueh, H. Chang, and S. Ramakrishnan, "Next generation wellness: A technology model for personalizing healthcare," in Healthcare Information Management Systems. Springer, 2016, pp. 355–374.

[12] J. Liu, X. Huang, and J. K. Liu, "Secure sharing of personal health records in cloud computing: ciphertext-policy attribute-based signcryption," Future Generation Computer Systems, vol. 52, 2015, pp. 67–76.

[13] E. Alkim, P. Jakubeit, and P. Schwabe, "Newhope on arm cortex-m," in International Conference on Security, Privacy, and Applied Cryptography Engineering. Springer, 2016, pp. 332–349.

[14] "Sample Medical Record: Monica Latte | Agency for Healthcare Research & Quality," Oct 2018, [accessed 1. Oct. 2018]. [Online]. Available: https://www.ahrq.gov/professionals/prevention-chronic-care/improve/system/pfhandbook/mod8appbmonicalatte.html

A Methodology for Synthesizing Formal Specification Models From Requirements for Refinement-based Object Code Verification

Eman M. Al-qtiemat*, Sudarshan K. Srinivasan*, Mohana Asha Latha Dubasi*, Sana Shuja†
*Electrical and Computer Engineering, North Dakota State University,
Fargo, ND, USA
†Department of Electrical Engineering, COMSATS University,
Islamabad, Pakistan
Emails: *eman.alqtiemat@ndsu.edu, *sudarshan.srinivasan@ndsu.edu, *MohanaAshaLatha.Duba@ndsu.edu,
†SanaShuja@comsats.edu.pk

Abstract—**Formal verification has become the bedrock for ensuring software correctness when dealing with safety-critical systems. One of the biggest obstacles in applying formal techniques to commercial systems is the lack of formal specifications. Software requirements are expressed only in natural language. We present a structured approach for synthesizing formal models from natural language requirements. Synthesizing formal specification models from natural language requirements is a hard problem. Our approach is structured in that, while our procedures do most of the work in the synthesis process, it allows for structured input from the domain expert. The uniqueness of this paper is the novel approach that can synthesize natural language requirements to formal specifications that are useful for refinement-based verification, a formal verification technique that is very effective for the safety-critical Internet of Things (IoT) embedded systems. A number of safety requirements for insulin pumps have been used to demonstrate the effectiveness of the approach.**

Keywords–requirements analysis; safety-critical IoT embedded devices; formal model; formal verification.

I. INTRODUCTION

Ensuring the correctness of control software used in safety-critical embedded devices is still an ongoing challenge. For example, from 2001 to 2017, the Food and Drug Administration (FDA) has issued 54 Class-1 recalls on infusion pumps (medical devices used to deliver controlled doses of fluid medications to patients intravenously) due to software issues [1]. Class-1 recalls are applied to medical device models whose use can cause serious adverse health consequences or death. With the advent of IoT, such safety-critical embedded devices incorporate a whole slew of additional functionality to interface with the network and other components, in addition to their core control functions. These additional functions significantly exacerbate the challenge of ensuring that the core functionality of the control software is correct and intact.

The use of formal verification has become an industry standard when addressing software correctness of safety-critical devices. There are many success stories and commercial adoption of formal verification processes. Examples include Intel [2], Microsoft [3] and [4], and Airbus [5].

Refinement-based verification [6] is a formal verification technology that has been demonstrated to be applicable to the verification of embedded control software at the object-code level [7]. In formal verification and refinement-based verification, typically the design artifact to be verified is called the implementation and the specification is a formal model that captures the correct functionality of the implementation. The goal of refinement-based verification is to mathematically prove that the implementation behaves correctly as defined by the specification. In refinement-based verification, both the implementation and specification are modeled as transition systems.

One of the key features of refinement-based is the use of refinement maps, which are functions that map implementation states to specification states. In practice, these refinement maps have a very favorable property in that they abstract out behaviors of the implementation not relevant to the specification, but only after determining that these additional behaviors do not actually impact the behaviors of the implementation relevant to the specification. This property of refinement maps makes the refinement-based verification very suitable for the verification of control software used in IoT devices as refinement maps can be used to abstract out the additional functionality of software in IoT devices; again, only after determining that these additional functionality are not impacting the behavior of the core functionality of the implementation as defined by the specification.

One of the crucial challenges in applying refinement-based verification to commercial devices is the availability of formal specifications. For commercial devices, typically, the specification of a device is given as natural language requirements. There are many approaches towards transforming natural language requirements to formal specifications, however none targeted towards refinement-based verification. In this paper, we present a methodology for transforming natural language requirements into formal specifications that can be used in the context of refinement-based verification.

The rest of the paper is organized as follows. An overview of the background is presented in Section II. Section III details the related work. A formal model describing the synthesis procedure is presented in Section IV. Section V details the case study. Section VI gives the verification results for the proposed formal model. Conclusions and direction for future work are noted in Section VII.

II. BACKGROUND

This section explores the parsing tree and the definition of transition systems as main topics related to our work.

A. Parsing tree

A parse tree is an ordered tree that pictorially represents how words in a sentence are connected to each other. The connection between each word in the sentence gives the *syntactic categories* for the sentence. The parsing process represents the syntactic analysis of a sentence in natural language. For example, when the parsing process is applied on a simple sentence like "Adam eats banana", the parse tree categorizes the two parts of speech: N for nouns (Adam, banana) and V for the verb (eats). Here N, V are the syntactic categories. The parsing process is considered to be a preprocessing step for some applications, where natural language should be converted into other forms. Usually, the system requirements are written in natural language, which needs to be converted into a structural form that can then be used to create the transition system(s) (explained in Section II-B). Enju [8] is an English consistency-based parser, which can process very long complex sentences like system requirements using an accurate analysis (the accuracy relation is around 90 percent of news articles and bio-medical papers). Besides, Enju is a high-speed parser with less than 500 msec per sentence. The output is the resulting tree in an XML format which is considered to be one of the commonly used formats by various applications. As will be described later, the case study used to describe the proposed methodology is from the bio-medical area, Enju was the perfect tool as the natural language processing (NLP) parser.

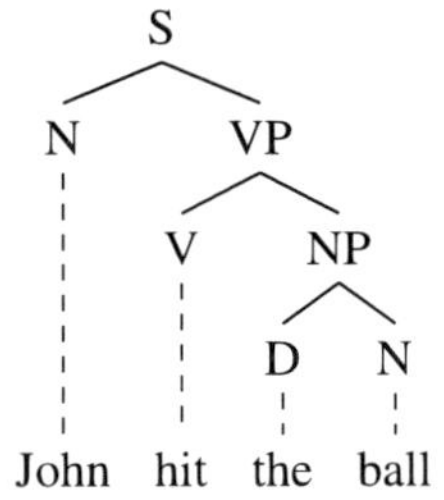

Figure 1. A simple example of a parsing tree using Enju parser [9].

Figure 1 shows a simple tree example using Enju. Here, Enju distinguishes between terminal nodes (John is a terminal node) and non-terminal nodes (VP is a verb phrase). The abbreviations of the syntactic categories of Figure 1 are: S stands for sentence (the head of the tree), N stands for noun, VP stands for verb phrase (which is a subtree), NP stands for noun phrase, V stands for verb, and finally D stands for determiner (comes with noun phrases). Using these syntactic categories, we have developed an extraction technique that would help in translating the natural language to a formal model of the requirements.

B. Transition systems

The implementation and specification in refinement-based verification are represented using Transition Systems (TSs) [6], [7]. The definition of a TS is given below:

Definition 1: A TS $M = \langle S, R, L \rangle$ is a three tuple in which S denotes the set of states, $R \subseteq SXS$ is the transition relation that provides the transition between states, and L is a labeling function that describes what is visible at each state.

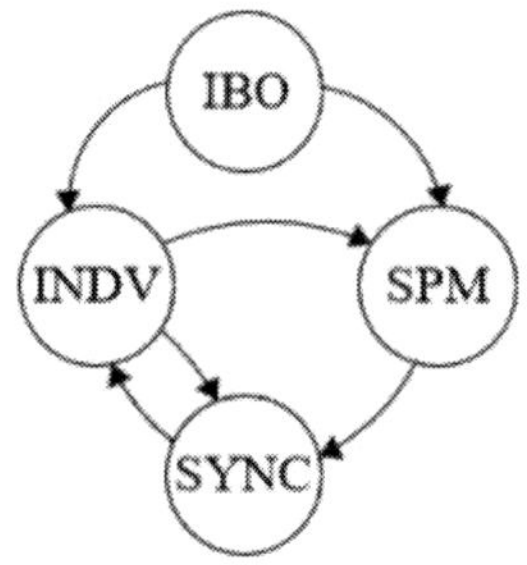

Figure 2. An example of a transition system (TS).

An Atomic Proposition (AP) is a statement that can be evaluated to be either true or false. The labeling function maps state to the APs that are true in every state. An example of a TS is shown in Figure 2. Here S = {IBO, SPM, SYNC, INDV}, R = {(IBO, SPM), (SPM, SYNC), (SYNC, INDV), (INDV, SYNC), (INDV, SPM), (IBO, INDV)} and, $L(SPM)$ represents the atomic propositions that are true for the SPM state. Similarly, labeling function can be applied to all the states in this TS.

III. RELATED WORK

In the last few years, there has been a tremendous growth in finding the optimal technique of requirement transformation into a formal model. While most of them proposed system-driven models, our approach is user-driven to ensure a safe product.

Automatic Requirements Specification Extraction from Natural Language (ARSENAL) [10] is a system based framework that applies some semantic parsers in multi-level to get the grammatical relations between words in the requirement. ARSENAL transforms natural language requirements into formal and logical forms expressed in Symbolic Analysis Laboratory (SAL) (a formal language to describe concurrent systems), and Linear Temporal Logic (LTL) (a mathematical language that describes linear time properties) respectively. The LTL formulas are then used to build the SAL model. Multiple validation checks are applied on Natural Language Processing (NLP) stage and LTL formulas to check for their correctness. However, ARSENAL records some inaccuracies in NLP stage that need a user intervention.

Aceituna et al. [11] have proposed a front end framework that builds a model to exhibit the system behavior (for synchronous systems only) and help in creating temporal logic properties automatically. This framework can be used before applying the model checking technique, it exposes accidental scenarios in the requirements. The framework is designed in a manner that helps in understanding the errors in a non-technical manner for users who do not have a formal background. In contrast, our work does not need the temporal logic in defining the specifications for a model.

A semantic parser has been developed by Harris [12] to extract a formal behavioral description from natural language specifications. The proposed semantic parser was employed to extract key information describing bus transactions. The natural language descriptions are then converted to verilog (a hardware description language) tasks.

Kress-Gazit et al. [13] have proposed a human-robot interface to translate natural language specification into motions.

This interface allows a user to instruct the robot using a controller. LTL formulas are employed to formalize the desired behavior requested by the user.

An approach supporting property elucidation (called PROPEL) has been introduced by Smith et al. [14], it provides templates that capture properties for creating property pattern. Natural language and finite state automation are used to represent the templates.

Two approaches have been proposed by Shimizu [15] to solve the ambiguity of natural language specifications using formal specification. The first approach simplifies the formal specification development for the popular PCI bus protocol and the Intel Itanium bus protocol. The second approach explains how formal specifications can help in automating many processes that are now done manually.

A natural language parsing technique has been used with the default reasoning, which is a requirement formalism to support requirement development, this work helps stakeholders to easily deal with requirements in a formal manner, in addition, a method has been proposed for discovering any existed requirements inconsistencies. A prototype tool called CARL was used for implementation and verification by Zowghi et al. [16].

Gervasi et al. [17] have also worked on solving the requirement's inconsistencies issues by using a well-known formalism called monotonic logic, it has been used especially for requirement's transformation. Multiple natural language processing tools [18]–[21] in additional to grammatical analysis methodologies for requirement's development have been done to get requirements in a formal manner.

However, the main advantages of our work over prior algorithms in requirements engineering is its ability to generate a full formal model directly from natural language requirements by an expert supervision to emphasis on the safety transformation. Also, our work does not require that the expert user know any temporal logic languages.

IV. FORMAL MODEL SYNTHESIS PROCEDURE

The first step to computing the TSs is to extract the APs from the requirements. We have developed three Atomic Proposition Extraction Rules (APERs) that work on the parse tree of the requirement obtained from Enju. The resulting APs are then used to compute the states and transitions. The APERs are described next.

A. *Atomic Proposition Extraction Rule 1 (APER 1)*

APER 1 is based on the hypothesis that noun phrases in a requirement correspond to APs. Each subtree of the parse tree with an NX root (called an NX head) corresponds to a noun phrase and hence an AP. Therefore, APER 1 computes the subtrees corresponding to NX heads. If NX heads are nested, then the highest-level NX head is used to compute the AP. The terminal nodes of the subtree are conjoined together to form the noun phrase. APER 1 returns AP-list, which is the set of APs corresponding to a parse tree.

We now describe the procedure corresponding to APER 1 in detail. Firstly, AP-List is initialized to the empty set (line 1). The procedure then iterates through each terminal node n (line 2). The head of a node is its parent. If a terminal node is part of an NX subtree, its level two head will be marked as NX, which

Procedure 1 APER1

Require: Parse-tree
1: AP-list $\leftarrow \emptyset$;
2: **for each** $n \in$ TerminalNodes(Parse-tree) **do**
3: Start-cat = head(head(n));
4: **if** Start-cat = NX **then**
5: X = Sub-tree(Start-cat);
6: **while** (head(X) = NX) $\vee$ (head(X) = COOD) $\vee$ (head(X) =NX-COOD) **do**
7: X = Sub-tree(head(X));
8: AP-list $\leftarrow$ AP-list $\cup$ TerminalNodes(X) ;

is checked in line 3. The level-two NX node of the terminal node is stored in variable State-cat. If the Start-cat is of NX category (line 4), a function called Sub-tree is used to get the resulting subtree (line 5), which is stored in variable X. A while loop is used to traverse the tree of X upwards checking if the head syntactic category is NX or COOD or NX-COOD (line 6). Only when one of the conditions is satisfied the subtree is stored in X (line 7). The terminal nodes of the resulting sub tree 'X' will be added to AP-List as a new suggested AP (line 8). Figure 3 gives a sub tree example for APER 1. Note that APER 1 may result in the same AP being duplicated. Duplicates are checked and removed from the AP list in the overall approach.

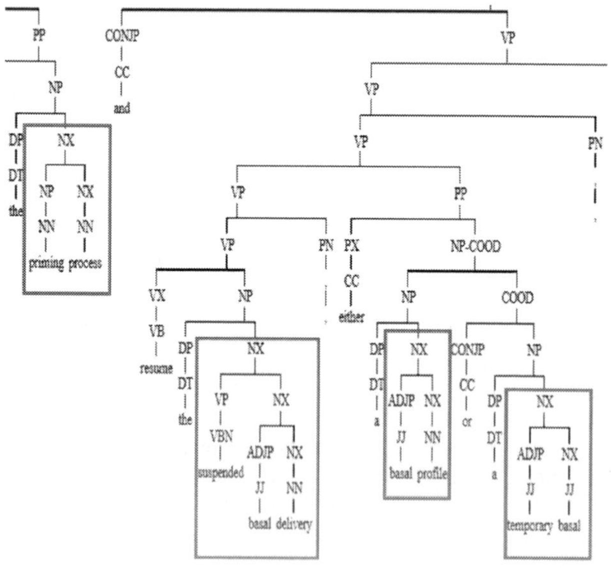

Figure 3. An Enju parsing tree portion shows some resulting APs by applying APER 1.

As shown in Figure 3, the terminal nodes 'the' and 'priming' does not have head(head(n)) = NX. The first terminal node that has the NX category is 'process'. Traversing upwards, the NX related categories gives us the subtree which contains 'priming process'. This now constitutes the first AP for this part of requirement. Applying the APER 1 rule on the visible part of the sentence in Figure 3 gives us the following APs: 'priming process', 'suspended basal profile', 'basal profile', and 'temporary basal'.

B. Atomic Proposition Extraction Rule 2 (APER 2)

APER 2 and APER 3 correspond to the two other parse tree patterns that also lead to noun phrases. APER 2 examines the parse tree for noun categories along with its upper verb head. APs will be the conjoined terminal nodes of the resulting sub tree. APER 2 states that APs are the terminal nodes under the head VP passing through NX (or its related phrases such as NX-COOD, COOD), NP (or its related phrases NP-COOD, COOD), and VX phrase. APER 2 is built on top of APER 1

Procedure 2 APER 2

```
Require: Parse-tree
1:  AP-list ← ∅ ;
2:  for each n ∈ TerminalNodes(Parse-tree) do
3:      Start-cat = head(head(n));
4:      X1 ← ∅;
5:      if Start-cat = NX then
6:          X = Sub-tree(Start-cat);
7:          while (head(X) = NX ) ∨ (head(X) = COOD)
                ∨ (head(X) =NX-COOD ) do
8:              X= Sub-tree(head(X));
9:          while (head(X) = NP) ∨ (head(X) = COOD)
                ∨ (head(X) = NP-COOD) do
10:             X1 = Sub-tree(head(X));
11:         if (head(X1) = VX) ∧ (head(head(X1)) = VP) then
12:             X = Sub-tree(head(head(X1));
13:         else
14:             if (head(X1) = VP) then
15:                 X = Sub-tree(head(X1);
16:         AP-list ← AP-list ∪ TerminalNodes(X);
```

to get atomic propositions for requirements that APER 1 is not able to collect. While APER 1 looks only for APs that are noun phrases, APER 2 looks for noun phrases that are further characterized by verb phrases. For example, if APER 1 finds the AP "suspended basal delivery," APER 2 will find "resume the suspended basal delivery."

APER 1 and APER 2 have the same algorithmic flow until finding the sub tree of X that is the top NX head (line 8). However, APER 2 does not consider the resulting X to be an AP like APER 1 does. Instead, X is the input of the next step. A while loop is used to search if the head category of X is in NP category or one of its related phrases (line 9). Only when the while loop condition is true, the new sub-tree is stored temporarily in the variable X_1 (line 10), where X_1 is a temporary variable initialized to null (line 4). This ensures that X does not change in this step for future use. The search for VX and VP categories is to be performed only when X_1 is not null.

On the successful completion of NP category search, the search for VX category followed by VP categories is performed (line 11). When the if condition is satisfied, X is updated with the new sub-tree (line 12). In the case of failure of the if condition in line 11, a new search for VP category is performed on the head of NP category sub-tree (line 14). On success, X is updated with the new sub-tree (line 15). If either of the if conditions (line 11 and line 14) fail, then X will remain as the sub-tree of NX category. The terminal nodes of the resulting subtree in X is appended to the AP-list (line 16). Figure 4 shows a resulting sub tree example by applying APER 2. Figure 4 shows that the procedure starts from left to right

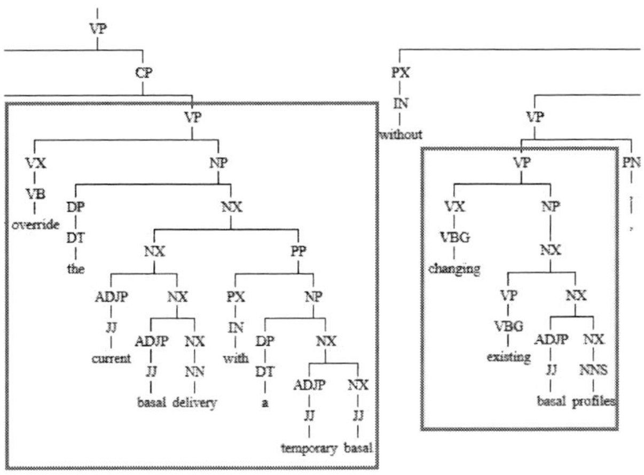

Figure 4. An Enju parsing tree portion shows some resulting APs by applying APER 2.

looking for level two NX nodes and traversing upward until higher NX nodes are accounted for. NP phrases are selected to expand the tree. Then choosing the upper level which is VP in this particular case (sometimes its VX → VP). The output of APER 2 for this tree portion is 'override the current basal delivery with a temporary basal', and 'changing existing basal profiles'.

C. Atomic Proposition Extraction Rule 3 (APER 3)

APER 3 is built on top of APER 2, it explores the verb head levels in the parse tree like APER 2, but APER 3 eliminates some verb phrases that is not part of APs. This elimination is done based on the head of the VP category as illustrated in Procedure 3 below. APER 3 and APER 2 have the same stream up to line 10. The algorithm starts with initializing temporary variables X_1 and Y to null (line 4). The search for syntactic categories start with the top NX phrase (line 7) and the resultant sub tree is stored in X (line 8). Then, the search begins for the top NP phrase (line 9) and the resultant sub tree is stored in X_1 (line 10) since the sub tree in X is needed for future use. As in APER2, the search for either VX phrase followed by VP phrase or just VP phrase is performed on X_1 and the resultant sub tree is stored in Y (lines 11-15). If and only if Y is not empty then the check on the head syntactic category is performed to ensure that it does not contain CP or COOD categories. In this case, X gets only the right child (line 16-18) i.e. the left child of Y is pruned. On the other hand, if Y has a CP or COOD head, X value will be updated to be equal to Y (line 20). Finally, terminal nodes of the resulting sub tree X will be saved in the AP-list as a new AP. The pruning process (line 18) is done to remove some action verbs which are not part of an AP.

Like APER2, APER3 also works on verb head categories. However, APER3 has some pruning techniques to remove parts of the sentence that should not be part of an AP. Consider the snippet in Figure 5, the sub tree "issue an alert" is subjected to left branch pruning to remove the verb 'issue' since such verbs do not add value in the AP. According to the algorithm, since the head node of VP is COOD, only the terminal nodes of the

Procedure 3 APER 3

```
Require: Parse-tree
AP-list ← ∅ ;
for each n ∈ TerminalNodes(Parse-tree) do
    Start-cat = head(head(n));
    X1 ← ∅ , Y ← ∅;
    if Start-cat = NX then
        X = Sub-tree(Start-cat);
        while (head(X) = NX) ∨ (head(X) = COOD)
                ∨ (head(X) =NX-COOD ) do
            X = Sub-tree(head(X));
        while (head(X) = NP) ∨ (head(X) = COOD)
                ∨ (head(X) = NP-COOD) do
            X1 = Sub-tree(head(X));
        if (head(X1) = VX) ∧ (head(head(X1)) = VP) then
            Y = Sub-tree(head(head(X1));
        else
            if (head(X1) = VP) then
                Y = Sub-tree(head(X1);
        if (Y ≠ ∅) then
            if head(Y) ≠ CP) ∧ (head(Y) ≠ COOD) then
                X = Sub-tree(RightChild(Y));
            else
                X = Y;
        AP-list ← AP-list ∪ TerminalNodes(X);
```

right child are considered as an AP. Applying APER 3 on the visible part of the requirement in Figure 5 gives the following APs: 'pump', 'an alert', and 'deny the request'. The proposed

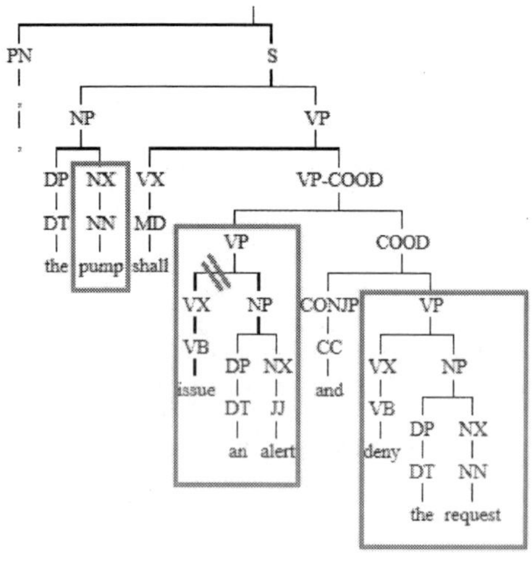

Figure 5. An Enju parsing tree portion shows some resulting APs using APER 3.

APERs may be used individually or in combination depending on the system requirement and model functionally. However, no one rule is considered to be the best for all models because of the natural language structure.

Procedure 4 Procedure for synthesizing TSs from system requirements

```
Require: set of requirements (System-requirements)
 1: TS-set ← ∅ ;
 2: for each Req ∈ System-requirements do
 3:     Parse-tree ← Get(Req_tree.xml);
 4:     AP-list ← APER(Parse-tree);
 5:     AP-list ← Eliminate_Dup(AP-list);
 6:     AP-list ← USR_IN(AP-List);
 7:     AP-truth-table ← Relation(AP-list);
 8:     AP-truth-table ← USR_IN(AP-truth-table);
 9:     S-list ← ∅;
10:     for each A ∈ AP-truth-table do
11:         S-list[i] = A_i ;
12:     S-list ← USR_IN(S-list);
13:     T ← CreateT(S-list);
14:     T ← USR_IN(T);
15:     TS ← CreateTS(T, S-list);
16:     TS-set ← TS-set U TS;
17:     return TS-set;
```

D. High-Level Procedure for Specification Transition System Synthesis

Procedure 4 shows the overall flow for computing the TSs. A set of system requirements in natural language are fed as input to the procedure. TS-set is the output of the procedure and will contain the set of transition systems that capture the input requirements as a formal model. TS-set is initialized to null (line 1). Each requirement is input to the Enju parser. The parser gives an xml file as output. A function called Get is used to obtain the xml file into the variable Parse-tree (line 3). The xml output in Parse-tree is subjected to the proposed APERs, which give the atomic propositions (APs) as output. APs are stored in the AP-list (line 4). Each requirement is subject to all APERs and the AP-list obtained is the union of the APs produced by each of the rules. The output obtained by using the APERs may contain duplicates, which are eliminated by using the function Eliminate_Dup (line 5). AP-list is then subjected to an expert user check, where the AP(s) might be appended, eliminated or revised based on the expert user's domain knowledge (line 6). Some of the APs maybe expressible as a boolean function of other APs.
Therefore, next, a truth table (AP-truth-table) is created, where each row corresponds to an AP from AP-list and each column also corresponds to an AP from AP-list (line 7). Each entry in the table is a Bolean value (true or false). Completing the truth table determines the relationship of each AP with the other APs in the AP-list. The truth table is completed by the expert user (line 8). The list of states for the input requirements are stored in the variable S-list. S-list is initialized to null (line 9). Each truth table entry (A) is defined to be a single state in the transition system (line 10). This heuristic has worked well in practice. S-list is subjected to expert user input (line 12).

The transitions of the TS are computed next. The list of transitions (T) is initialized to a transition between every two states using function 'CreateT' (line 13). The transition list is subjected to expert user input (line 14). A transition system (TS) is constructed using the CreateTS function, which takes the transitions (T) and the list of states (S-list) as input (line

15). This transition system (TS) is then added to the transition system set (TS-set) (line 16). The procedure finally returns a set of transition systems for all the requirements in an application (line 17).

V. CASE STUDY: GENERIC INSULIN INFUSION PUMP (GIIP)

Insulin pump is a medical device that delivers doses of insulin 24 hours a day to patients with diabetes. It is typically used to keep the blood glucose level in an acceptable range. Overdose of insulin can lead to low blood sugar that can lead to coma/death. Therefore, the insulin pump is a safety-critical device.

Requirement 1.8.2: *When the pump is in suspension mode, insulin deliveries shall be prohibited. Any incomplete bolus delivery shall be stopped and shall not be resumed after the suspension.*

The Generic Insulin Infusion Pump (GIIP) has been proposed [22], which lists a set of safety requirements for insulin pumps. We use these safety requirements for our approach.

As an example, consider requirement 1.8.2 (from [22]) which is needed to address a hazard that may happen in the suspension mode of the pump. Suspension mode can occur when the pump may be in refill or priming or insulin delivery processes. The insulin pump has two type of insulin deliveries: bolus and basal. Bolus is a high insulin rate that is recommended in case of low blood glucose level. From safety requirement 1.8.2, it is clear that the pump should not resume a suspended bolus automatically after returning from suspension since they would be an unexpected amount of insulin.

Requirement 1.8.5: *When the pump resumes from suspension, calculations shall be performed to synchronize insulin used and remaining reservoir volume.*

Requirement 1.8.5 is an extension of how the pump should function after returning from the suspension mode. Here two requirements are needed to address one safety hazard. When algorithm 4 is applied on these two requirements, the first step is collecting the APs by using the extraction rules. Applying APER 2 on 1.8.2 gives: "pump", "suspension mode", "insulin deliveries", "incomplete bolus delivery", and "suspension". Applying APER 2 on 1.8.5 gives: "pump", "suspension", "calculations", and "synchronize insulin used and remaining reservoir volume". Next, duplicate APs are to be removed. This eliminates 'pump' and 'suspension' from the AP-list. Now, the expert user intervenes for manipulating the AP-list, where APs can be deleted, modified or even inserted based on the expert user's domain knowledge. This yields the final AP-list as "suspension mode" (SPM), "insulin deliveries" (INDV), "incomplete bolus delivery" (IBO) and "synchronize insulin used and remaining reservoir volume" (SYNC). Next, the AP-truth-table to define relations between APs is constructed as shown in Table I.

Here, each row represents a state. For example, SPM represents a state where suspension mode is true, IBO is false, INDV is false, and SYNC is also false; which emphasizes that insulin bolus should not be active during suspension. Finally, Procedure 4 applies transitions between every two states as shown in Figure 6a. The expert user will approve or remove some unacceptable transitions. Figure 6b shows the final transition system.

TABLE I. AP-TRUTH-TABLE FOR REQUIREMENT 1.8.2 AND 1.8.5 FROM AP-LIST

APs → ↓	SPM	INDV	IBO	SYNC
SPM	T	F	F	F
INDV	F	T	F	F
IBO	F	T	T	F
SYNC	F	F	F	T

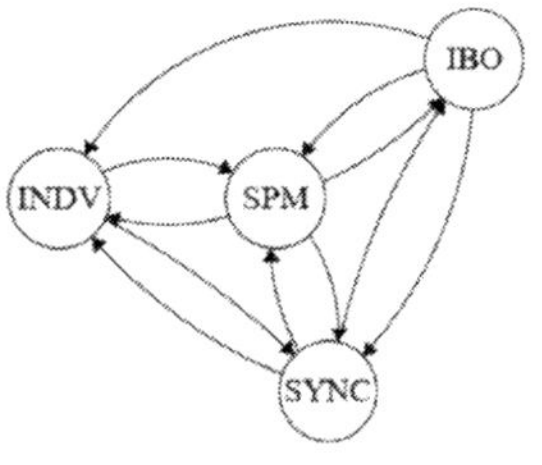

(a) TS with all suggested transitions.

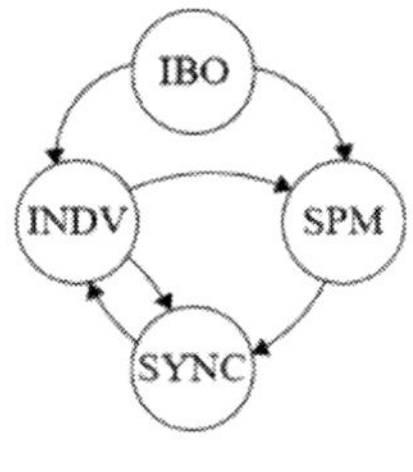

(b) TS after removing some transitions.

Figure 6. Finite state machine for pump suspension requirements (1.8.2, 1.8.5).

VI. RESULTS ANALYSIS

Evaluation of the presented approach is performed using the NuSMV model checker. A model checker is a tool that can check if a TS satisfies a set of properties. The properties have to be expressed in a temporal logic. Here, we have used CTL to express the properties. The CTL properties were written manually for each of the requirements that were subjected to our approach. NuSMV was used to check if the TSs synthesized by the presented approach satisfied the CTL properties corresponding to that requirement.

Table II shows the results of applying Procedure 4 on a number of GIIP requirements. The requirement numbers in the table are from [22]. All the final TSs satisfied their corresponding CTL properties. Each requirement or set of requirements (listed in column 1) have been subjected to the extraction rules (column 2), where column 3 shows the total number of APs resulting from each extraction rule. Column 4 gives the number of APs after removing the duplicate APs. In addition, a record of the suggested expert user intervention for adding, removing or modifying the APs is shown in column 5. The final number of APs, states, and transitions are shown in column 6.

As shown in the table, when a requirement is subjected to the APERs, the resultant output from each APER may be different even though the number of APs is the same. For requirements 1.8.2 and 1.8.5, although applying APER1, APER2, and APER3 give the same number of APs, APER1 gives different list of APs from APER2 and APER3.

VII. CONCLUSION AND FUTURE WORK

The key ideas of our approach for transforming requirements into transition systems are the following. The extraction rules work on the parse tree to get an initial list of APs. The AP truth table is used to establish relationships between the initial list of APs. For example, an AP may be expressible as a conjunction of two other APs. The initial expert user pruned

TABLE II. RESULTING TRANSITION SYSTEMS BY APPLYING THE GENERAL ALGORITHM AND APERS ON A SET OF SYSTEM REQUIREMENTS

Req. NO.	APER	Total No. of APs	No. of APs Without DP	User input			Final		
				AP added	AP removed	AP modified	APs	states	transitions
1.1.1	1	10	10	0	6	0	5	4	5
	2	10	10	0	5	0			
	3	10	10	0	6	0			
1.1.3	1	7	7	0	3	2	4	4	4
	2	7	7	0	3	2			
	3	7	7	0	3	1			
1.2.4 , 1.2.6, 1.2.7	1	24	12	3	5	1	10	10	14
	2	24	18	0	8	0			
	3	24	16	2	8	0			
1.3.5	1	11	6	1	3	0	4	4	4
	2	11	8	0	4	1			
	3	11	8	1	5	0			
1.8.2, 1.8.5	1	9	7	1	3	1	4	4	5
	2	9	7	0	3	0			
	3	9	7	0	3	0			
2.2.2, 2.2.3	1	6	6	0	3	1	3	3	4
	2	7	6	0	3	1			
	3	7	6	0	3	2			
3.1.1	1	15	14	0	9	0	5	3	3
	2	14	12	0	7	0			
	3	14	13	0	8	0			
3.2.5	1	10	9	0	7	2	3	3	3
	2	7	7	0	4	1			
	3	7	7	0	4	1			
3.2.7	1	4	4	0	1	0	3	3	3
	2	4	4	0	1	1			
	3	4	4	0	1	0			

list of APs gives insight into the states of the transition system. We have found empirically that having one state for this initial pruned AP list is a good heuristic to compute the states of the transition system. Transitions are applied between every two states and then pruned by the expert user.

Transforming natural language requirements into formal models is quite a hard problem and hard to get right without input from domain expert. Our approach sets up a very structured process, where the tool does lot of the work in analyzing and synthesizing TSs, but also allows for input from domain expert. The proposed methodology has worked very well in practice for the GIIP requirements. All the TSs computed for the requirements satisfied their corresponding CTL properties. For future work, we plan to address requirements with real-time constraints. The corresponding formal model will be timed transition systems.

ACKNOWLEDGMENT

This publication was funded by a grant from the United States Government and the generous support of the American people through the United States Department of State and the United States Agency for International Development (USAID) under the Pakistan - U.S. Science & Technology Cooperation Program. The contents do not necessarily reflect the views of the United States Government. The authors would like to acknowledge Dr. Vinay Gonela for helping with proofreading the paper.

REFERENCES

[1] FDA, "List of Device Recalls, U.S. Food and Drug Administration (FDA)," 2018, last accessed: 2018-09-10. [Online]. Available: https://www.accessdata.fda.gov/scripts/cdrh/cfdocs/cfRES/res.cfm

[2] R. Kaivola, et al., "Replacing testing with formal verification in intel coretm i7 processor execution engine validation," in Computer Aided Verification, 21st International Conference, CAV 2009, Grenoble, France, June 26 - July 2, 2009. Proceedings, ser. Lecture Notes in Computer Science, A. Bouajjani and O. Maler, Eds., vol. 5643. Springer, 2009, pp. 414–429. [Online]. Available: https://doi.org/10.1007/978-3-642-02658-4_32

[3] T. Ball, B. Cook, V. Levin, and S. K. Rajamani, "SLAM and static driver verifier: Technology transfer of formal methods inside microsoft," in Integrated Formal Methods, 4th International Conference, IFM 2004, Canterbury, UK, April 4-7, 2004, Proceedings, ser. Lecture Notes in Computer Science, E. A. Boiten, J. Derrick, and G. Smith, Eds., vol. 2999. Springer, 2004, pp. 1–20. [Online]. Available: https://doi.org/10.1007/978-3-540-24756-2_1

[4] K. Bhargavan, et al., "Formal verification of smart contracts: Short paper," in Proceedings of the 2016 ACM Workshop on Programming Languages and Analysis for Security, PLAS@CCS 2016, Vienna, Austria, October 24, 2016, T. C. Murray and D. Stefan, Eds. ACM, 2016, pp. 91–96. [Online]. Available: http://doi.acm.org/10.1145/2993600.2993611

[5] D. Delmas, et al., "Towards an industrial use of fluctuat on safety-critical avionics software," in International Workshop on Formal Methods for Industrial Critical Systems. Springer, 2009, pp. 53–69.

[6] P. Manolios, "Mechanical verification of reactive systems," PhD thesis, University of Texas at Austin, August 2001, last accessed: 2018-10-10. [Online]. Available: http://www.ccs.neu.edu/home/pete/research/phd-dissertation.html

[7] M. A. L. Dubasi, S. K. Srinivasan, and V. Wijayasekara, "Timed refinement for verification of real-time object code programs," in Working Conference on Verified Software: Theories, Tools, and Experiments. Springer, 2014, pp. 252–269.

[8] Tsujii laboratory, Department of Computer Science at The University of Tokyo, "Enju - a fast, accurate, and deep parser for English," 2011, available from http://www.nactem.ac.uk/enju, [accessed: 2018-07-10].

[9] V. Ágel, Dependency and valency: an international handbook of contemporary research. Walter de Gruyter, 2003, vol. 1.

[10] S Ghosh, et al., "Automatic requirements specification extraction from natural language (ARSENAL)," SRI International, Menlo Park, CA, Tech. Rep., 2014.

[11] D. Aceituna, H. Do, and S. Srinivasan, "A systematic approach to transforming system requirements into model checking specifications," in Companion Proceedings of the 36th International Conference on Software Engineering. ACM, 2014, pp. 165–174.

[12] I. G. Harris, "Extracting design information from natural language specifications," in Proceedings of the 49th Annual Design Automation Conference. ACM, 2012, pp. 1256–1257.

[13] H. Kress-Gazit, G. E. Fainekos, and G. J. Pappas, "Translating structured English to robot controllers," Advanced Robotics, vol. 22, no. 12, 2008, pp. 1343–1359.

[14] R. L. Smith, G. S. Avrunin, L. A. Clarke, and L. J. Osterweil, "Propel: an approach supporting property elucidation," in Proceedings of the 24th International Conference on Software Engineering. ACM, 2002, pp. 11–21.

[15] K. Shimizu, "Writing, verifying, and exploiting formal specifications for hardware designs," Ph.D. dissertation, PhD thesis, Stanford University, 2002.

[16] D. Zowghi, V. Gervasi, and A. McRae, "Using default reasoning to discover inconsistencies in natural language requirements," in Software Engineering Conference, 2001. APSEC 2001. Eighth Asia-Pacific. IEEE, 2001, pp. 133–140.

[17] V. Gervasi and D. Zowghi, "Reasoning about inconsistencies in natural language requirements," ACM Transactions on Software Engineering and Methodology (TOSEM), vol. 14, no. 3, 2005, pp. 277–330.

[18] W. Scott, S. Cook, and J. Kasser, "Development and application of a context-free grammar for requirements," in SETE 2004: Focussing on Project Success; Conference Proceedings; 8-10 November 2004. Systems Engineering Society of Australia, 2004, p. 333.

[19] X. Xiao, A. Paradkar, S. Thummalapenta, and T. Xie, "Automated extraction of security policies from natural-language software documents," in Proceedings of the ACM SIGSOFT 20th International Symposium on the Foundations of Software Engineering. ACM, 2012, p. 12.

[20] Z. Ding, M. Jiang, and J. Palsberg, "From textual use cases to service component models," in Proceedings of the 3rd International Workshop on Principles of Engineering Service-Oriented Systems. ACM, 2011, pp. 8–14.

[21] C. Rolland and C. Proix, "A natural language approach for requirements engineering," in International Conference on Advanced Information Systems Engineering. Springer, 1992, pp. 257–277.

[22] Y. Zhang, R. Jetley, P. L. Jones, and A. Ray, "Generic safety requirements for developing safe insulin pump software," Journal of diabetes science and technology, vol. 5, no. 6, 2011, pp. 1403–1419.

Static Stuttering Abstraction for Object Code Verification

Naureen Shaukat*, Sana Shuja*, Sudarshan Srinivasan†, Shaista Jabeen* and Mohana Asha Latha Dubasi†
*Department of Electrical Engineering
COMSATS University, Islamabad , Pakistan
Email: nsawan23@gmail.com, sanashuja@comsats.edu.pk, shaista.sj@comsats.edu.pk
†Department of Electrical and Computer Engineering
North Dakota State University, Fargo, USA
Email: sudarshan.srinivasan@ndsu.edu, mohanaashalatha.duba@ndsu.edu

Abstract—**The biggest challenge in the formal verification of an embedded system software is the complexity and large size of the implementation. The problem gets even bigger when the embedded system is an Internet of Things (IoT) device that is running intricate algorithms. In Refinement-based verification, both specification and implementation are expressed as transition systems. Each behavior of the implementation transition system is matched with the specification transition system with the help of a refinement map. The refinement map can only project those values that are responsible to label the current state of the system. When the refinement map is applied at object code level, several instructions map to a single state in the specification transition system called stuttering instructions. The concept of Static Stuttering Abstraction (SSA) is a novel idea that focuses on filtering common multiple segments of these stuttering instructions. The patterns are then replaced by mergers that preserve the behavior of the original object code and extensively reduce the size of the object code. The smaller code size also gives the lesser number of stuttering transitions and eventually more discernible matching between the specification and implementation of transition systems. We have implemented SSA technique on two platforms using infusion pump as a case study and the technique has proved consistent in considerably reducing the size and complexity of the implementation transition system.**

Keywords–Formal verification; static stuttering abstraction; stuttering instructions; refinement map; infusion pump.

I. INTRODUCTION

One of the pivotal entities in the ecosystem of Internet of Things (IoT) is an embedded system due to its capability of receiving data from sensors and making decisions independently. From a cell phone to an automobile, all are comprised of an embedded system; that collects, and senses data received, collates that data to be analyzed, and consequently perform necessary functions. The functionality of the embedded system not only encompasses basic I/O, but it also involves complex communication protocols that consent other indispensable peripherals to communicate over shared buses and gateways. Hence, with IoT embedded devices are built on intricate algorithms, which make the verification process even more complicated. Safeguarding these embedded systems against errors is an inevitable task especially in those devices that prevent life-threatening ailments like pacemakers and insulin pumps. Such devices can cause severe consequences if the software or hardware malfunctions, making these medical devices safety critical. For example, from 2001 to 2017, the Food and Drug Administration (FDA) has issued 54 Class-1 recalls on infusion pumps due to software errors [1]. Hence, an embedded system which is a thing on the IoT running complex algorithms, techniques need to be devised for reducing the complexity and the capacity of verification efforts.

An embedded system is comprised of a hardware and a software. The software is a complex piece of code that is prone to errors due to the translation process that converts the high-level code to assembly code. Assembly code is the object code, which is larger in size and complexity as compared to its high-level counterpart. The biggest challenge in the application of formal verification techniques is the large size of the code being executed on the embedded system. Therefore, the success and efficiency of formal verification techniques are highly dependent on the reduction of the size of the code leading to the need for an abstraction technique to minimize the length of the code.

The abstraction technique is a transformation of the object code that will significantly reduce the complexity of the verification process. In this paper, we propose a novel abstraction technique called Static Stuttering Abstraction (SSA). As the name suggests, this technique is applied to the object code directly. The abstraction is developed in the context of refinement-based verification, a formal verification technique. In refinement-based verification, both the specification and the implementation of the system are expressed as Transition Systems (TS). The specification TS is the behavior of the system expressed as states and transitions, whereas the implementation TS is obtained after the software is symbolically simulated at the object code level. The implementation TS is therefore very large as compared to the specification TS, as several transitions of the implementation TS map to a single transition of the specification TS. These several transitions of the implementation TS that map to a single transition of the specification TS are called stuttering transitions. Stuttering transitions usually arise from the execution of stuttering instructions, which are instructions that do not directly modify the state of the system as is visible at the specification level.

The idea with stuttering abstraction is that a finite sequence of stuttering instructions can be merged into one. Such a merger will still preserve the functional behavior of the original implementation TS but will be reduced in size. We call the segment obtained due to the merger an abstracted stuttering segment. Also, we call the reduced TS obtained using such mergers as the abstracted implementation TS. In this paper, we present a methodology to apply abstractions on the stuttering instructions of the implementation TS named static stuttering abstraction (SSA).

The rest of this paper is organized as follows. Background is presented in Section II. Section III details related work. The abstraction technique is described in Section IV. Section V details the case studies and gives verification results. Conclusion and future work are noted in Section VI.

II. Background

In refinement-based formal verification, both the implementation and specification are expressed as a TS. A TS is defined as follows [2].

Definition 1: A TS $\mathcal{M}$ is a 3-tuple $\langle S, R, L\rangle$, where S is the set of states, R is the transition relation, which is the set of all state transitions, and L is a labeling function that defines what is visible at each state. A state transition is of the form $\langle w, v\rangle$, where $w,\ v \in$ S.

MM_S and MM_I denote the specification TS and implementation TS respectively. MM_S is an explicit representation of the requirements of the system thus containing the minimal number of states and transitions. On the other hand, in MM_I a single execution of an instruction in the object code makes up for one or more transitions in MM_I. Therefore, in refinement-based formal verification techniques, the biggest challenge is matching a small set of transitions of MM_S to a large set of transitions of MM_I.

The abstraction technique is developed in the context of Well-Founded Equivalence Bisimulation (WEB) refinement [2]. A key idea in WEB refinement is the notion of refinement maps, which are functions that map implementation states to specification states. The specification TSs are constructed simple and the states include only the predicates relevant to the property being verified. Whereas, the implementation states for object code comprise all the registers in the target micro-controller and memory locations of relevance. Therefore, there is big difference in the abstraction-level of the specification and implementation. Refinement maps essentially extract the relevant variables from the implementation state to construct the corresponding specification state.

The idea with WEB refinement is to match transitions of the implementation with transitions of the specification. Given an implementation transition $\langle w, v\rangle$, checking if this transition matches with a specification transition is achieved by applying the refinement map function $r()$ to both states of the implementation transition. The resulting transition $\langle r(w), r(v)\rangle$ should correspond to a specification transition. However, there are four possibilities. The first possibility is the one mentioned above, that when the refinement map is applied, the implementation transition does correspond to a specification transition. Such an implementation transition is called a non-stuttering transition. The second possibility is that one or both of $r(w)$ and $r(v)$ do not map to any valid specification state. This points to a bug. The third possibility is that both $r(w)$ and $r(v)$ map to the same specification state. In this situation, $\langle w, v\rangle$ is still considered to be a correct transition, but one that is not making visible progress w.r.t. the specification TS. Such a transition is called a stuttering transition. The fourth possibility is that both $r(w)$ and $r(v)$ map to specification states, but $\langle r(w), r(v)\rangle$ does not correspond to any specification transition and $\langle w, v\rangle$ is not a stuttering transition (as described above). The fourth case again corresponds to a bug in the implementation.

The common operations in high-level code are translated to the same set of instructions in the assembly code. Thus, a single set of instructions may have large multiple numbers of occurrences, which correspond to a large piece of the assembly code. The idea of SSA is to identify common multiple occurrences of two or more stuttering instructions named as patterns and reduce the length of the pattern by replacing it with a merger that is a single line instruction but encompasses all the operations performed by the list of instructions in the pattern. Therefore, a pattern comprising of 3 stuttering instructions occurring 100 times in the code will reduce 200 lines of the code and consequently the size of MM_I.

III. Related Work

There are a number of previous approaches that exploit the notion of stuttering to improve verification scalability. An algorithm is presented by Groote and Wijs [3] to check the equivalence between two transition systems based on stuttering. Ray et al. [4] show how to verify concurrent programs using refinement-based on stuttering trace containment. A method for the functional correctness of hardware and low-level software is developed based on refinement-based testing by Jain and Manolios [5]. Stuttering is introduced in the context of probabilistic automata by Delahaye et al. [6]. While the above approaches employ stuttering, they do not apply it to static object code, which is the focus of our work.

Timed Well-Founded Simulation (TWFS) refinement for verification of real-time Field Programmable Gate Array (FPGA) is presented by Jabeen et al. [7]. Reachable states of the FPGA are identified using manually generated invariants, without employing abstractions. This approach is feasible for FPGA only and not for object code with a very large number of instructions as the manual characterization of reachable states for object code is impractical.

Theory of automata is employed to stimulate discrete timed systems and continuous timed systems by Rabinovich [8]. The concept of stuttering is described, but stuttering abstraction is not addressed.

Stuttering invariant properties are expressed using specification languages by Etessami [9] and Dax et al. [10]. The properties distinguish behaviors of systems regardless of their stuttering or non-stuttering nature. The properties can be verified using a model checker.

A similar idea of stuttering abstraction is presented by Nejati et al. [11], but static abstraction is not considered.

Stuttering equivalence is employed in the context of the model checking to present an abstraction technique by De-Leon and Grumberg [12]. This abstraction technique is applied dynamically to the transition system and not statically to the object code.

Our abstraction is applicable to recurring patterns of object code instructions that are responsible for millions of transitions in real-time systems. Refinement-based verification, which is a general form of equivalence verification is known to scale well for low-level design artifacts. As can be seen from the experimental results, the object code that constitutes the implementation TS is considerably reduced. Next, we explain SSA.

IV. Automatic Static Stuttering Abstraction

A. *Static Stuttering Abstraction (SSA)*

The need to develop an abstraction technique for the object code is to ensure efficiency and scalability of the verification process. One of the challenges in refinement-based verification is the complex behavior of the object code. SSA ensures that the object code is transformed into a comparatively smaller piece of code; which consequently reduces the complexity and effort involved in the verification process. SSA is applied after the high-level code is translated to object code, then patterns comprising of stuttering instructions s_i called stuttering patterns s_p with the multiple numbers of occurrences are identified. The pattern is called a stuttering pattern because none of the instructions in the pattern update the values projected by the refinement map. Let's take stepper motor as an example for the specification transition system. The pins of the embedded system (LPC1768) that are responsible for rotating a 4-lead stepper motor and changing the current state is connected to the 4 rightmost pins of general purpose I/O, i.e., LPC_GPIO1. So as long as the assembly instruction does not change the contents of the register associated with LPC GPIO Port 1 (LPC_GPIO1), the instruction is a stuttering instruction s_i. An example of a segment containing a non-stuttering instruction is given below:

```
0x0000067A  2001  MOVS  r0,0x08
0x0000067C  4953  LDR   r1,[pc,332] ; @0x000007CC
0x0000067E  6388  STR   r0,[r1,0x38]
```

The first instruction in the above segment moves the binary 1000 in r0, the second instruction loads the base memory address of the peripheral registers of LPC1768. The third instruction is a store instruction that stores a value of the binary 1000 in rightmost 4 bits of LPC_GPIO1 (to the address calculated by adding an offset of 38 to the base address of 0x000007CC in order to access the address of GPIO Port1 register). Moving a value of 4 in LPC_GPIO1 asserts the leftmost lead of the stepper motor, and hence the stepper motor will take a step and the implementation transition system gets a new state. The STR instruction is hence a non-stuttering instruction n_i, as it has changed the state of the system. This implementation state can be matched to a specification state by employing the refinement map and extracting the rightmost four bits of the register LPC_GPIO1 and mapping them to the specification states. The reason for not abstracting a segment with a non-stuttering instruction n_i is to preserve the independence and behavior of the system, as in a merger a single instruction is supposed to depict multiple parallel operations.

The stuttering patterns s_p on the other hand, comprise of stuttering instructions s_i only. These patterns are observed and are replaced by mergers that preserve the functional behavior of the original MM_I, but will be reduced in size. Below is an example of s_p,

```
0x00000622  4968  LDR   r1, [r3,416]; @0x000007C4
0x00000624  2001  ADDI  r1, 0x04,
0x00000626  6008  STR   r1, [r3,416]
```

The above pattern is a set of instructions that essentially update the contents of a memory location 0x000007C4 by adding 4 to it. Modern processors are not equipped to do such operations in 1 clock cycle. However, we replace these 3 instructions with a single merger as given below,

```
0x00000622  7968125  LAS  [r3,416], 0x04
```

The merger is given a new name LAS abbreviated from Load-Add-Store and is assigned a new opcode for reference. Merger LAS is updating the contents of a memory location 0x000007C4 by directly adding 4 to it in a single instruction. An interesting thing to note here is that the original pattern occupies addresses 0x00000622 to 0x00000626, whereas the merger is only contained at 0x00000622. If each instruction in the original code gives rise to 100 stuttering transitions thus causing a total of 300 stuttering transitions, the merger only corresponds to 100 stuttering transitions. In SSA, we are not concerned with the implementation of the merger on the actual processor. Rather the merger is the abstraction that enables more scalable verification. A library is maintained for stuttering patterns and the corresponding mergers with the type of operation, name of instruction and the opcode shown in Table I.

B. Procedure of SSA

Algorithm 1 shows a procedure that applies SSA to the object code. The inputs to the procedure are,

1) Initial object code file($init\_obj\_code$)
2) A matrix ($path\_opc\_mat$) that contains information regarding opcode of instructions involved in each pattern is shown in Figure 1.

$$M = \begin{bmatrix} LDR, STR & 01001 & 01100 & X & X \\ MOV, STR & 1111000001001111 & 01100 & X & X \\ LSLS, STR & 00000 & 01100 & X & X \\ MOVS, LDR, STR & 00100 & 01001 & 01100 & X \\ MOVS, MOV, STR & 00100 & 1111000001001111 & 01100 & X \\ LDR, LDR_reg, COM, BNE & 01001 & 01101 & 00101 & 11010 \\ LDR, LDR_reg & 01001 & 01101 & X & X \\ TLR, STR & 10000100 & 01100 & X & X \\ LDR, STR(32Bit) & 01001 & 1111100011000001 & X & X \\ LST, TLR & 01110110 & 10000100 & X & X \\ MOV(32Bit), LDR_reg & 1111000001001111 & 01101 & X & X \\ LST, LST & 01110110 & 01110110 & X & X \\ OMS, OMS & 01111001 & 01111001 & X & X \\ TLR, CBNZ & 10000100 & 10111 & X & X \\ OMS, LST & 01111001 & 01110110 & X & X \end{bmatrix}$$

Figure 1. Patterns Opcode Matrix

Each row contains information about the pattern. The first column depicts the instruction types in a pattern. The first row in M contains the pattern LDR-STR, which based on the observation and research has the highest number of frequency in the assembly file. The second column of pattern LDR-STR (row 1) contains the opcode of LDR, the third column contains the opcode of STR. As this pattern only contains 2 instructions so rest of the columns get no opcode values (X). Similarly, row 2 has pattern MOV-STR that has the second highest number of occurrences, second and third columns of row 2 get opcodes values for MOV and STR respectively. Same goes for the rest of the rows and columns.

3) Refinement map ($ref\text{-}map$)

The procedure $Stutt\_Abs$ outputs the updated object code upd_obj_code, which reflects the abstracted implementation TS. The total number of patterns $count$ is calculated statically through a function $No\text{-}of\text{-}Rows$ (line 2). It is equal to the total number of rows in matrix $patt\_opc\_mat$. N_c keeps a record of the number of patterns that have been abstracted so far in the algorithm. Its initial value is 0 and maximum value must be equal to $count$. Value of N_c will be incremented by one when the search for a pattern starts in $init\_obj\_code$ (line 4). It will be incremented when the search for a pattern in object code completes. s_p is the number of lines in each pattern. It is computed through a function $patt\_size$ (line 6). Function counts the total number of numeric values in each row. Its value must be greater than 2. N_{opc} is a variable that is used to keep track of the number of lines in each pattern (line 7). Function $Next-Ins-Fetcher$ is used to find the Next instruction I_c in $init\_obj\_code$ (line 8). Opc represents the opcode of an instruction I_c and is calculated through function $Opc{-}Cal$ (line 9).

In order to abstract the instructions, Opc must match with already defined opcode in $patt\_opc\_mat$ (line 10). If both opcodes are matched (line 10), the instruction I_c is stored in $buff$ (line 11) else algorithm will set N_{opc} to 0 (line 26), initialize the buffer $buff$ again, and go to step 6 (line 28) to find the pattern in rest of the object code. To abstract instructions stored in the $buff$, N_{opc} must be equal to s_p (line 12). It indicates that all the required instructions in a pattern are stored in the $buff$. If $s_p \neq buff$, control will go to step 6 again (line 23).

In order to abstract instructions stored in the $buff$, it is required that they all should be stuttering instructions. The stuttering or non-stuttering nature of instructions is computed using a function ref_map (line 13). Output res of function ref_map will be '1' if instructions in the $buff$ are stuttering and '0' in case of non-stuttering instructions. If instructions in the $buff$ are stuttering (line 15), $init\_obj\_code$ is updated by abstracted instruction through a function mrg (lines 16-17). Instructions in $buff$ cannot be abstracted if they are non-stuttering (line 18) and the algorithm will start searching for a pattern in rest of the object code (lines 19-20). obj_code_end is representing the end of an object code. It is computed using function $code\_comp$ (line 27) and the initial value is 0. The algorithm will repeat until each pattern consisting of stuttering instructions is not abstracted in whole object code (line 28). The whole algorithm will repeat until N_c become equal to $count$ (line 29).

The abstracted Object Code depicts the functionality of the original object code and it does not change the essence of the original object code.

V. Case Study and Results

We have implemented SSA on the object code of an infusion pump. The basic functionality of an infusion pump is to inject medicine, which is done using a stepper motor. This behavior is modeled on an ARM Cortex-M3 based NXP LPC1768 microcontroller, and the assembly code is obtained. The number and type of patterns observed and caught by the automatic SSA are given in Table II. The assembly file is comprised of 335 lines of code for one cycle of execution, which after applying SSA is reduced to 234 instructions.

The result confirms that stuttering abstraction reduces 30.3% of the object code. To show that the algorithm can work consistently on another platform, infusion pump object code was developed for another platform ATMega382P microcontroller. In this case, 26.1% of object code is reduced through SSA. The results in Table II depict that SSA consistently reduces the size of the object code, this is for one execution cycle of the code, whereas in real-time systems the object code is executed in an infinite loop. Also, the reduction in object code will considerably reduce the number of stuttering transitions, which is a huge problem in refinement-based verification.

```
1: procedure Stutt_Abs(init_obj_code, patt_opc_mat, ref−map)
2:     count = No−of−Rows(patt_opc_mat)
3:     repeat
4:         Nc++;
5:         repeat
6:             sp ← patt− size(patt_opc_mat(Nc, :));
7:             Nopc++;
8:             Ic ← Next−Ins−Fetcher(init_obj_code);
9:             Opc ← Opc−Cal(Ic);
10:            if [Opc = patt_opc_mat(Nc, Nopc)] then
11:                buff(Nopc) ← Ic;
12:                if [sp = Nopc] then
13:                    res ← ref − map(buff)
14:                    N_opc = 0;
15:                    if [res = 1] then
16:                        upd_obj_code ← mrg(buff, init_obj_code);
17:                        init_obj_code ← upd_obj_code;
18:                    else
19:                        buff − initialized − again;
20:                        again − go − to − step6;
21:                else
22:                    again − go − to − step6;
23:            else
24:                N_opc = 0;
25:                buff − initialized − again;
26:                again − go − to − step6;
27:            obj_code_end ← code_comp(init_obj_code);
28:        until !(obj_code_end = 1)
29:    until !(Nc = count)
30: return upd_obj_code
```

Figure 2. Procedure for Static Stuttering Abstraction

VI. Conclusion and Future Work

We have developed SSA and shown that the technique can be effectively applied to object code. We have demonstrated static abstractions on object code of infusion pump controller implemented on two different micro controller platforms to reason about the consistency and efficiency of the proposed algorithm. The results demonstrate that static abstraction once applied on stuttering instructions is capable of reducing one-third of the object code, which exponentially reduces the number of stuttering transitions in the implementation transition system. In the context of model checking, several other abstraction techniques have been developed but they have not targeted a very large state space like object code.

In the future, we plan to explore the combination of dynamic stuttering abstraction and static stuttering abstraction and experimentally evaluate this combination. Dynamic stuttering abstraction is the technique where the abstraction is applied to the transition system obtained by symbolically simulating

TABLE I. PATTERNS AND THE MERGERS OF AN LPC1768 OBJECT CODE FOR INFUSION PUMP

Serial Number	No of Instructions in Pattern	Frequency Of Pattern	No. of Lines Reduced	Instruction Type	Instruction Opcode	Abstracted Merger Label	Merger Opcode (ASCII)	Merger Opcode (Binary)
1	2	13	13	LDR (PC) STR	[01001] [01100]	LST	768384	01110110
2	2	3	3	MOVS STR	[00100] [01100]	MST	778384	01110111
3	2	2	2	LSLS STR	[00000] [01100]	STL	838476	10000110
4	3	15	30	MOVS LDR (PC) STR	[00100] [01001] [01100]	OMS	797783	01111001
5	3	2	4	MOVS MOV (32 Bit) STR	[00100] [F04F] [01100]	VMS	867783	10000110
6	4	9	27	LDR (PC) LDR (REGISTER) CMP BNE	[01001] [00100] [00101] [11010001]	BCL	666776	01100110
7	2	7	7	LDR (PC) LDR (REGISTER)	[01001] [00100]	TLR	847682	10000100
8	3	3	6	LDR (PC) LDR (REGISTER) STR	[01001] [00100] [01100]	RSL	828376	10000010
9	2	2	2	LDR (PC) STR (32 Bit)	[01001] [F8C1]	DLS	687683	01101000
10	2	4	4	LST (User Defined) TLR (User Defined)	[01110110] [10000100]	NLT	787684	01111000
11	2	1	1	MOV (32-Bit) LDR (Register)	[F04F] [00100]	CML	677776	01100111
12	2	2	2	LST (User-Defined) LST (User-Defined)	[01110110] [01110110]	ELT	697684	01101001
13	2	2	1	OMS (User-Defined) OMS (User-Defined)	[01111001] [01111001]	FOS	707983	01110000

TABLE II. RESULTS OBTAINED ON LPC1768 AND ATMEGA382P

Metrics	LPC1768	ATMEGA382P
Number of Lines in Original Object Code	336	524
Number of Lines reduced in Original Object Code	102	139
Number of Lines in Abstracted Object Code	234	385
Total Number of patterns that are abstracted in Object Code	13	21
Percentage of Object Code Abstraction	30.3%	26.5%

the object code.

ACKNOWLEDGMENT

This publication was funded by a grant from the United States Government and the generous support of the American people through the United States Department of State and the United States Agency for International Development (USAID) under the Pakistan - U.S. Science & Technology Cooperation Program. The contents do not necessarily reflect the views of the United States Government.

REFERENCES

[1] "Medical Device Recalls," 2017, URL: https://www.fda.gov/MedicalDevices/Safety/ListofRecalls/ucm535289.htm [accessed: Nov,2018].

[2] P. Manolios, "Mechanical verification of reactive systems," PhD thesis, University of Texas at Austin, 2001.

[3] J. F. Groote and A. Wijs, "An O(m log n) Algorithm for Stuttering Equivalence and Branching Bisimulation," CoRR, vol. abs/1601.01478, 2016.

[4] S. Ray and R. Sumners, "Specification and Verification of Concurrent Programs Through Refinements," J. Autom. Reasoning, vol. 51, no. 3, 2013, pp. 241–280.

[5] M. Jain and P. Manolios, "An Efficient Runtime Validation Framework based on the Theory of Refinement," CoRR, vol. abs/1703.05317, 2017.

[6] B. Delahaye, K. G. Larsen, and A. Legay, "Stuttering for Abstract Probabilistic Automata," J. Log. Algebr. Program., vol. 83, no. 1, 2014, pp. 1–19.

[7] S. Jabeen, S. Srinivasan, and S. Shuja, "Formal verification methodology for real-time Field Programmable Gate Array," IET Computers & Digital Techniques, vol. 11, no. 5, 2017, pp. 197–203.

[8] A. M. Rabinovich, "Automata over continuous time," Theor. Comput. Sci., vol. 300, no. 1-3, 2003, pp. 331–363.

[9] K. Etessami, "Stutter-Invariant Languages, omega-Automata, and Temporal Logic," in Computer Aided Verification, 11th International Conference, CAV '99, Trento, Italy, July 6-10, 1999, Proceedings, 1999, pp. 236–248.

[10] C. Dax, F. Klaedtke, and S. Leue, "Specification Languages for Stutter-Invariant Regular Properties," in Automated Technology for Verification and Analysis, 7th International Symposium, ATVA 2009, Macao, China, October 14-16, 2009. Proceedings, 2009, pp. 244–254.

[11] S. Nejati, A. Gurfinkel, and M. Chechik, "Stuttering Abstraction for Model Checking," in Third IEEE International Conference on Software Engineering and Formal Methods (SEFM 2005), 7-9 September 2005, Koblenz, Germany, 2005, pp. 311–320.

[12] H. De-Leon and O. Grumberg, "Modular Abstractions for Verifying Real-Time Distributed Systems," Formal Methods in System Designg, vol. 2, 1993, pp. 7–43.